Natural Science Education, Indigenous Knowledge, and Sustainable Development in Rural and Urban Schools in Kenya

Cultural and Historical Perspectives on Science Education: Research Dialogs
Volume 6

Series editors

Kenneth Tobin
The Graduate Center, City University of New York, USA

Catherine Milne
Steinhardt School of Culture, Education, and Human Development, New York University

Research dialogs consists of books written for undergraduate and graduate students of science education, teachers, parents, policy makers, and the public at large. Research dialogs bridge theory, research, and the practice of science education. Books in the series focus on what we know about key topics in science education – including, teaching, connecting the learning of science to the culture of students, emotions and the learning of science, labs, field trips, involving parents, science and everyday life, scientific literacy, including the latest technologies to facilitate science learning, expanding the roles of students, after school programs, museums and science, doing dissections, etc.

Natural Science Education, Indigenous Knowledge, and Sustainable Development in Rural and Urban Schools in Kenya

Toward Critical Postcolonial Curriculum Policies and Practices

Darren M. O'Hern
The Council for International Culture and Education, NY, USA

and

Yoshiko Nozaki
Waseda University, Tokyo, JAPAN

SENSE PUBLISHERS
ROTTERDAM/BOSTON/TAIPEI

A C.I.P. record for this book is available from the Library of Congress.

ISBN: 978-94-6209-540-3 (paperback)
ISBN: 978-94-6209-541-0 (hardback)
ISBN: 978-94-6209-542-7 (e-book)

Published by: Sense Publishers,
P.O. Box 21858,
3001 AW Rotterdam,
The Netherlands
https://www.sensepublishers.com/

Printed on acid-free paper

For Jessica, Lindsey, Maya, Corryn, and Elsie
For Kazumi and Takeji Nozaki

TABLE OF CONTENTS

FOREWORD TO NATURAL SCIENCE EDUCATION, INDIGENOUS KNOWLEDGE, AND SUSTAINABLE DEVELOPMENT IN RURAL AND URBAN SCHOOLS IN KENYA

Aside from the very evident economic and political crises that we are facing in education, we are also in the midst of what can only be called an epistemological crisis. With the rise of *audit cultures* (Apple, 2006; Leys, 2003), schools, teachers, and students are seen as "good" along only one measure—test scores. A good teacher is one who produces ever increasing average student test scores. A good student is one who does the same. And entire school systems are to be judged by comparative scores on the PISA ratings. Evidence is of course needed in judging education. But in the rush to install such regimes of accountability, too little thought is given to whether the knowledge that is supposedly measured by such tests is itself what students, communities, and nations actually need. What can be measured too often replaces what should be taught. An active critical examination and debate over what knowledge is needed, especially in a time of severe environmental crisis, is either delayed or seen as unnecessary or too costly. So too is the question of where such knowledge might come from. This is where *Natural Science Education, Indigenous Knowledge, and Sustainable Development in Rural and Urban Schools in Kenya: Towards Critical Postcolonial Approaches to Educational Policy and Practice* enters.

Let me situate this volume in the larger context of critical educational theory and practice. In *Can Education Change Society?* (Apple, 2013), I detail nine tasks of the critical scholar/activist in education. Among them were the following three tasks:

1. Bearing witness to negativity. That is, one should engage in describing what is actually happening in education that reproduces relations that do not support a more equal and sustainable society.
2 Illuminate the spaces of possible counter-hegemonic educational work. That is, point out the spaces and resources that already exist where a more critically democratic education can go on.
3. Act as a critical secretary. That is, critically describe the educational actions, the curricular knowledge, the teaching, and the people who are actually engaged in filling these spaces so that our efforts do not simply have the effect of increasing both cynicism and the feeling that "nothing can be done."

Darren M. O'Hern and Yoshiko Nozaki's insightful book engages in all three of these tasks. The aims of the volume are clear in the following quotation from their introductory chapter:

[W]hat kind of knowledge, or whose knowledge, is currently considered legitimate to be taught in natural science education in Kenya? How is such knowledge taught in schools and under what kinds of social, cultural, and economic conditions? How do Kenyan students and teachers view alternative (e.g., indigenous) kinds of knowledge and their exclusion from (or possible inclusion in) formal curricula and pedagogical content, forms, and contexts?... [D]rawing upon theoretical insights from critical and postcolonial perspectives in varied social, cultural, and educational settings, this volume argues for the need to overcome the dichotomization and entrenched binary representations of Western and indigenous systems of knowledge on nature, environment, and sustainability in order to create a contextualized and empowering natural science education for Kenyan students.

These are crucial questions both ideologically and pedagogically for Kenya. But they are equally significant for every nation that is concerned with the relationship between education and the creation of an environmentally sustainable future for its people.

In and of itself, this would be sufficient to make O'Hern and Nozaki's volume a worthy contribution. But it also makes a substantive contribution to a major focus of critical education. The book is situated within a set of much larger debates about what is considered to be "legitimate" or "official" knowledge (see, e.g., Apple, 2014). From the vast universe of possible knowledge that might be taught in schools, only some is considered worthy of the imprimatur of the state, while other knowledge is considered "popular" or less worthy. Indeed, it is a conceptual requirement for the constitution of the concept of official knowledge that there be its opposite, its constitutive outside, called popular knowledge.

The epistemological and political implications of this have their roots in the concerns expressed by the noted critical cultural theorist Raymond Williams when he demonstrated how the creation of a "selective tradition" was closely connected to the legitimation of relations of dominance and subordination in the larger society (Williams 1961). Since that time, an extensive critical literature has developed on the politics of "tradition," on the defense and loss of collective memory, and on the sociology of school knowledge (see, e.g., Bernstein, 1977; Bourdieu, 1984; Apple, 2004; Apple, 2014; Apple, Au, & Gandin, 2009).

Yoshiko Nozaki has already contributed to this literature in important ways with her well-received book, *War Memory, Nationalism and Education in Postwar Japan, 1945-2007* (Nozaki, 2008). That book detailed the history of a very significant struggle over memory and what dominant groups decided was to be official knowledge. The book you are about to read by O'Hern and Nozaki takes up the issues surrounding the question of whose knowledge should be taught right now. It directs our attention to the conflicts over one of the most important curriculum areas—natural science and its relationship with teaching about sustainability. *Natural Science Education, Indigenous Knowledge, and Sustainable Development in Rural and Urban Schools in Kenya* brings us inside a number of schools. It provides us with an insightful picture of the contradictory interpretive frames that teachers and students employ to make decisions about what is legitimate science and should be taught and what is popular and "indigenous" and hence seems less important.

Their analysis shows how curriculum decisions are produced and lived out in daily realities. But the book goes further in that O'Hern and Nozaki also illuminate the ways in which the realities of gendered specificities work in the curriculum and pedagogies of the schools and in the interpretive frames used to understand the issues surrounding what is considered important knowledge.

In response to these complicated dynamics, compromises, and conflicts over curriculum and pedagogy in classrooms and in the lives of teachers and students, O'Hern and Nozaki call for a new way of engaging with educational policy, curriculum, and pedagogy, one based on critical postcolonial approaches. The result is a very nuanced picture of what is happening in the teaching of knowledge that is supposed to help us honestly deal with one of the most significant sets of issues we face nationally and internationally. In the process, they challenge us to rethink the ways we understand the importance of "indigenous knowledge" (see also Smith 2012). They have produced a volume that is a very thoughtful contribution to the ongoing construction of more epistemologically and socially responsive models of educational theory and practice.

Michael W. Apple
John Bascom Professor of Curriculum and Instruction
and Educational Policy Studies
University of Wisconsin, Madison

REFERENCES

Apple, M. W. (2004). *Ideology and Curriculum*, 3rd ed. New York: Routledge.
Apple, M. W. (2006). *Educating the "Right" Way*, 2nd ed. New York: Routledge.
Apple, M. W. (2013). *Can Education Change Society?* New York: Routledge.
Apple, M. W. (2014). *Official Knowledge*, 3rd ed. New York: Routledge.
Apple, M. W., Au, W., and Gandin, L. A. (Eds.). (2009). *The Routledge International Handbook of Critical Education*. New York: Routledge.
Bernstein, B. (1977). *Class, Codes and Control, Volume III*. New York: Routledge and Kegan Paul.
Bourdieu, P. (1984). *Distinction*. Cambridge, MA: Harvard University Press.
Leys, C. (2003). *Market-Driven Politics*. New York: Verso.
Nozaki, Y. (2008). *War Memory, Nationalism and Education in Postwar Japan, 1945-2007*. New York: Routledge.
Smith, L. T. (2012). *Decolonizing Methodologies*. London: Zed Books.
Williams, R. (1961). *The Long Revolution*. London: Chatto and Windus.

ACKNOWLEDGEMENTS

Darren M. O'Hern thanks his spouse and best friend, Jessica, for her infinite love and support. He would like to give sincere thanks to Lois Weis and Bob Stevenson for their helpful critique and thoughtful suggestions during the various phases of his research. He is also deeply indebted to his Kenyan colleagues and friends for their tremendous generosity and assistance. They include Jimmy Mwangi and his entire family, Dr. Mary Ngolovoi, Samuel Irungu, John Kahura, and Lucas Mwakisha. Charles Njuguna and Dr. Dorothy McCormick at the Institute for Development Studies at the University of Nairobi provided the institutional support that allowed this project to proceed. Finally, Darren thanks all the teachers and students he had the distinct pleasure of meeting and interacting with during his time in the Taita Hills and Nairobi.

Yoshiko Nozaki expresses her heartily appreciation to her family members, friends, colleagues, and students for their support, kindness, and encouragement in the last several years. In particular, she would like to acknowledge that she would never be able to thank enough Hiro Inokuchi, her spouse, for his love and strength in these years.

Finally, O'Hern and Nozaki thank Tom Benson at the Council for International Culture and Education for his generosity and friendship, and Susan Johns for her kind support and editorial assistance. Special thanks are due to Michel Lokhorst, Bernice Kelly, and other staff members of Sense Publishers for their patient and kind assistance, and the anonymous reviewer(s) for their helpful comments and suggestions.

INTRODUCTION

Sustainability, Development, and Natural Science Education

Acquiring appropriate knowledge about the natural environment through education is one of the most vital components in our global efforts for a sustainable future; however, we—whether we are educators, researchers, policy makers, or community activists—often face challenges, contradictions, and adversaries at local levels when planning and practicing such education.[1]

There is a pressing need to conduct research on the content of, and pedagogical approaches to, education for sustainability, since questions about how—and, indeed, if—the human race can sustain the globe and its societies have become topics of critical concern and debate in nearly all regions of the world in recent years.[2] To meet the challenge, the United Nations General Assembly has designated the years from 2005 to 2014 as the Decade of Education for Sustainable Development, suggesting that the process of education and educational institutions (e.g., schools) are crucial for ensuring the world's sustainable future. As Kazuhiko Takemoto (2011), program director and senior fellow at the United Nations University,[3] puts it:

> In order to ensure a sustainable future, people of all ages and walks of life need to start thinking and acting more responsibly towards our environment. But it is impossible to ask this of anyone without first making sure that people understand a right choice from a wrong choice and that they have the information and skills needed to follow through on whatever choice they make. (para. 4)

For Takemoto, education is "the answer," as it transforms people's views and behaviors and provides the knowledge and skills they need for building a sustainable future. He further contends that, in order to succeed in education for sustainability, we need to understand local needs, values, and insights and take bottom-up, grassroots approaches, since "we will never be able to change people's behaviors by simply telling them what to do" (Takemoto, 2011, para. 8). In other words, it is vital to listen to local voices that often go unheard in discussions of educational policy and implementation and comprehend layers of perspectives on teaching and learning about the natural environment.

THE PRESENT VOLUME: PURPOSE AND SIGNIFICANCE

The present volume explores natural science education, as it is practiced at the secondary level in rural and urban Kenya, in order to gain critical perspectives for equality and sustainability in postcolonial, developing countries. In particular, the volume examines the perceptions of students and teachers concerning the knowledge and skills taught in natural science subject areas such as agriculture, biology, and geography.[4] The volume, by analyzing their narratives regarding knowledge gained inside and outside of schools about nature, the environment, and sustainability, explicates their views on two kinds, or systems, of knowledge: knowledge encountered through teaching and learning in secondary institutions that offer ecological, environmental, and natural concepts and the knowledge gained through local activities, ethnic traditions, and/or interactions with their family members and relatives. In what ways do students and teachers in rural and urban Kenya explain and valuate—or devaluate for that matter—these two kinds of knowledge, their uses, and teaching and learning of them? As we discuss below, it is significant to examine the views on science education and knowledge in relations to critical questions, including those concerning equality, social justice, sustainable development, and globalization.

Natural Science Education and Epistemological Tensions of School Knowledge

Presently, the study of grassroots views on natural science education for sustainable development is critically important in countries such as Kenya, where dramatic environmental degradation has occurred over the past twenty years. As natural resources continue to deteriorate from deforestation in coastal (Fondo & Martens, 1998) and interior (Kironchi & Mbuvi, 1996) areas, industrial pollutants accumulate (Jumba, Kisia, & Kock, 2007), and greenhouse gas emissions skyrocket (Bailis, Ezzati, & Kammen, 2003), Kenyan education must offer natural science knowledge and skills that promote sustainable development to enable Kenyan students and young adults to fashion appropriate responses to such crises.

Historically, however, concerted efforts and initiatives that address the need for education focusing on sustainability have received scant attention and inadequate support in Kenya. Some researchers (e.g., Ho, 1998) even suggest that such efforts, if actually designed and implemented, would ultimately be derailed given the pervasive pressures of formal syllabi and credentialing examinations. Critical questions of school curriculum and knowledge (e.g., Apple, 1979; Whitty, 1985) should be raised here: what kind of knowledge, or whose knowledge, is currently considered legitimate to be taught in natural science education in Kenya? How is such knowledge taught in schools and under what kinds of social, cultural, and economic conditions? How do Kenyan students and teachers view alternative (e.g., indigenous) kinds of knowledge and their exclusion from (or possible inclusion in) formal curricula and pedagogical content, forms, and contexts?

The academic literature concerning science education in Kenya (and beyond), however, tends to lack critical inquiries into the issues of curriculum, pedagogy, and assessment of educational knowledge about nature, environment, and sustainability (and the epistemologies behind such knowledge). In particular, little research has juxtaposed the viewpoints of the state and those of students, teachers, and local communities on these issues, despite the invaluable insights such research can offer for bottom-up approaches to sustainability education.

To fill the gap, the present volume directs its attention to two kinds of educational knowledge: one taught through instruction in natural science classrooms in schools and the other learned through experiences in localized and out-of-school contexts. It explores the ways various actors such as the state (in its curriculum and policy texts), students, and teachers talk about the two by identifying and analyzing the epistemological tensions—and dichotomization—that exist in the texts and narratives of these actors.

In recent decades, knowledge held by local people and communities—sometimes referred to as "indigenous knowledge" (Ogunniyi & Ogawa, 2008)—has received considerable attention from donor agencies and non-governmental organizations alike, as it can play a critical role in the empowerment of local peoples and the development of rural (and, to a lesser extent, urban) areas. Volumes have been compiled that chart the usage of such knowledge in specific contexts and promote the preservation of non-Western epistemologies and practices (e.g., World Bank, 2004). Once exclusively oral in nature, this kind of knowledge has increasingly been categorized and cataloged (as recorded, written texts) under the pretext of "knowledge sharing" (Agrawal, 2002). Although we should welcome the attention to indigenous knowledge, as it represents a paradigm shift to grassroots approaches to (international) development and sustainability, we should be cautious. Research needs to be conducted to see if the two kinds of knowledge are still misleadingly represented in binary terms,[5] where Western knowledge is cast as objective, neutral, and scientific and pitted against the contextually-derived and situated nature of indigenous knowledge.

Despite the fact that several studies examine indigenous knowledge in various Kenyan educational contexts (e.g., Gitari, 2006; Kithinji, 2000), indigenous knowledge has yet to be regarded as part of formal natural science education. Remarkably absent are analyses that investigate students' and teachers' responses to the official knowledge (e.g., Apple, 2000) of natural science education vis-à-vis their perceptions of indigenous knowledge about nature, environment, and sustainability. The present volume is not content with knowing the views of adults or community professionals regarding indigenous knowledge, nor does it investigate indigenous knowledge in Kenya in an effort to "catalog" the information for natural science education in schools. Instead, drawing upon theoretical insights from critical and postcolonial perspectives in varied social, cultural, and educational settings, this volume argues for the need to overcome the dichotomization and entrenched binary representations of Western and indigenous systems of knowledge on nature, environment, and sustainability in order to create a contextualized and empowering natural science education for Kenyan students.

The State, Inequality, and Globalization

Research into the broad category of science education is voluminous and diverse in attention. Problems that are explored range from curricular issues concerning testing formats (e.g., Peyton, 2010) or conceptual retention of specific topics (e.g., Franco & Taber, 2009) to social issues such as the engagement of various student populations with science instruction (e.g., Barton, Tan, & Rivet, 2008). Sub-fields of science education, such as natural science or environmental education, can further expand angles of focus to include the interplay of humanistic factors and social, political, and economic influences with science education (e.g., Strife, 2010). The concept of education for sustainability entails even more complex entanglements of natural science and human science dimensions and includes not only issues of the environment but also those of economy, culture, society, peace, and justice (Gadotti, 2010).

Education for sustainability, therefore, can be seen as a more expansive concept that goes beyond the existing notion (and academic boundaries) of science education or natural science education. As such, the issues of curriculum, pedagogy, and assessment of educational knowledge about nature, environment, and sustainability and the views of students and teachers regarding these issues need to be situated in local, national, and global contexts that recognize social, cultural, and economic dynamics.[6] It is in these contexts that differential powers operate and influence and narratives are constructed relaying the interactions of human dynamics and power.

To investigate the contradictions and complexities of natural science education for sustainability at grassroots levels, the lenses of critical social and cultural theories (e.g., Apple, 1979; Weis, Fine, & Dimitriadis, 2009) must be used to examine the issue relationally. In Kenya, one of the most critical dynamics of education is the strong state control over local schools. State education policies that target the content, organization, and implementation of natural science curricula have numerous consequences on practices at the classroom level that are often unaccounted for by such policy initiatives. Critical examinations of these policies and practices can reveal the unseen difficulties, contradictions, and negotiations that must be traversed by administrators, teachers, students, parents, and community members during the pursuit of comprehensive and appropriate natural science knowledge and skills at local sites.

Kenya's social and historical context as a de-colonized, developing country with notable internal diversity and occasional eruptions of violent conflicts presents another dimension for considerations of natural science education for sustainable development. The country's rural and urban disparities, which are manifest in the science-oriented schooling of pupils, appear to be widening despite efforts by the state to promote uniformity through centralized syllabi and the reliance on national testing in natural science subjects.[7] In a national context where uneven development—whether in terms of economic, educational, or physical resources—has a profound effect on the natural environment and the health and well-being of citizens, critical inquiry must uncover difficulties in the natural science education of students. Important questions include: In what ways do conceptions of science and knowledge about the natural environment differ across social and cultural differences (such as class, gender, and race/ethnicity), geographic locations, and generations? How should educators deal with such diversity in their practices? How can recent social and cultural theories (such as critical and postcolonial theories) inform new practices of science education that will promote sustainable development for all Kenyans?

To envision a critical and contextualized sustainability education for all Kenyan students today, we cannot overlook gender dynamics operating in social, cultural, and educational contexts in Africa. Stambach's (2000) and Mungai's (2002) volumes detail the challenges faced by women (predominantly in rural locations) in their pursuit of education and are important ethnographic studies of community life and schooling in Tanzania and Kenya, respectively. Researchers who explore the issues of gender, curriculum, and pedagogy can move beyond the works that focus on classic issue of gender gaps in education to comparatively examine gendered knowledge in increasingly disparate and distanced rural and urban areas across the African continent. The present volume sheds light on the gender dimension and gendered conception of natural science knowledge in Kenya (and Africa) by understanding the perspectives of teachers and students in single-sex and mixed-sex institutions in rural and urban locations.

Finally, an analysis of the narratives of Kenyan students and teachers provides an understanding of the changing climate of natural science education and environmental knowledge in non-Western, postcolonial contexts. These perspectives are especially valuable in the era of globalization, as national education systems attempt to implement decentralized models of curricular administration (Astiz, Wiseman, & Baker, 2002) and many students in developing countries are increasingly interested in acquiring knowledge and skills in science and technology and participating in the global knowledge economy. By analyzing students' and teachers' views on science and knowledge about the natural environment, this volume offers postcolonial dynamics of "lived perspectives" (Nozaki, 2005) for natural science education for sustainability.

ETHNOGRAPHIC, QUALITATIVE STUDY: VIEWS FROM STUDENTS AND TEACHERS

The present study employs ethnographic, qualitative research methods and methodologies to explore challenges, contradictions, and struggles that contemporary policies and practices involving natural science education pose for students and teachers in Kenya—and elsewhere by implication. Through the use of ethnographic data, the study offers empirical insights into the ways students and teachers speak to curricula, pedagogies, and assessments of Kenyan natural science education vis-à-vis their views on indigenous knowledge, local practices, ethnic beliefs, and folklore. The data, collected by O'Hern with Nozaki's supervision at three distinctive schools in Kenya from April to November in 2005,[8] are regarded as "thick" layers of interpretation (Geertz, 1973).[9] As such, the present study makes unique contributions to educational research in general, and critical education studies in particular (e.g., Apple, 1995, 2000, 2004; Apple & Weis, 1983; Apple, Au, & Gandin, 2009; Weinstein, 1998; Pedroni, 2007).

5

First, it focuses on the data and analysis on daily practices of schools, students, and teachers. Although the topics of science education and Western and non-Western knowledge have been addressed in works discussing education in African contexts (e.g., Cleghorn, Merritt, & Abagi, 1989; Gitari, 2006; Jegede, 1997; Ogunniyi & Ogawa, 2008), few volumes have included the ethnographic data registering daily practices of schools with descriptions of local contexts and conditions of living from grassroots perspectives. For example, Gitari (2006) examines the topics of health and healing in a rural location through discussions with local residents in Kenya. This work demonstrates that several contextual processes (such as "inner sensing") and the use of localized objects (e.g., plant and animal products) are important for individuals when developing knowledge concerning health and healing. Gitari also notes that such contextual components and objects are not embraced in formal science instruction. Gitari's study provides excellent narrative information from adults and elders in the community; however, the attitudes and perspectives of teachers and students towards such methods of learning for concepts in health and healing are not considered.[10]

In the contexts of research on Kenyan education, albeit limited in number, important studies exist that employ qualitative methods as they investigate topics such as classroom conversations (e.g., Pontefract & Hardman, 2005) and teachers' understandings of democracy and democratic citizenship (e.g., Kubow, 2007).[11] However, such studies do not necessarily focus on the voices of students and teachers concerning the practical utility and intellectual instrumentality of knowledge held by local people and communities and their views on the exclusion and inclusion—pros and cons—of such local and communal knowledge in formal natural science instruction. It could be argued that it is necessary to intensively interact with rural and urban students, teachers, and administrators as they perform their daily educational duties in their respective schools in order to gain in-depth understanding of different perspectives concerning educational knowledge taught in schools and communities.

In studies of Kenyan society and cultures, although attention has been paid to the kinds of knowledge circulating among local people and communities (Munguti, 1997; Watson, Adams, & Mutiso, 1998), most studies focus almost exclusively on societal views of, and adult interactions with, such kinds of knowledge.[12] The present volume shifts the focus from actors outside of educational institutions (typically rural adults and communities) to students and teachers in secondary schools and targets schools and classrooms as crucial sites for understanding the perspectives of educational stakeholders on natural science knowledge. With the help of ethnographic data from Kenyan rural and urban adolescents, educators, and classrooms, the present study allows us to begin a critical debate concerning the current state of natural science education, the role of knowledge held by local people and communities, and the (possible) merits of diverse epistemologies in the future of sustainability education.

DATA COLLECTION: MULTI-SITED ETHNOGRAPHIC WORK

For the present study, data collection, conducted by O'Hern with Nozaki's supervision, took place in three Kenyan secondary schools, each with the designation of "provincial school" by the Kenyan Ministry of Education (MOE, hereafter). Although the nuances of instruction and learning concerning issues of natural science education for sustainability can certainly be gained through the investigation of natural science education in any primary, secondary, or post-secondary educational institutions, the present study centers on natural science education in secondary schools for two reasons. First, secondary school students are usually better equipped than primary school students to discuss their interactions (as frequent or infrequent as they are) with grandparents' and elders' indigenous practices and beliefs pertaining to natural sciences or the environment. Second, Kenyan students at this level, as opposed to students at post-secondary levels, have daily interactions with natural science education in schools and, thus, are better candidates for expressing—with their own stories of daily experiences—their views on natural science education and indigenous knowledge.

Multi-sited, multi-case study

The present study is a multi-sited, or multi-case, ethnographic study—a research design that meets methodological challenges in the era of globalization. This is because it allows qualitative researchers to demonstrate that seemingly independent events at one site are indeed connected to events at other sites at deeper levels (Weis, Fine, & Dimitriadis, 2009), and suits well for registering heterogeneity, subtlety, and complexity that exist within a society and culture (e.g., Inokuchi & Nozaki 2010). That is, the data that include the narratives of both rural and urban Kenyan students and teachers from three distinctive sites not only present the alarming disparity that exists in the science-oriented schooling of pupils in these populations (despite the uniformity of centralized syllabi and national testing in the natural sciences),[13] but also show the heterogeneity of the forces, language, and ideas that work to preserve social, cultural, and economic inequalities though teaching specific kinds of school knowledge and maintaining the binary of the West and indigenous (Kenya in this study) relationship.

Using the multi-sited, or multi-case, approach, the present study is designed not to overlook the differences, compromises, and negotiations—or "variations, multiplicities, and contradictions" (Nozaki, 2009, p. 486)—that exist within Kenyan society in general, and its natural science education for sustainability at grassroots levels in particular, in order to avoid—as much as possible—creating another binary. For cross-cultural studies, it is critical to "elucidate a complex and uneven topography" (Said, 1993, p. 318) within a nation, region, or geography to see the connections between peoples, cultures, histories, and societies, while understanding the relative autonomy of its intricate socio-historical experiences and conditions of living. In this sense, we would argue, the present volume offers "a fresh imaginary" for critical research methods and methodologies (Weis, Fine, & Dimitriadis, 2009, p. 437) that help us capture the "rippling effects" (p. 438) of actions in one place influencing those in another place in the age of an increasingly globalizing world.[14]

Ethnographic approach

Ethnographic approaches were taken for the data collection. Qualitative research, according to Bogdan and Biklen (2003), requires an approach to social phenomena that is open-ended and "allows the subjects to answer from their own frame of reference rather than from one structured by pre-arranged questions" (p. 3). In the field of education, qualitative approaches can be referred to as "naturalistic because the researcher frequents places where the events he or she is interested in naturally occur" (Bogdan and Bilken, 2003, p. 3). Ethnographers in the field of education usually observe students, teachers, and their interactions in school, while participating in the activities at school (and in its communities). The ethnographic researcher's aim is the demonstration of plausibility and validity of assertions in his/her analysis, and, for that aim, it is necessary for the researcher to collect data not only from interviews but also from observations and to triangulate the situation (Erickson, 1986). Recording observations consisting of concrete descriptions in social processes and contexts is important. The researchers should record observations and write them up with care and self-conscious awareness, though, in any form of recording method (field notes, audio-taping, video-taping and filming), one can never record everything, as some selection must be made (Hammersley & Atkinson, 1983).

The ethnographic research actions of sitting in classrooms (and conducting interviews) cannot be undertaken without prior consideration of the methodological issues involved with field research in an international setting. Here, it is noteworthy to comment on the challenges associated with representing the thoughts, feelings, and actions (or perspectives) of participants without forcing informants' experiences into a mode that is utterly foreign to them, an issue Bogdan and Biklen (2003) termed the "participant perspectives" problem (p. 23). Understanding the lived perspectives is not an easy task (Nozaki, 2006)—and understanding those of rural and urban secondary students and teachers in an analysis of natural science education in a developing country is no exception. There are multiple ways to interpret student experiences and interactions in classrooms and on school compounds. By privileging student perspectives and attempting to understand their point of view in regards to the use and value of natural science knowledge, their experiences with such knowledge may be distorted. Yet, as Bogdan and Biklen (2003) contend, "approaching people with a goal of trying to understand their point of view, while not perfect, distorts the informants' experience the least" (p. 23).

One way to minimize distorting effects is to observe interactions among students and between students and teachers or administrators inside and outside classrooms. It is understood that researchers' roles and (perceived) identities as outsiders may preclude them from fully observing or comprehending interactions in classroom and school environments, such as those occurring in natural science classes in rural and urban Kenyan schools. However, preconceptions about discussion topics, schooling in rural and urban areas, and, more broadly, contemporary education in Kenya, can (and should) be continually challenged in an attempt to dislodge these very preconceptions—or "bracket" them (Ely, 1991, p. 50)—and try to interpret layers of meanings students and teachers in three schools make through their experiences with the acquisition, prioritization, and valuation of various natural science knowledge.

To be sure, although the data collection methods for the present volume did not depart radically from the classic paradigm of ethnographic study, the authors have keenly been aware of the power relations that are both inherent and created between field researchers and research participants. We would contend that, as researchers (either native or from outside) become visible and active in their target communities and engage the researched in detailed conversations, the researchers must reflect on their position as holders of specific knowledge and investigators of complex phenomena. They should understand the ways their position influence, or otherwise impact, the research, and remain open to alternative research methodologies (e.g., action research, participatory evaluation, and participatory action research [PAR]) that can disrupt established power relations in conducting research. (For further discussion, see Chapter Three).

Study Sites Selections

In the early stages of designing the research, it was envisioned that O'Hern's contacts at individual schools would be established prior to his arrival in Kenya with the aid of pre-arranged institutional relationships. However, most, if not all, of the legwork for the data collection was carried out in Nairobi in early April 2005 because of the difficulties involved in the long distance negotiations, which included coordinating his Research Associate position at the Institute for Development Studies at the University of Nairobi, obtaining government research clearance for the duration of the fieldwork through the MOE, initiating contact with the urban schools and gaining permission for the research activities at each institution, and arranging for housing in both the rural and urban locations.

While it is not uncommon for foreign researchers to be met with some obstacles when initiating fieldwork, the challenges O'Hern faced resulted in a number of minor, yet noteworthy, alterations to the original data collection plan for the present study. For example, originally observations and interviews were to be conducted at two sites—one non-boarding school in a rural location and one in an urban location. Non-boarding schools were sought because students enrolled at such institutions typically live near the school and therefore could perhaps be classified as rural or urban students with less difficulty than students who may have been raised in a rural region but attended boarding school in an urban environment. Furthermore, it was assumed that non-boarding students—both in rural and urban contexts—might have had more consistent interactions with grandparents and community elders, individuals who practice indigenous natural science knowledge. Yet, as research

9

preparations took shape in Nairobi, it became apparent that finding a non-boarding co-education institution in Nairobi was difficult, since single sex, full-boarding secondary institutions were far more common in the greater Nairobi area. Most of the students in such schools were, however, fully urban coming from nearby areas.

After a good deal of considerations and negotiations, three schools were selected as research sites. The first institution, Forest Secondary School (pseudonym), was located in rural Taita-Taveta District in the Coast Province of southeastern Kenya. The school rested approximately ten kilometers (6.2 miles) from Wundanyi, the largest town in the Taita Hills and district headquarters for Kenyan government offices. The hilly areas surrounding Wundanyi were populated mainly by small-scale farmers and lack electrification, running water, and paved roads. The school enrolled both males and females, either boarding students or "day scholars" (students who returned home after each day's classes). The second and third research sites were situated on the outskirts of Nairobi's Central Business District, within 10 kilometers of one another. The first urban school, Uhuru Girls Secondary (pseudonym), was boarding institution for females, while the second, Central Boys Secondary (pseudonym), was an all-male boarding school. Enrollments at the urban schools are nearly double that of the rural school. Most of the urban students are from Nairobi Province or regions within close proximity to the capital city.

Data collection at all three schools progressed under similar timeframes and with few difficulties. At each school, a set of qualitative research methods used to collect observational and interview data included: participant observation in agriculture, biology, and geography classes, semi-structured, open-ended interviews with students and teachers, and the administration of short questionnaires with the interviewees. In addition, documents were also collected from ministry resources and Kenya's main English-language daily newspapers that pertained to secondary education, testing, or syllabi. However, there were some discernable differences in the ways that students, teachers, and community members responded to presence of O'Hern in each setting. Such reactions, whether they occurred on school compounds or in other locations, undoubtedly shaped the interactions with each community and also affected the recorded observations of teaching and learning in rural and urban schools (for further discussion on the issues of research processes and decisions, see Chapter 3: Methods and Methodology).

OVERVIEW OF CHAPTERS

Chapter Two reviews the literature that informs this research and identifies theoretical debates that are used during the analysis of the ethnographic data collected in rural and urban schools. This chapter examines works that interrogate natural science education using critical perspectives in numerous social and national contexts, including Kenya as well as other countries in Africa. The second chapter includes a review of the literature that delineates Western scientific knowledge and indigenous knowledge. The second chapter also explores theories of curriculum that aid in reconceptualizing natural science education in Kenyan secondary schools. Chapter Three discusses the methods and methodology employed for the present study. It situates this study within the tradition of critical educational studies, but goes beyond that to argue for a multi-sited ethnographic study with an international focus.

Chapter Four begins with a discussion of the history and organizational structure of the formal education system in Kenya and also contains information on curriculum development and textbook selection for the natural sciences, evaluation at the secondary level, and pedagogical practices in secondary science classrooms. The chapter provides an analysis of formal education in Kenya, beginning with a discussion of the historical context of formal schooling and tracing the development of the education system through the pre-colonial, colonial, and postcolonial periods. The fourth chapter also includes an examination of contemporary issues facing schools and the education system in Kenya and the influences that globalization has on the Kenyan system. We conclude with an overview of state agencies that are tied to the administration of schooling in Kenya, the development of curricula, the assessment of school knowledge at the secondary level, and the impact of these agencies on daily practices in schools.

The next three chapters present ethnographic case studies from rural and urban schools and document interactions with students and teachers who live and work in two highly disparate areas in Kenya. The chapters document the daily instructional practices in the natural sciences at each school and provide observational and narrative accounts of instructors' and students' interactions with, and perspectives of, school science and environmentally-oriented indigenous knowledge, beliefs, and practices. Chapter Five focuses on these processes at Forest Secondary School in rural Taita-Taveta District. Chapter Six examines natural science education at Central Boys Secondary, an all-male institution located in Nairobi, while Chapter Seven discusses Uhuru Girls Secondary, an all-female school situated in close proximity to Nairobi's central business district.

The final chapter of the volume, Chapter Eight, begins by relating the implications of this study for efforts and discussions that address the issues of sustainability and natural science education, especially in African contexts. The chapter also discusses the narratives of rural and urban teachers and students concerning indigenous and schooled natural science knowledge and highlights historical factors, formal and structural arrangements, and new realities wrought by globalization that contribute to the current marginalization of indigenous knowledge in science education in Kenya. Finally, we use critical and postcolonial insights to propose effective pedagogy that displaces the dichotomization of Western scientific and indigenous knowledge about the natural environment and produces a contextually-relevant and globally-connected sustainability education for all students.

NOTES

[1] Although we recognize debates concerning the conceptual notions attached to terms such as "education for sustainability" and "education for sustainable development (ESD)" (e.g., Gadotti, 2010), in the

present volume the terms "education for sustainability," "education for sustainable development," and "sustainability education" are used interchangeably.

2   In this volume, "science education" means "natural science education." By that we do not mean to ignore the existence of social and human sciences as sciences in a broader sense, but they are usually not part of "science education" taught in schools.

3   Takemoto is also Senior Advisor to the Japanese Minister of the Environment.

4   This volume employs the term "natural science" to separate out the subjects of agriculture, biology, and geography, as these are the actual subjects that teach about the natural environment. Other science classes exist in secondary schools in Kenya: computer science, social science classes (like economics or political science/government), and, of course, physical science (physics). The volume uses the term "natural science" because it includes all classes about the natural environment but not all Kenya's science classes. For example, it includes geology if the schools teach it, but it never includes physics or chemistry because, although these subjects have practical applications in the natural world and are fundamental to understanding our natural surroundings, their content mastery involves more mathematics than it does an understanding of ecological, environmental, and/or natural concepts. We use natural science to include science classes that specifically focus—at one time or another, like biology does in its "ecology" and "botany" units—on some aspect of the natural environment.

5   For further discussion on the two kinds, or systems, of knowledge, see Chapter Two.

6   The concept of "education for a sustainable future" involves both natural science and human science dimensions. For example, the United Nations Educational, Scientific, and Cultural Organization (UNESCO) lists the following natural science and human science dimensions as part of "Education for Sustainable Development": Biodiversity, Climate Change, Cultural Diversity, Indigenous Knowledge, Disaster Risk Reduction, Poverty Reduction, Gender Equality, Health Promotion, Sustainable Lifestyle, Peace and Human Security, Water, and Sustainable Urbanization.

7   A more detailed explanation of the selection of research sites for the present study is provided briefly in Chapter One. Chapter Three: Methods and Methodology contains supplemental information concerning research methodology, data collection at each site, and data analysis.

8   From 1996 until 1998, O'Hern also worked in the Taita-region of Kenya as a volunteer with the U.S. Peace Corps. As an agroforestry extensionist, he worked with community groups, schools, and churches on reforestation projects and other conservation and environmental education projects.

9   Nozaki did not visit Kenya; however, she and O'Hern maintained on-and-off communications by emails (and fax once) throughout the data collection phase. There were some intense communications at the beginning and, again, at the ending phase. This experience suggests that, with today's technological advances, field researchers can collaborate while being in different places.

10   Other studies employ qualitative methods to examine Kenyan education policies and interactions in classrooms and focus on science education (e.g., Cleghorn, Merritt, & Abagi, 1989) and, more specifically, indigenous knowledge and science curricula and education (e.g., Gitari, 2003, 2006).

11   For example, Pontefract and Hardman (2005) is a study of classroom discourse in Kenyan primary schools that involves an evaluation of English, mathematics, and science lessons in nine schools spread across urban and rural areas. In order to intensively analyze the discourse variations by teachers and the nature of participation by primary students aged approximately five to thirteen, entire lessons were audio-taped and the researchers later performed discourse analyses. Although Pontefract and Hardman also add layers of information by interviewing teachers and administering a survey questionnaire, their study relies heavily on audio recordings, and not classroom-based observations or interviews, as the primary data source.

12   For example, some studies spotlight the use of indigenous and Western knowledge in agricultural-related activities and natural resource management (e.g., Wane & Chandler, 2002), while others target the usage of indigenous botanical or herbal knowledge in the treatment and prevention of disease (e.g., Sindiga, 1994). Gitari (2003) provides a thorough critique of the secondary biology syllabus and the extent to which indigenous knowledge concerning the topics of health and healing are incorporated into formal schooling in a rural location. These and other studies, however, fail to include the roles of young Kenyans in these practices and their perspectives concerning indigenous knowledge about nature and environment.

13   Chapter Three contains supplemental information concerning the specific schools that were selected as research sites, as well as data collection at each site and data analysis.

14   For further discussion, see Chapter Three.

NATURAL SCIENCE EDUCATION IN NON-WESTERN NATIONS AND CRITICAL AND POSTCOLONIAL PERSPECTIVES

A Literature Review

Science education, including natural science education, has been studied and debated across the globe for more than half a century. As such, there are a number of works that review this large body of literature from various perspectives.[1] Few such reviews, however, focus on works that contain, or lead to, critical analyses of natural science education in Kenya, Africa, and the United States.[2] In order to begin a reconceptualization of natural science education in Kenyan schools—and, by implication, elsewhere—for a sustainable future, it is necessary to examine existing literature from critical and postcolonial perspectives. The questions here include: How has the literature addressed the influences and meanings of state policies that define the official knowledge of science education? How are the implications these policies have on classroom practice in several intra- and international contexts viewed? To what extent and in what ways has the literature addressed the challenges of science education policies and practices in relation to contemporary issues such as diversity, social justice, globalization, and sustainable development? How has the literature conceptualized and examined Western scientific knowledge and indigenous knowledge and analyzed the relationships between the two?

THE STATE, SCHOOLS, AND NATURAL SCIENCE CURRICULUM AND PEDAGOGY

Michael Apple's (1995, 2000) work on relationships between knowledge, power, and society offers us a starting point. From Apple's perspective, the knowledge of a subject area that is deemed most worthy or legitimate is the official knowledge that is embodied in the formal curriculum. An exploration of official knowledge can reveal not only the types of knowledge that find their way into curricula and schools, but also the processes through which knowledge and values are legitimated by individuals or groups in positions of power in society. Through the definition, legitimization, and dissemination of official knowledge by groups of social and economic elite—by direct state power or though various cultural practices that are commonsensical and hegemonic—societal inequality can be maintained. It follows that if there is a predominance of content aligned with a specific kind of knowledge (e.g., the Western scientific tradition) in the agriculture, biology, and geography curricula, or if there is a struggle over official knowledge sanctioned for these subject matters, it raises questions concerning the societal power granted to different groups by promoting or marginalizing certain kinds of knowledge. We would suggest, however, that national contexts play a role in terms of where we observe manifestations of such politics of official knowledge and what particular aspects (e.g., policies, topics, and themes) become contentious. This is not to suggest that external (e.g., global) influences cannot play significant roles in the selection and de-selection of certain types of knowledge by certain groups within national contexts (as we address the interplay of globalization and education policy and practice more fully in Chapter Four), but that global influences are always situational within a given national and regional context.

NATURAL SCIENCE EDUCATION IN KENYA AND AFRICA: STATE POLICIES AND EVERYDAY PRACTICES

In Kenya, an examination of the syllabi organized by the Kenya Institute of Education (hereafter KIE, 2002) for secondary agriculture, biology, and geography—the major subject areas that constitute what we refer to as "natural science education"— reveals the significance assigned to the study of scientific disciplines in general, and these subject areas in particular. For instance, the general objectives listed in the agriculture syllabus read: "Create awareness of the role of agriculture in industrial and technological development" and "Demonstrate that farming is a dignified and profitable occupation" (p. 97). Similarly, all secondary students enrolled in biology should be able to "Demonstrate resourcefulness, relevant technical skills and scientific thinking necessary for economic development" and be aware that "Biology is the precursor of biotechnology which is a tool for industrial and technological development" (p. 80). Geography students, furthermore, are required to "Recognize different types of environments and manage them for individual, national and international development" (KIE, 2002, p. 144).

It is clear that Kenya's natural science syllabi also acknowledge the importance of natural science education in achieving desired social goals. The agriculture syllabus aims to "Promote health consciousness" through the use of agricultural activities and implores teachers to present farming as respectable and profitable, while also warning school leaders that "Agricultural and other related activities must not be used as punishment for wrong doers" (p. 97). Likewise, the study of biology "Enables the learner to appreciate humans as part of the broader community of living organisms" (p. 79). Aside from the desired outcomes concerning the economic well-being, social consciousness, and responsibility of individuals, the Kenyan government also seeks to promote the study of science through the natural science coursework mandated in the national syllabi—agriculture, biology, and geography students should "[a]cquire a firm foundation of relevant knowledge, skills and attitudes for further education and for training in related scientific fields" (KIE, 2002, p. 80).

The fundamental objectives and specific goals listed in the natural science syllabi, of which those listed above are only a sample, address a wide spectrum of issues, including numerous subject-related skills, overarching conceptual understandings, issues of social justice and inequality, and general attitudes towards individual subjects and schooling. When the goals of natural science education, as defined by the KIE, are looked at more broadly, it is clear that the Kenyan government views the study of agriculture, biology, and geography as important in terms of the economic and social development of the country—and, therefore, defines the official knowledge of these subjects. (For more comprehensive discussions of the interplay of official knowledge and education policy, see Apple [1995] and Apple [2000].)

While studies that consider the impact of state-propagated policies on natural science instruction and learning in Kenya are limited in number, there are some analyses that aim to examine conflicts between state policies and school practices.[3] For example, Gitari's (2003) inquiry into types and characteristics of knowledge held by rural communities and the secondary biology curriculum in Kenya furnishes an analysis of the theoretical and practical relations between government education policies and the natural science education that is practiced in schools. Gitari argues that, despite stated government intentions to indigenize the secondary science curriculum, knowledge and principles of local communities, particularly in the area of health and healing, are not accounted for in the science education that students receive in a rural area of Kenya. Her critique illuminates a rift between the national curriculum and the rural knowledge and skills of health and healing that community members practice. Gitari concludes that unless the knowledge and skills practiced at local sites are integrated into formal schooling, many Kenyan secondary students who do not advance to post-secondary education will be unable to make "positive epistemological contributions to the rural community" (p. 195).

Some studies have examined the nexus of government language policy and science instruction in Kenyan schools. For example, in their research on primary school education, Cleghorn, Merritt, and Abagi (1989) probe the difficulties encountered by teachers and students in regard to the national policy advocating English-Swahili bilingualism in science education. According to Kenyan government directives, the emphasis on English instruction is intended to unify instruction in primary-level sciences and prepare students for the system's English language national tests. However, the study suggests that variations in individual schools and student populations alter the conceptual and linguistic input from students during instruction and that the policy, in general, disadvantages rural students who benefit from increased opportunities for "mother tongue science instruction" (p. 38).

The hindrance of conflict between state policies and everyday local practices is ubiquitous in African contexts[4]. Take for example, the work of Sanders and Ngxola (2009), which is applicable to the study of Kenyan natural science education. Their research offers insight into the disjuncture between science-related policies prescribed by the state and the effects of such policies on teaching and learning in classrooms through a salient critique of the "radical, new" (p. 122) *Life Sciences* (biology) curriculum (finalized in South Africa in 2008). This particular curriculum initiative entails the comprehensive teaching of evolution in secondary biology, a significant departure from the previous official stance on the topic. Although these authors approach their analysis of this reform from a viewpoint of curriculum change (p. 123), their examination also considers the systemic change from a critical perspective. In doing so, it details a number of issues related to the conflict between government-sanctioned curricular knowledge and the practice of education in classrooms, including the controversy generated by the topic of evolution, teacher apprehension due to personal belief systems,[5] and student resistance to the subject.

Difficulties in the practical implementation of education policy are clearly illustrated by Engida (2002), who discusses teacher reaction and sentiment concerning an Ethiopian curriculum amendment that initiated chemistry instruction in grade seven, when students are approximately 13 years old. Research with primary school chemistry teachers in Addis Abba indicates that serious difficulties arise in classrooms due to the inclusion of highly abstract concepts in the new curriculum, contradictory suggestions in the chemistry curriculum guide, and a lack of adequate representation of advanced chemistry concepts in textbooks. Probyn (2006) also describes the challenges that South Africa's Language-in-Education Policy (LiEP) produces for teachers and students as they attempt to meet the policy goals of bilingualism with English as the language of learning and teaching despite rural and township students' lack of interaction with English speakers or English-language materials outside of school.

The studies discussed above clearly suggest that educational policies of the state that target the content, organization, and implementation of natural science curricula in Kenya and other African countries—while they might be well conceived and intended—result in conflicts and consequences at the classroom level that are often unaccounted for by such initiatives. The studies, however, seem to overlook the possibility that dominant cultural practices of curriculum and pedagogy in schools can invite struggles (perhaps between schools/teachers and students). In other words, a part of the problem facing Kenyan natural science education may well be one of "cultural hegemony" (e.g., Apple, 1978), rather than the sheer imposition of state power over official knowledge. Here, it is useful to review works in the area of science education in the United States, as they have approached the issues of science teaching and learning in schools from diversity and social justice perspectives. We would refer to such approaches as "multiculturalist," borrowing the term from other subject areas such as literacy and social science education.

SCIENCE EDUCATION AND MULTICULTURALIST APPROACHES IN THE UNITED STATES: THE ISSUES OF DIVERSITY AND SOCIAL JUSTICE

In the United States, the passage of the National Defense Education Act in 1958 marked a noteworthy government-led effort to increase funding for, and participation in, science-related subjects at all levels of schooling. While the motivations behind this particular piece of legislation were couched in the Cold War and the changes to the college-bound demography in the United States, the added emphasis on the development of science-related knowledge and skills reflected the idea that science education is important for national defense as well as economic and social development (Anderson, 2007; Harris & Miller, 2005). Since the National Defense Education Act of 1958, the rationale for promoting science education has often been coupled with economic arguments concerning the preparation of workers for participation in the competitive world economy and international business (Carter, 2008; Drori, 2000; Rutherford & Ahlgren, 1990).

In recent decades, some critics have attempted to rethink science education critically, suggesting social justice goals, such as equitable educational opportunities for diverse populations of students (Barton, 2002; Lee & Fradd, 1998), and making arguments that consider science education in terms of broader human concerns that occur in everyday life and culture (Aikenhead, 2005; Varelas, Becker, Luster, & Wenzel, 2002).[6] We should note that the major concern here—especially among critical educators and scholars—has often been the persistent science achievement gaps between the majority, mainstream (i.e., White) students and minority students. In other words, the problem of science education is the disarticulation of science education in schools and students' experiences at home. A number of studies have suggested that science curricula and pedagogy in schools be made responsive and relevant to the social and cultural contexts and experiences of urban students (i.e., minority students in general and African American and Latino/a students in particular).

For example, in a study of a "low performing" urban elementary school, Buxton (2006) investigates the ways minority youth employ a student-centered model of scientific inquiry that values their lines of reasoning and helps to create contextually authentic science.[7] Through the use of this model, a collaborative approach to inquiry is utilized that resonates with the cultures and experiences of urban students outside the classroom, but also taps into the strengths of canonically authentic science inquiry. Buxton argues that this approach helps authenticate scientific learning for these urban children because it begins with their interests, perspectives, and needs, suggesting that youth empowerment must be advocated and valued if schooling should promote social justice as well as the content of science education.

Research on science education from diversity and social justice perspectives also focuses on teaching and learning strategies that teachers and students can use to merge their social lives and experiences from outside the school with the content and practices of science education that they encounter in the science classroom and laboratory. For example, through their research with African American and Latina girls in three low-income, urban middle schools, Barton, Tan, and Rivet (2008) demonstrate the ways students create "hybrid spaces" that allow them to "reshape the landscape of science education, rendering it less foreign" (p. 99). To create such spaces, students and teachers forge creative interactions in the science classroom that connect the spaces of science education and the home to open the hybrid space that contains aspects of both school and home. Such emerging science practices and hybrid spaces also serve to welcome students who are not fluent in the school-acknowledged language and views of the science classroom and help to redefine student participation and the role of the teacher in science instruction. Through this research, these authors look beyond the abundantly studied issue of the achievement gap in sciences for minority students to focus on the responsiveness of formal science instruction to students' lives and cultures outside the schools.[8]

Another example of research that interrogates science education using diversity and social justice perspectives can be found in Gilbert's (2002) work in a predominantly Hispanic urban high school in the southwestern United States. In this research, Gilbert suggests that the use of "non-traditional" approaches (including the use of pedagogical approaches informed by multicultural, feminist, indigenous, or non-traditional science)[9] by science instructors increases student participation in science and allows them to recognize the importance of science in their daily lives.[10] In addition, Verma's (2001) research with White and African American seventh graders in an urban setting shows the impact of a "contextualized science curriculum (an alternate science curriculum)" on student acquisition of, and attitudes toward, scientific content in the classroom (p. 5). These and other studies (e.g., Seiler, 2001; Zuniga, Olson, & Winter, 2005) concerning the science education of various student populations demonstrate that science education in schools fails to make its content (whether it be natural, life, or physical science information) relevant or responsive to the life experiences, perspectives, and cultures of students outside schools.[11]

The studies discussed above suggest that an examination of natural science education in rural and urban areas of Kenya may also need to raise questions of engagement and relevance for secondary students in these locations. Such an investigation should identify lines of inquiry that problematize and examine the disarticulation of students' community experiences and schools' teaching practices. Research on Kenyan education has pointed out the top-down, prescriptive national syllabi and standardized assessment process that is followed by each and every public secondary school in the country; however, it has not fully explored the (possible) conflicts between teachers and students in terms of their views on the legitimate knowledge to be taught in schools.

Indeed, these studies suggest that tremendous challenges exist for educators and those interested in promoting scientific literacy among youth to remake science education responsive and relevant to students' experiences, views, and interests. Part of the challenges may not only be cultural in nature, but may also involve political aspects as well. Thus, critical examinations of such challenges can help teachers conceive and develop new approaches to curricula and pedagogies for education in general, and natural science education in particular, for sustainability in Kenya.

Here, we would argue, critical perspectives are more than helpful, as they provide us with theoretical tools to stir the debate over the relations between the kind of knowledge that is taught—and should be taught—in schools and the maintenance of existing social, cultural, and economic structure(s) that enable certain groups within society to subjugate and marginalize others.

NATURAL SCIENCE EDUCATION AND CRITICAL PERSPECTIVES

Critical Practice of Education: Pedagogy of the Oppressed and Counter-hegemonic Curriculum Making

Paulo Freire (1970), envisioning a critical, transformative role for education, argues that schooling should not seek to "integrate" students into a structure of oppression, but to transform the structure so that they can become "beings for themselves" (p. 74). Freire fundamentally opposes the prevailing form of education that involves interactions between teachers and students that are dominated by a "banking" concept of education. This concept, which positions students as containers into which the knowledge of the teacher can be deposited on a daily basis, is completely insufficient and will "never propose to students that they critically consider reality" (p. 74). The banking concept of education, which Freire sees as mechanistic and alienating, enables certain groups in society to more easily dominate other groups by regarding them as marginal or on the outside.

Freire also envisions knowing not merely as an individual process, but as a social, collective process. According to his theory, education needs to be a series of conscious acts in which educational content can be analyzed and understood by both the teacher and student, thus overcoming the conflict, or dichotomy, that exists between the two parties and their epistemologies. Freire's pedagogy calls for the transformational relationship between teacher and student to be accompanied by collective consciousness-raising that taps personal and communal situations and daily lives to provide powerful knowing processes and growth.

In Freire's view, it is not necessary to reference exotic spaces in order to generate opportunities for study; instead, topics for learning can be found in the reality that surrounds oppressed groups. In using such resources, the epistemological curiosity and interest of the oppressed will allow them to construct their own knowledge using their lived experiences. In other words, Freire proposes a powerful bottom-up approach to education that starts with the knowledge produced by students and teachers through the examination of their immediate conditions of existence.

R. W. Connell, in *Schools and Social Justice* (1993), further develops critical theories and perspectives for education of socially and culturally disadvantaged students.[12] Connell's arguments regarding curricular organization, presentation, and assessment suggest that the very process of formalized schooling creates the potential for broad social consequences that are, in the end, divisive. Connell contends that once social divisions are well established in society and schools (through numerous other mechanisms aside from the process of schooling), then "academic splitting" drives a wedge between work deemed "academic" and work that is seen as practical or vocational. He states:

> The latter (learning that occurs in an engineering shop, a bakery, or a steno pool) comes to be treated as a subordinated or inferior kind of curriculum, associated with the education of subordinated social classes. (1993, p. 33)

Connell argues for counter-hegemonic curriculum making. As he puts it, "the position of those who carry the burdens of social inequality" serves as "a better starting-point" for the construction of knowledge about society than "the position of those who enjoy its advantages" (p. 39). "At its simplest," he argues, the standpoint(s) of the socially subordinate "[yield] experiences and information not normally available to the dominant groups, and therefore overlooked or marginalized in their constructions of knowledge" (p. 39). In other words, the traditional mainstream curriculum excludes the knowledge of the socially subordinate groups, whereas a counter-hegemonic curriculum inverting hegemony brings out that knowledge. In Connell's view, the latter is at least better than the former in being "more comprehensive, truer to life 'as it really happened'" (p. 40). For example, a school history curriculum that includes histories of socially subordinate groups (e.g., ordinary people and women) is more comprehensive than the traditional school history curriculum centering on the deeds of famous men.

Connell points to the assembly and dispersal of curricula that appropriate "bits of hierarchically-organized abstract knowledge" as being intricately linked to schisms between social classes within society and in schools (1993, p. 34). Couple such curricula with forms of assessment that are exclusively measured through individualized and competitive testing, and the resulting "hegemonic curriculum . . . helps generate and reinforce class hierarchy in society as a whole" (p. 34). Although Connell discusses this point in terms of social class, his theory of building a counter-hegemonic curriculum can be applied to other socially subordinate groups (Nozaki, 2006), including, we argue, the rural population in Kenya.

Possibilities of Critical Educational Studies and Practices in Kenya

As we have discussed, the Kenyan government exerts significant, unitary control over education in general, and natural science education in particular, in classrooms across the nation. While the state creates a uniform education for students, neoliberal economic policies transcend international boundaries and processes associated with globalization in the current era appear to widen the rural-urban divisions. In this context, an examination of educational practices that take place in Kenyan schools and classrooms becomes important to the nation's sustainable future.

Critical educational theories problematize the relationships between and among the knowledge sanctioned for, or taught in, natural science education in schools, the standpoints and epistemologies of the teachers, and those of the students in

20

Kenya. These theories present a paradigm of educational research to assist in the exploration of the social and economic elements of educational action in natural science classrooms in rural and urban Kenya. Critical educational theories offer a framework for conceptualizing an education for all Kenyan students, leading to a more transformative and sustainable society. And envisioning such an education requires research that generates critical and empirical insights into system- and school-level education policy and practices and the nature of natural science education itself. Such insights—while often opaque at best—must seek to clarify the processes through which natural science syllabi are constructed, how individuals or groups are charged with the organization and content of syllabi, and how formal natural science syllabi treat the knowledge and practices of individuals and groups that are often seen as marginalized.

For example, practical, indigenous knowledge about nature, the environment, and sustainability may be seen by dominant groups as belonging to members of a lower-class, or subordinate group—e.g., those residing in rural areas—and thus unworthy of inclusion in the formal curriculum. The critical point here is that educational research must examine whether the curricular content taught in schools and the knowledge gained through out-of-school contexts are tagged to specific groups who, through their ascent or stagnation in the educational system, are separated into social strata.

As Apple (e.g., 1995) also reminds us, school knowledge and curriculum in their stated and practiced forms cannot be considered neutral. On the contrary, knowledge that is deemed legitimate results from complex power relations and struggles among identifiable groups in society. Hence, following Apple, a series of questions can be raised to explore, including: Whose individual or societal goals are represented by the stated objectives for natural science education? Whose interests are being met through the current content and form of natural science education in Kenya? Is it the interests of students? Is it the interests of a particular segment of Kenyan society (e.g., those who live in urban areas) and are in positions whereby they can form policy and draft syllabi? Or, are both of these groups' (or others') interests being met?

Critical theories in education also provide guiding principles for ways to (re)organize the curriculum and pedagogy of Kenyan natural science education and put them into practice.[13] For example, Freire insists that critical communal knowledge and local understandings—or what we may call "indigenous knowledge"—are essential to the education of the oppressed. Gadotti relates Freire's position on mathematics and natural science education. As Freire states:

> What is called today surveying the local environment should also be made by the pupils, with the help of their teachers. I can't see how mathematics can fail to be taught by examining the environment. I can't see how biology and natural sciences can fail to be taught by observing the environment. (Gadotti, 1994, p. 117)

Connell (1993) suggests that curriculum making should be undertaken using the "inverting hegemony" approach, which "seeks a way of organizing content and method that builds on the experience of the disadvantaged, but generalizes that to the whole system, rather than confining it to an enclave" (p. 38). According to this strategy, utilization of the experiences and knowledge of the subordinate (e.g., rural students in Kenya and the practitioners of indigenous knowledge) will provide a path toward the reconstruction of curriculum and pedagogy in schools, including natural science education. Through such a reconstruction, the socially and culturally disadvantaged students would not be granted advantages; instead, this process would initiate grassroots approaches toward the epistemological transformation of curriculum and pedagogy that would benefit all students.

There are, however, some issues that merit further consideration. First, critical educational theories, challenging the vertical dialogue of society's elite and the relationship between the knowledge of the dominant and that of the subordinate, use examples and references drawn from specific cultural and scholarly contexts. For example, Freire's theory suggests that it is possible to reconstruct natural science education of Kenyan secondary school students based on the knowledge and skills the students acquire in their local communities. It is still an open question to what extent the aspects of Freire's theory—or other critical analyses for that matter— translate to the situations surrounding Kenyan state control of curricular content, pedagogical practice, and the image of indigenous knowledge that we uncover in agriculture, biology, and geography in both rural and urban classrooms.

Second, and perhaps more problematic, is the retention, however nuanced, of epistemological dichotomization between the oppressor and the oppressed, or the colonizer and the colonized. Freire's replacement of oppressive education with education that is liberating begins with a critical theory of knowledge that is seeded with the interests of the oppressed and grants them the opportunity to reorder their knowledge and therefore acquire new knowledge. Such substitution is also clear in Connell's arguments for the liberating and socially-empowering nature of counter-hegemonic curriculum making and implementation. In this picture, the knowledge of the oppressor, or that of the socially subordinate, is seen as more coherent than it actually is. Two bodies of knowledge are represented as mutually exclusive categories.

However, the critical theories in education discussed above do not seem to direct adequate attention to the dilemmas and contradictions—or, say, "epistemological tensions"—that exist within the experiences and knowledge of the socially and culturally subordinate (Nozaki, 2006). This is not to suggest that it is unimportant to ask whose knowledge is—and should be—taught in schools; however, it is to question if a dichotomy lurks in that question; if so, such a question can be misleading. Postcolonial perspectives, by making us aware of heterogeneity, hybridity, inauthenticity, and incoherence of histories, cultures, and experiences of the colonized (e.g., Bhabha, 1994; Said, 1979, 1993), urge us to critically examine the dichotomy. In order to propose the future of natural science education in diverse school settings, it seems essential to examine the interplay of these issues and tensions and how students and teachers in science classrooms talk about them.

Note that the dichotomization of knowledge also can exist between separate classifications of knowledge, such as Western scientific knowledge and indigenous knowledge. This particular rift is vital to the discussion of natural science education in Kenya (and elsewhere by implication). Below, we closely examine the notions of Western scientific knowledge and several important notions of non-Western knowledge, since the focus of this volume is the epistemological tensions between, and dichotomization of, the two kinds of knowledge in the context of Kenyan secondary schools. By investigating these tensions, we seek to unearth their manifestations in policy documents, school curricula and pedagogies, and the voices of teachers and students in regard to natural science education.[14]

WESTERN SCIENCE, COLONIAL POWER, AND INDIGENOUS KNOWLEDGE

Western Scientific Knowledge and Colonial Power

Over the past thirty years, discussions on the formation of (Western) science disciplines have proliferated in the anthropological, educational, and international development literature. Although reviewing this literature in its entirety is beyond the scope of the present study, it is helpful to discuss prevailing conceptions of Western scientific knowledge and how research regarding science education in developing countries interacts with critical discussions of knowledge, power, and the subordination, or colonization, of non-Western peoples.

Park and Daston (2006) trace the history of the Aristotelian framework and its influence on the rise of mechanical philosophies, natural philosophies, and the Newtonian experience and summarize the significant advances in what is often termed "scientific knowledge" during the scientific revolution of the Sixteenth and Seventeenth Centuries. Other studies explore the histories of particular disciplines during the early stages of the scientific revolution, such as medicine (e.g., Siraisi, 2007). These works provide a foundational understanding of the scientific knowledge that shaped the development of Western civilization.

Western scientific knowledge is described as the product of centuries-old traditions of analytical thought emphasizing literate, didactic communication and an objective, reductionist view of natural phenomena and processes (Sillitoe, 2002). The production of such knowledge is argued to be "self-contained, self-sustaining, handy, convenient, and even tinged with a sense of righteousness" (Rains, 1999, p. 317). Furthermore, the development of Western knowledge is thought to occur more or less independently of the ongoing production of more contextually specific types of knowledge of local, non-Western people (Maurial, 1999).[15] Through its insular production, authoritative claims, and positivistic foundations, Western scientific knowledge positions locally-, culturally-, and environmentally-bound knowledge of non-Western people and communities as substantively and functionally inferior.[16]

Several studies in Kenya (e.g., Lillis & Lowe, 1987; Merryfield, 1986) that specifically tackle the topic of Western knowledge's influence on educational content and practice in schools do not concentrate on kinds of knowledge in natural science per se. Researchers also associate the predominance of generalized Western perspectives in schools with numerous characteristics of the education system itself, such as variable enrollment rates (e.g., Buchmann, 2000) and diminished participation by girls (e.g., Ndunda & Munby, 1991).

In recent years, relations between the concepts and principles that are represented in formal science education curricula in schools—which may be termed "school science"[17]—and Western scientific knowledge have been explored in great detail, with numerous analyses concentrating on science education in developing nations (e.g., Agrawal, 1995; Cobern & Loving, 2001; George, 1999). Analyses of Western science and schooling in the context of the developing world typically evoke discussions regarding the role schools played when large swaths of Central and South America, Africa, and Asia were colonized by European powers. In particular, critical studies such as Linda Tuhiwai Smith's (1999) help to uncover the ways that various Western disciplines, transmitted through the formal colonial system of schooling, not only subvert existing knowledge systems of the colonized but also serve to assimilate their cultural practices and languages into the colonial system.

Smith (1999) argues that the colonized nations must "de-colonize" the ways—"methodologies" in her words—they produce knowledge in order to become truly liberated. But how should we conceptualize and define such knowledge produced and used locally—especially in a country such as Kenya?

Primitive, Local, and Indigenous Knowledge

Questions regarding the delineation of specific kinds of knowledge and the means by which such kinds of knowledge are produced have been deliberated for centuries. During the second half of the twentieth century, numerous debates addressed, among other topics, the epistemological differences between Western scientific knowledge and its alternatives. To discuss all the nuances of every epistemological debate is not our intention here; however, we would like to examine three major conceptions that emerge from such debates—"primitive," "local," and "indigenous."

The Savage Mind (Levi-Strauss, 1966) juxtaposes the knowledge systems of so-called "primitive" and modern cultures by suggesting that primitive societies are more intimately bound with their environments and surroundings than modern societies are. Levi-Strauss' usage of the term "primitive" is not synonymous with inferior or backwards. On the contrary, the kinds of knowledge these societies generate and employ are advanced and valuable in their situated contexts. Yet, as he sees it, the epistemological foundations of such kinds of knowledge are complicated by the associations between primitive knowledge and magical thought (p. 11). Through his theoretical comparison of the "bricoleur" (handyman or craftsman) and engineer, Levi-Strauss deliberates the nature of understanding and knowledge between the "savage mind" and the scientific mind. He posits that the knowledge constructed by the savage mind in primitive cultures is not easily detached from its context, but instead is given form and order mainly in accordance with the needs of the culture.

The Savage Mind legitimates primitive knowledge, positioning it as an independent, developed system of knowledge. Primitive knowledge is different from Western knowledge, but is equally valuable and worthy of consideration. The position here is a foundational and formative theoretical move to relativize Western and primitive knowledge systems. *The Savage Mind* has made enormous contributions to the field of anthropology (and other academic fields such as literature, sociology, political sciences, and education) and inspired numerous studies by focusing specifically on the separation of Western and non-Western knowledge systems. For example, Berkes (1993) provides detailed distinctions between ecological knowledge held by native people (in his words, "traditional knowledge") and (Western) scientific ecological knowledge. Similarly, Maurial (1999) argues that non-Western people's knowledge exists in everyday cultural practices, unlike the archived, tested, and manipulated disciplinary knowledge of the West.

Levi-Strauss' arguments concerning the nature of knowledge produced and used by native people are followed by a series of analyses that explore how such knowledge systems are culturally bound and contextually constructed and reconstructed. For example, Geertz (1983) refers to it as "local knowledge" to argue for the need to draw upon the knowledge, beliefs, and ideas of a local culture when exploring its contextual practices. According to Geertz:

> [T]he shapes of knowledge are always ineluctably local, indivisible from their instruments and their encasements. One may veil this fact with ecumenical rhetoric or blur it with strenuous theory, but one cannot really make it go away. (p. 4)

If Geertz's assertions constitute an accurate depiction of how knowledge is constructed across different cultural contexts, then the frameworks that people use to make sense of their world and construct their knowledge are local, specific, and highly valued and entangled with local histories and experiences. These local experiences, interpretations, and interactions—with people, objects, or natural processes—thus have greater merit to these groups than associations of abstracted or detached concepts, theories, or formulas. Hence, some critics (e.g., Hobart, 1993) argue that local knowledge appears to be more about "knowing how" than "knowing that" or "knowing as," and may be more sensitive to particularities of place, occasion, and circumstance (Hobart, 1993, p. 4). Moreover, individuals and communities can perform certain practices without actually knowing the science that underlies or explains the practices.

For Geertz, universalist judgments and dense analyses of local knowledge cannot dislodge the local, situated nature of local knowledge and their importance to those who develop and use them. Note that he made his argument in the context of anthropology in which Western scholars conduct research on non-Western cultures. Yet, in examining the origins, assembly, practice, and valuation of local knowledge and specific populations existing in a particular space and time, Geertz's theorizing leads us to ask: Can we apply discussions about local knowledge to numerous contexts such as schools and communities in the West? Are deliberations regarding local knowledge in one culture even transferrable to another? Is the notion of local knowledge keen enough to point to the nexus of knowledge and colonial power?

"Indigenous knowledge" is another term that is prevalent in contemporary anthropological, sociological, and educational literature which refers to contextualized, situated, or experience-informed knowledge of native people (e.g., Bollig, 1999; Ogunniyi & Ogawa, 2008)—and is perhaps the best term to refer to such knowledge held by Kenyan people locally. Definitions of indigenous knowledge, in broad terms, often incorporate notions of groups of peoples creating knowledge-producing systems based on historical and cultural understandings of themselves in relation to their bio-physical surroundings for the purposes of long-term human adaptation (Purcell, 1998, p. 260) and the enhancement of their livelihood and existence (Semali & Kincheloe, 1999, p. 3). In other words, the nature of indigenous knowledge is more dynamic than is often assumed or acknowledged.

In recent years, indigenous knowledge has been associated with national or regional populations in postcolonial and less developed countries (e.g., Kassam, 2002; Whitt, 2009). However, as Purcell (1998) notes, the notion of indigenous knowledge can be (and has been) expanded to encompass "territorially non-indigenous communities and nations acting on their own behalf, in accordance with the dictates of their own history and political culture" (p. 260). Using this perspective, the notion of indigenous knowledge can be used beyond so- called "indigenous peoples" and instead can be more functionally tied to humans' interactions with their surroundings and their social, political, economic, ideological, and religious practices. In this sense, it becomes similar to the notion of local knowledge as offered by Geertz (1983); however, the term evokes more political and critical meanings because of its origins in colonial and postcolonial struggles, which, indeed, fits into Kenyan contexts well.

Research on Indigenous Knowledge

The existence of indigenous knowledge systems, including locally-informed and contextually-appropriate ways of knowing, is well documented and established through the work of Brokensha, Warren, and Werner (1980), Hess (1995), and Sillitoe (1998). This topic is moderately dispersed through anthropological literature and predominantly focuses on the use of indigenous knowledge in science-related livelihood activities, such as agriculture (e.g., Dewalt, 1994), medicine (e.g., Sindiga, 1994), and nutrition (e.g., Mwadime, 1999). Deliberations of indigenous knowledge are also included in other bodies of literature, including educational studies (e.g., Kubow, 2007) and sociology (e.g., Gair, Miles, & Thomson, 2005).

Numerous publications consider historical and contemporary issues concerning indigenous knowledge in Africa. Harries' (2007) book is a wide-ranging account of how European intellectuals categorized local African knowledge and how local Africans, in turn, incorporated foreign epistemologies and practices into their societies during the early colonial period. Falola's (2000) text also investigates bodies of indigenous knowledge, and, like a number of other works, does so by tapping into locally-constructed narratives by adults and elders regarding African history and historical knowledge. Marchand and Kresse's (2009) edited publication includes a variety of perspectives examining practical applications of accumulated knowledge in Sub-Saharan Africa using examples from traditional healers, community leaders, and artisans. Although historical accounts like Harries' research (2007) thoroughly document the subjugation of peoples (and kinds of knowledge they held) during the colonization of the African continent, many volumes that trace the intersections of indigenous and Western cultures do little to dispel or interrupt the dichotomization of these epistemologies.

In the field of Kenyan studies, scholarly investigations of indigenous knowledge, although relatively few in number, yield thoughtful debates concerning various theoretical and practical issues surrounding the usage and maintenance of such ways of knowing and their applicability in diverse contexts. In most of these analyses, investigators focus on the indigenous knowledge of adults and typically confine their scope to specific geographies or ethnicities. Wane and Chandler's (2002) work typifies this limited body of research. Through their exploration of the indigenous and cultural environmental knowledge of rural adult women in a specific location, they contend that such contextual knowledge, while complex and localized, can and should be used as an untapped resource for the broader teaching of environmental concepts within Kenyan society.[18] In their view, indigenous knowledge can provide alternative, even oppositional, sets of knowledge to the Western scientific knowledge.

Some studies focus on the interactions of indigenous and Western knowledge systems in Kenyan contexts. These inquiries predominantly address two themes: the use of indigenous knowledge in modern agricultural-related activities and natural resource management (e.g., Wane & Chandler, 2002; Watson, Adams, & Mutiso, 1998) and indigenous botanical or herbal knowledge usage in the treatment and prevention of disease (e.g., Munguti, 1997; Sindiga, 1994).

Other studies examine practical issues surrounding the co-existing or complementary relationships of Western scientific and indigenous knowledge systems in practical contexts in Kenya and Africa. For example, Sibisi (2004) highlights examples from agricultural practices and healthcare initiatives in Africa that illustrate the richness of indigenous knowledge systems and their contributions to science and technology. O'Donoghue (2003) describes how game rangers in South Africa's Umfolozi Game Reserve utilize both the practical experiences of indigenous game guards and university-based ecological training to establish management practices for the fledgling reserve. In O'Donoghue's (2003) example, the interplay between the Nguni (indigenous) "knowledge of the interconnected ways of the wild and game ranger scientist as interpretive mobilizer of ecological patterns that connect" help to create mutually enriching interactions for the reserve's first game guards and rangers (p. 62).

In the field of educational research, Ogunniyi and Ogawa (2008) review bold attempts to reflect elements of indigenous knowledge in science classrooms in South Africa and Japan and discuss the challenges in the development and implementation of indigenized science curricula in both countries. Ogunniyi and Hewson (2008) analyze a teacher-training course in South African that seeks to enhance their understanding of indigenous knowledge systems (IKS) and improve their ability to integrate IKS into their science classrooms.[19]

Studies that specifically address the potential use of indigenous knowledge in Kenyan schools are extremely limited. Gitari's (2003) research focuses on the theoretical compatibility of indigenous knowledge and science education, but is limited to the particular topic of health and healing, which is addressed in the form four biology syllabus. Her study, while helpful in interrogating the disparities between school offerings and everyday offerings regarding this topic, overlooks input from students and teachers regarding these epistemologies.

Kithinji's study (2000), which focuses on views concerning health and healing through an analysis of retrospective accounts of formal science instruction from adults (mostly women) in Kenya's Meru District, specifically suggests the integration of the non-Western knowledge produced and circulated among Kenyans into the secondary science curriculum. By using these and other sources, the study recounts how school science becomes the definitive knowledge of human health in Kenya, supplanting indigenous ways of healing which encompass an individual's physical, spiritual, social, and emotional dimensions of life. Kithinji's research demonstrates how externally-developed, Eurocentric changes to secondary science education fail to produce significant improvements in existing life conditions in Kenya.[20] In her conclusion, she suggests that the secondary science curriculum "must aim to give adequate attention to the principles and processes that are used in everyday problem solving in rural areas" (p.250).

The academic works reviewed above have advanced the debates concerning the role of indigenous knowledge in the natural science education of youth in Kenya, as well as other African countries, by exploring ways of supplementing current science curricula with indigenous perspectives (e.g., Gitari, 2003; Kithinji, 2000; Ogunniyi & Ogawa, 2008). Indeed, their scholarly contributions go beyond the boundaries of education research, since the subject of Western scientific knowledge and indigenous knowledge is now woven through conversations and arguments of various scholarly fields that span the spectrum of anthropological and sociological thought and analysis. A question arises, however, from the perspectives of postcolonial theories (e.g. Said, 1979): While enormously helpful to rethink natural science education in Kenya and, by implication, elsewhere, do the studies discussed above reify, consciously or unconsciously, the binary of Western scientific knowledge and indigenous knowledge? In this binary, Western scientific knowledge is viewed, rightly or wrongly, as authoritative (and reductionist) and indigenous knowledge is suggested as the (oppositional) alternative.

In other words, one may wonder if, in their arguments, many studies reviewed above adopt theoretical positions that tend to dichotomize Western scientific knowledge and indigenous knowledge. Is the binary of Western versus indigenous the only perspective that can be employed when discussing the relationships and roles of these epistemologies? How can we overcome the dichotomy of indigenous and Western knowledge systems? To what extent do critical theories in education, such as those offered by Freire and Connell, help us transcend the binary of the two epistemologies prevalent in natural science education in Kenya? How can we develop a discussion of curriculum theories that provides a framework for linking (as opposed to adding to or substituting) Western scientific knowledge and indigenous knowledge?

It is important to note that there also seems to be a vacuum in educational research on the subject of the dichotomization of the indigenous and Western bodies of knowledge. In particular, scant empirical attention has been paid to the perspectives of youth and their teachers concerning their views on, and experiences with, the two systems of knowledge discussed above. To be sure, the dichotomy between Western scientific knowledge and indigenous knowledge has been, to some extent, questioned in anthropological and educational debates for decades; however, the focus of much of the literature on this topic is theoretical in nature. It is here that we argue that there is considerable merit in the (re)conceptualization of bottom-up approaches to natural science education and the exploration—with a critical lens—of students' and teachers' interaction with, and perceptions of, Western scientific knowledge and/or indigenous knowledge.

The investigation of student and teacher interactions with, and perspectives on, indigenous knowledge—when viewed with a critical lens—can yield a reconceptualization of natural science education in Kenya (and beyond). Such exploration involves a series of essential questions: What are students' and teachers' views on indigenous knowledge? How do individuals within these groups articulate the relationship between indigenous knowledge and knowledge taught through formal schooling? Do discussions of indigenous knowledge within the context of specific subjects, such as those in natural science education, create enhanced possibilities for framing the interactions with or of indigenous knowledge and school knowledge? Do individuals from different socioeconomic groups and different geographic locations such as those located in rural or urban areas have similar or different perspectives of indigenous knowledge and those practicing such knowledge?

With these (and other related) questions in mind, it is worthwhile to examine the relationship between indigenous knowledge and school curriculum of a specific subject or group of related subjects in diverse locations within a particular country, such as Kenya. In the next chapter, we detail the historical development of formal schooling in Kenya and discuss the strong role of the state in the natural science education of secondary students in modern Kenya.

NOTES

[1] For example, Lawson (1985) reviews the research on science education to explore the role of formal reasoning in the teaching of science, while Bowen (1992) analyzes the predominant themes in science education literature to examine the usage of scientific practices in solving educational problems (e.g., questions about curricular content or instructional practices). Critical questions can be raised regarding the entanglement of indigenous and Western knowledge and their (co)production, representations, engagement, and usage. For example, Bang and Medin (2010) question the lack of cultural orientation of education in science, technology, engineering, and mathematics (STEM), and Jegede and Aikenhead (1999) examine contemporary goals of science education through cognitive understanding of the cross-cultural experiences students encounter. While we must acknowledge the importance of understanding how students come to know such knowledge, how they construct it, or how they store and access it, the present study focuses on the ways in which students view and conceptualize indigenous and Western systems of science knowledge vis-à-vis their formal schooling in agricultural, biological, and geographical sciences.

[2] There is a substantial body of scholarly work that investigates various topics surrounding science education in other Western contexts, such as Lithuanian teens' attitudes towards species protection (e.g., Lamanauskas, Gailien, & Vilkonis, 2006), the work of environmental non-governmental organizations in education initiatives in southeastern Europe (e.g., Turnock, 2004), and innovations in science education that target stale pedagogies and disengaged teachers (e.g., Willingale-Theune, Manaia, Gebhardt, De Lorenzi, & Haury, 2009). Despite this excellent body of work, we highlight critical analyses of science education in the United States not only because of their theoretical perspectives, but also due to their utility in drawing parallels between the perceived incompatibilities of science education for some (mostly urban) students in the United States and the similar incompatibilities that were observed in Kenya.

[3] The body of literature that focuses on "science education" is voluminous given the differentiation of sciences into broad categories (such as natural, physical, or social) and individual disciplines (such as biology, chemistry, or geology). However, it is important to note that researchers have investigated myriad policy and practical issues in relation to science subjects, such as physics and chemistry, in numerous national contexts, such as England (e.g., Franco & Taber, 2009), Spain (e.g., Solbes & Traver, 2003), and the Czech Republic (e.g., Škoda & Doulik, 2007).

[4] To be sure, a number of notable studies have also examined conflict in education in African contexts, however not specifically between state and local entities or actors. Some of these studies have addressed, critically or otherwise, points of contention related to issues of colonization, decolonization, and Western influence upon, or westernization of, education. For example, Ottevanger, Akker, and Feiter (2007) examine a group of academic disciplines, namely science, mathematics, and information and communication technology (ICT) in secondary schools located in ten Sub-Saharan African countries. Bassey's (1999) book investigates the ways that Western education has been used by Africa's political and economic elite to marginalize and dominate Africa's poor. While both of these publications offer in-depth critiques and critical analyses of education in various African contexts, they do so broadly, focusing on multiple disciplines in national education systems and wider social processes, such as socialization and the accumulation of political and economic capital.

[5] Sanders and Ngxola (2009) note that, prior to 1994, South Africa's government implemented a Christian National Education policy that disallowed the teaching of subjects that were viewed as either anti-Christian or unchristian. Such a national policy could have produced a generation of teachers that now struggle to reconcile their Christian-influenced upbringing and education with the evolutionary principles that they are required to teach (a conflict that, these authors suggest, is fed by misconceptions between the two and the portrayal of evolution and religion as being mutually-exclusive). In fact, these authors note that many of their study's participants would skip or omit

entire sections dealing with genetics or evolution; this behavior was not only due to their personal beliefs about evolution, but also their lack of understanding of the topics prior to (and after) the implementation of the new curriculum and their uncertainty about how to teach the topics. Griffith and Brem (2004) and Downie and Barron (2000) also address issues and controversies surrounding the teaching of evolution in the United States and Scotland, respectively.

[6] As we see it, this position suggests that science education curricula be made from broader, critical perspectives of societal transformations, rather than its knowledge and skills being offered simply as technical tools for economic success of the nation and individuals. Furthermore, such critical science education curricula should be offered to all students. As such, this position is, indeed, close to the notion of science education for sustainability, as both attempt to deal with such issues as equality, justice, and peace. It is interesting (and important) to realize the recent shift of language here from "transformation" to "sustainability."

[7] Buxton (2006) refers to contextually authentic science as approaches to science that begin with the interests and needs of learners and seek to discover "ways that science learning can be taken up and negotiated within and against the canonical world of science, but rarely within the setting of school science" (p. 702). In using such an inclusive approach, science instruction can de-center the "expert" paradigms that characterize canonically authentic science and provide learning in science that is collaboratively constructed and uniformly stresses "both the relevant science learning experiences themselves and the social issues/actions that are embedded in those science experiences" (p. 719).

[8] "Culturally relevant or responsive pedagogy" has been one of the key theories of multiculturalist education for some time (e.g., Ladson-Billings, 2009), and the studies discussed here suggest that the theory applies to science education also. For a useful and concise review of the theory, see Sleeter and Cornbleth (2011, pp. 2-5).

[9] In Gilbert's (2002) research, he defines indigenous science as "a philosophical orientation of science knowledge which values responsibility, care, and respect concerning the rights of all living things, the earth, the universe, and all matter within it" (p. 21). He continues: "My use of this term represents an effort to broaden the notion of what science should be as opposed to what has been accepted and forwarded by western mindsets" (p. 21).

[10] The studies referred to in this section typify many of the science education-related analyses, in that they tend to concentrate on specific aspects of science education, such as achievement, attainment, or teaching practices, in or with individual communities. Broader investigations of science education in the United States and elsewhere that use a critical perspective are scarce; however, notable exceptions are Kincheloe (1997), Kincheloe (2001), and Lee and Luykx (2006).

[11] It is critically important to consider the ways that science education connects not only with students' lives outside classrooms, but also with different groups of students themselves. Research that investigates the ways that formal, curricular-based science knowledge contributes to the positioning of individuals from different backgrounds, locations, and ethnicities into socioeconomic groupings in Kenya needs to be one of the important foci of future studies. Many thanks to Lois Weis and Robert Stevenson for their comments on this point.

[12] For a more thorough analysis of Connell's work as it relates to the nexus of curricula development and power, knowledge, and ideology, see Nozaki's (2006) chapter in Weis, McCarthy, and Dimitriadis' (2006) edited volume.

[13] Another perspective used to evaluate the nature of natural science education in rural and urban Kenyan secondary schools is derived from Michael Apple's (1995, 2000) critical work on relationships between knowledge, power, and society. From Apple's perspective, the knowledge of a subject that is deemed of the most worth or legitimacy is the official knowledge that is embodied in the formal curriculum of that subject. In the exploration of official knowledge, one may reveal not only the types of knowledge that find their way into curricula and schools, but also the processes through which knowledge and values are legitimated by individuals or groups in positions of power in society. Through the definition, legitimization, and dissemination of this knowledge by the social and economic elite, societal inequality can be maintained. In the Kenyan context, the predominance of knowledge aligned with the Western scientific tradition in the agriculture, biology, and geography curricula raises questions concerning the ascension and marginalization of certain types of knowledge and the power granted to specific groups to select school knowledge.

[14] This chapter examines the bodies of knowledge that are most commonly referred to as "indigenous" knowledge. As demonstrated during the course of the literature review, various names have been used to address various types of knowledge, including "primitive," "local," and "non-Western." For the purposes of theoretical clarity, this volume uses the term indigenous, as it is the most popular term used to refer to such knowledge in the literature. It should be noted, however, that the term "traditional knowledge" was used in the data collection (i.e., interviews and discussions primarily with rural and urban students) in order to tack such knowledge to the practices and traditions of elders in their families and the community. Yet, for the remainder of the present study, the term indigenous is used when discussing this kind of knowledge.

[15] The concept of indigenous knowledge will be discussed later in this chapter.

[16] "Western science" is actually the product of knowledge contributions from many non-Western cultures (see Bernal [1987] and Turnbull [1997]). le Grange (2008) argued that by considering all kinds of knowledge to be local in nature, Western science is de-centered and, therefore, more conceptually comparable to indigenous knowledge. In leveling the two epistemologies, Western science's claims of objectivity, rationality, and universality are weakened (p. 819).

[17] The term "school science" is coined based upon Whitty's (1985) notion of "school knowledge," which he refers to as a selection of knowledge that is carved "from a much vaster range of knowledge" (p. 1). Accordingly, in this volume, the term is used to connote the natural science knowledge that is bound by the Kenyan national curriculum and that does not account for indigenous knowledge or indigenous natural science.

[18] Kithinji (2000) and Gitari (2003) make similar arguments regarding the potential benefits of increased access and acceptance of indigenous knowledge, but also attempt to link the indigenous knowledge of a specific topic (health and healing) to the teaching of the topic in schools.

[19] According to Ogunniyi and Ogawa (2008), Indigenous Knowledge Systems (IKS) refers to "a conglomeration of knowledge systems" that is "a redemptive, holistic, and transcendental view of human experience with the cosmos" (p. 178).

[20] Gitari's (2003) research findings were similar to Kithinji's (2000) analysis. In essence, both researchers argued that the formal curriculum in health and healing did not incorporate indigenous concepts that, according to these authors, were vital to the health maintenance of the rural communities where their research occurred.

METHODS AND METHODOLOGY

Multi-Sited Ethnographic Study

Qualitative research examines local, contextualized settings in order to understand lager, macro social phenomenon (e.g., Neuman, 2006). No doubt critical educational studies, by employing qualitative, including ethnographic, methods and methodologies, have strived for gaining such understandings of micro-macro linkages and offered strong empirical and theoretical insights into social and cultural dynamics operating in and through everyday practices (e.g., Willis, 1981; Weis, 1990, 2004: McNeil, 1988, 2000; Pedroni, 2007). The tradition of critical educational studies, however, has seldom examined natural science knowledge, or views on such knowledge, taught and circulated in schools and communities. This is unfortunate, to say the least, since conducting research on natural science education and its policies and practices has become enormously important, as our societies are more and more depending on scientific and technological innovation, knowledge, and skills.

Qualitative research allows us to examine—both closely and critically—complexities of local struggles over natural science education and the policies and practices of sustainable development in the context of larger struggles. The sciences, broadly defined, have been linked to national (and now global) development initiatives for decades (Jegede, 1997) and have received considerable attention at conferences (such as the World Conference on Science, held in Budapest, Hungary in 1999) and from organizations such as UNESCO (Holbrook, 2009). In recent years, natural science education offered in schools and educational institutions have increasingly become arenas in which global, regional, national, and local forces struggle. At the heart of local conflicts over particular development and sustainability initiatives often lie challenges and contradictions of natural science education, since any such education disseminates particular bodies of knowledge through formal and informal curricula inside schools and in communities.

Qualitative research methods and methodologies in the field of critical educational studies have met new challenges of globalization, however. How should we examine micro-macro linkages in the era of globalization without succumbing to a quick assertion that everything local is global? In (re)considering qualitative method in a period of shifting times from a critical perspective, Weis, Fine, and Dimitriadis (2009) recognize the need to re-conceptualize the methods and methodologies. As they put it, "[t]he increasingly interconnected world . . . demands a fresh [research] imaginary, one that enables/encourages us to capture the rippling effects of actions in one place as they impact on another" (437-438). One of research designs of their interest is multi-sited ethnographic work. They contend:

> [M]ultisited ethnographic work—even work focused on a single, strategically selected locale—challenges us to rethink fundamentally our "research imaginary" in ways that push the borders and the interior complexity of the home-school-economy nexus. "Demographics" such as class, gender, immigration status, and so forth are theorized as vibrant embodied practices, and social movements and popular culture are theorized as electrified rhizomes of knowledge, resistance, and culture. (p. 443)

Multi-sited, ethnographic research design is not just powerful tool to capture rippling effects from one place to another. The research design allows researchers to conduct a study from postcolonial perspectives effectively. Although it is possible to take postcolonial perspectives to conduct research at only one site, having multiple sites gives researchers good opportunities to examine local contexts and actions comparatively and help them come up with explanations keen to hybridity, ambiguity, heterogeneity, adversarial opposition, variation, contradiction, tension, or inauthenticity that exists within a nation, culture, society, or curriculum making (Nozaki, 2006, 2009). By this research design, critical educational studies can fully appreciate and take advantages from postcolonial perspectives.

For example, postcolonial perspectives ask researchers to overcome binary representations of culture and knowledge systems. Efforts to bolster the uniqueness and appropriateness of indigenous or local knowledge (through oral dissemination or extraordinary reports in popular media) in the past might have actually helped marginalize indigenous epistemologies further, as ordinary citizens (e.g., Kenyans with access to media outlets) frame judgments regarding these kinds of knowledge through the prevailing (and dominant) terms of modernity, development, and progress. The past research efforts might have invoked racist, classist, tribal, or geo-spatial viewpoints that subjugate non-Western knowledge as inferior and non-Western peoples as backwards, undeveloped, and unmotivated for social, economic, and political improvement.

To be sure, binary representations can sometimes be used strategically to the benefit of groups that live beyond the centers of power within society. For example, in the contexts of resistance and independence struggles in colonial countries, essentialized images of a nation helped forge alliances for liberation (e.g., Spivak, 1990). However, such images tend to obscure intra-group differences and often fortify the hegemonic knowledge (e.g., Western knowledge) that is promoted by the policymaking elite through the strengthening of the binary forms of knowledge and worldviews (e.g., "indigenous versus Western" knowledge) (e.g., Inokuchi & Nozaki, 2010; Muller, 2000; Nozaki, 2000, 2007, 2009; Nozaki & Inokuchi, 1998; Young, 2008). Although the debates over epistemology, curriculum, and educational policy will continue, multi-sited research design can help overcome—or at least minimize—negative effects of essentializing tendencies that segment contexts (e.g., "rural" and "indigenous") into distinct entities. Some powerful techniques for resisting or overcoming the essentializing tendencies of any binary representation include, for example, to stress the "variations, multiplicities, and contradictions" (Nozaki, 2009, p. 486) within a nation, culture, society, or place, including sites of natural science instruction in Kenya and to show "embeddedness" of dichotomized systems of knowledge (Young, 2000, p. 193).

Educational research casts an eye towards the new reality of globalization through the use of juxtaposition highlighting rural-urban disparities found multi-sited settings, which enables us to tether analyses of modern perspectives and realities concerning education to the contexts found in developing East Africa. Cumulatively, data gathered at multiple sites concerning formal science instruction, indigenous knowledge, modern education systems, and student and teacher perspectives would enable us to offer complex analysis of globalization effects upon local schools, communities, and human actions, given the dramatic shifts globalization has wrought, the increasing scarcity of elders and community leaders who still make use of indigenous knowledge, and the staggering changes in land use and land cover in local communities. Given these changes, and the widespread movements that globalization is precipitating in other contexts across the globe, multi-sited ethnographic methods and methodology are timely—and indeed vital—for future educational researchers and practitioners in the field of critical educational studies.

This is not to suggest that multi-sited ethnography is the only tool needed to advance critical postcolonial understandings of local and global linkages and struggles. It is crucial for contemporary ethnographic researchers—whether they identify themselves as critical or not—to frame what they observe, record, and ultimately analyze with an understanding of larger social and economic processes that can have subtle and complex yet noteworthy effects on views about education and the processes involved with schooling. Globalization, with its increases in the internationalization of information and knowledge (among other economic, social, and cultural forms), does not make obsolete discussions of research method that can be more finite in scope or practice. Rather, methodological debate and theorizing remains important in the global milieu, now perhaps more than ever due to explosions in connectivity and residence within shared spaces (whether real, imagined, or virtual) of similar and dissimilar populations around the world.[1]

METHODOLOGIES, RESEARCH PROCESSES, AND DESCRIBING THE METHODS

Researchers have debated over many methodological issues in general, and those concerning the validity, or generalizability, of claims made through qualitative studies in particular. Although it is extremely important to critically examine, and debate over, the (vexing) methodological issues of qualitative research, such methodological examinations and debates should not be used to keep researchers from actually conducting qualitative research. Since the methodological examinations and debates will—and should—continue, one of the most productive contributions field researchers can make is to record and report the research processes and decisions. As Bogdan and Biklen (2006, p. 116) put it, "describe what you did" rather than using the imprecise and abstract methodological terminologies.

To give a description of "what you did" is not so simple, however. For one thing, eliminating all terminologies would be impossible and might perhaps be undesirable. It is, therefore, worth trying to discuss methodologies with a description of research methods, processes, and decisions. For it allows us to explore the methodological issues not only in practical and contextual but also more meaningful and reflexive ways.

Participant Observations

Participant observation provides researchers the opportunity for developing a quality of trust with local people and places undergoing investigation, and acquiring the status of trusted person allows them to see patterns of behavior, hear voices and stories that otherwise they might not hear, and learn local meanings of words and deeds. Participant observation "ranges across a continuum" from a complete observer to a full participant (Glesne & Peshkin, 1992, p. 40). On this continuum, it seems important that researchers place themselves, following more what their "judgment tells . . . [them] is fitting" than "what is established as right" (p. 41).

Wherever researchers position themselves on the continuum, the act of conducting research using participant observation as one of the chief methods necessarily complicates the settings under study, and regardless of precautions taken to ensure the naturalness of interactions and observations, even the most un-intrusive actions influence the very phenomenon that is the focus of study (for further discussion, see also Ely, 1991). It is critical to acknowledge this intrusion and conceptualize the different dimensions of researcher role as observer/participant/interpreter of the social reality under scrutiny, while remaining focused on the ordinary life that unfolds before them (Bostis, 1988, p. 338).

For the data collection phase of the present study, O'Hern adopted a participant observer role that mirrored Wolcott's (1988, p. 194) conception of a "limited observer." By assuming such a role, he was positioned as a pseudo-outsider to Kenyan culture while observing classroom and school-based interactions and behaviors, asking questions, and establishing trust with the rural and urban communities over a period of weeks and months. It should be noted here that, as discussed below, he found himself "at different points [on the continuum] at different times in the data collection process[es]" (Glesne & Peshkin, 1992, p. 40).

The participant observation took place mostly in school compounds and classrooms, since they were crucial sites for the development of student perspectives concerning two different epistemological approaches to natural science knowledge (i.e., indigenous knowledge and Western science knowledge). Attention was particularly paid to the ways students intellectually, verbally, and physically interacted with formal natural science content in classrooms and how teachers presented the material contained in the national agriculture, biology, and geography syllabi. Student-student and student-teacher interactions outside the classes were also detailed, especially in regards to natural science issues. Although the observations took place primarily during natural science lessons, biology laboratory sections and other "non-natural science" subjects, including English, computer, and chemistry were observed. Several activities that took place outside of rural and urban classrooms, such as sporting competitions, special ceremonies, and field trips were also observed. Notes concerning these events focused on the interactions of the participants (students, teachers, and, occasionally, administrators) with the natural environment and also centered on the ways that various types of natural science knowledge were represented during activities.

At the onset of observations at the three schools, an abbreviated lesson was scheduled for an introduction of research and a general question-answer session in each class observed. The questions generated by students ranged from geographical inquiries about the United States to questions about race relations, politics, and the organizational structure of U.S. education. These discussions served to position O'Hern as an in-class resource for students and teachers in topics such as English pronunciation and geo-political relationships. As a courtesy to the instructors that had been observed and befriended, any requests for supplemental or tangential information (even if those requests meant that class was disrupted or topics were discussed that were not directly related to the content being taught) were obliged. On these occasions, and others, the working relationships that were established with teachers and students were maintained in order to make the research processes meaningful and productive.

However, maintaining the exclusive role of researcher in Kenyan secondary schools was a delicate process that was confronted on several occasions. For example, on the first official day of observations at Forest Secondary School, the upcoming research activities were announced to the entire school community during a special assembly that included remarks by the headmaster and the science teachers that were to be observed, as well as a brief welcome song performed by a group of students. This formal introduction, while culturally appropriate, immediately positioned the researcher as an outsider that required special attention. During the first weeks of fieldwork at the school, students were often reluctant to initiate conversations and spent more time examining O'Hern from afar than accepting repeated attempts at informal interactions. While the rural pupils' behavior and reactions were not entirely the result of the ceremonial introduction, the formal and public acknowledgement of the research activities perhaps manufactured some distance between O'Hern and the students.

In addition, in-class observations at the rural school (Forest Secondary) seemed to create a modest distraction to both students and teachers, despite verbal assurances to the contrary before and during the observations. Throughout lessons, students occasionally turned around in their seats to peer at O'Hern (who sat at the rear of the classroom) or would attempt to follow the notes that were scribbled in an observational notebook. Teachers also focused students' attention on the presence of the researcher by asking for topical information relating to the United States or for assistance with the English pronunciation of assorted words. These frequent interchanges not only disrupted the lesson but also defined the researcher's position in the classroom and school community as an "expert" in areas such as the English language, North American history, and global atmospheric sciences.

At Central Boys Secondary and Uhuru Girls Secondary in urban Nairobi, the presence of O'Hern in classrooms and around the school compounds was not as disquieting as it had been at Forest Secondary as urban students seemed less distractible as than their rural counterparts. This may be due, in part, to the cosmopolitan nature of Nairobi and urban dwellers' frequent exposure to individuals from diverse nationalities. The pervasiveness of satellite television, international news, and the existence of urban-based white Kenyans, coupled with the palpable presence of international organizations and foreign aid agencies, made pupils from these schools desensitized to the research activities that were undertaken at their schools. In fact, a temporary instructor from a European country was teaching foreign language classes at one of the urban institutions for the 2005 school year. Therefore, less attention was drawn from the urban adolescents that were met as a result of their social interactions with Westerners and whites on a daily basis.

It should also be noted here that frequent and consistent access to classrooms proved difficult in both rural and urban locations for a number of reasons. First, not only were individual natural science teachers at Forest Secondary responsible for instruction in their specific subject, but they also taught laboratory sections or individual classes in other subject areas, such as chemistry or commerce. The resulting teaching burden complicated the master teaching timetable for these individuals and presented challenges for arranging regular observational sessions. In the urban schools, teaching schedules were even more complex than Forest Secondary's due to the number of subjects taught at each institution and the number of instructors required to teach in each individual subject (due to enrollments). Second, observational periods in the three sites often involved the cancellation of lessons by individual teachers who had external activities or obligations to attend to. In both rural and urban environments, attempts were made to spend entire days at a single institution in order to promote consistency and visibility and perhaps increase the "naturalness" of observations. Yet, entire days occasionally became uneventful as teachers left the school premises and assigned readings or note taking for their classes. In addition, the shift in research locations to urban Nairobi from the single rural site required a split in observational time equitably between Uhuru Girls Secondary and Central Boys Secondary School.

Semi-structured, Open-ended Interviews

Ethnographers also interview the students and teachers in school. While direct observation can be considered to be the heart of field research, interviewing which must be used to provide context or meaning is a special mode of inquiry suited to the study of human beings (Schatzman & Strauss, 1973). The researchers should construct ways that would enable them to access the context and meaning they want. Qualitative interviews differ in the degree to which they are structured—they can be placed somewhere on the structured-unstructured continuum. At one end are interviews "focused around particular topics or may be guided by some general questions" to get comparable data across interviews; at the other end are "very open-ended," "free-flowing" ones that allow interviewees to define the content of the interviews and structure the topics at hand (Bogdan & Biklen, 2003, p. 96). Researchers can/should choose a type of interviews on the continuum depending on their research goals and situations.

We should note that the researchers' identities play a role in how people in the field react to them and what people tell them. Therefore, they have to think of or deal with these effects consciously. The use of interviews, whether in-depth, interactive, or structured interviews, presents both conceptual and practical issues that require careful attention. In particular, the difficulties associated with "insider-outsider" roles, which may be present in all types of interviewing, are almost always prevalent in cross-cultural interviews. As Ryen (2002) notes, in using the interview as one of the primary sources of data collection in a cross-cultural context, the interviewer attempts to engage a respondent in a discussion that illuminates their social realities. These realities, in fact, are culturally stored and independent of the interviewer-interviewee relationship. In attempting to capture and (re)present such realities, a researcher must take appropriate steps to avoid the marginalization of the interviewee (through the use of jargon and abstract concepts and representations) and to recognize the power relations that are involved in "outside" researcher-respondent interactions.

For the present study, interviews were semi-structured (see Appendix A and B for interview protocols). The interviews were conducted with sixteen students at Forest Secondary School (ten individual and three interviews with a pair of students), with seven students at Central Boys Secondary (five individual and one interview with a pair of students), and with eight students at Uhuru Girls Secondary (four individual and two interviews with a pair of students). At the three schools, both individual and group (pair in this case) interviews were instrumental in unearthing student perspectives of the natural science knowledge they interfaced with in the classroom and outside of school. The views that rural and urban adolescents harbored about their grandparents' knowledge and practices could not be observed through classroom interactions. All interviews in both rural and urban locations were conducted on school grounds, in English, after daily classes had ended, with the exception of one Form Two female from Forest Secondary, which was conducted at the student's home on a weekend. It was considered imperative to engage in semi-structured open-ended conversations with individual students or pairs of students. The pair interviews of the same sex students were used as a means to offer a more comfortable atmosphere for individuals who seemed somewhat reluctant or shy about being interviewed. For

39

the pair interviews, a space was created where peers could interact with each other as they discussed formal and indigenous natural science knowledge.

The initial list of interviewees was based upon observations in natural science classes and informal communications on school compounds during the first three weeks of fieldwork in each location. Interviews were then requested with students who exhibited some degree of comfortableness with an outsider in the midst of their school and community. These young men and women would open informal conversations before or in-between classes or in public spaces after the day had ended. Once classes had been attended and a rapport had been developed with individual instructors, the teachers were asked to recommend students from the list whom they thought would be talkative and engaging in conversations about natural science knowledge and personal experiences. By interviewing the students that had been suggested by teachers, the interview list at each school was narrowed quickly and, subsequently, an interview timetable was constructed in a short period of time. Second, as natural science teachers were enlisted to assist in the selection of student participants, the nature of the research was explicated more clearly to both instructors and potential student interviewees, thus allowing for both groups to reflect more fully on their interactions with indigenous and school natural science knowledge. It turned out that many of the students whom were eventually interviewed were the first individuals to initiate conversations after the preliminary introduction at the rural and urban institutions.

The interviews first asked the student's family background and details of their home environment and experiences with their natural surroundings. Pupils were also asked about their interactions with extended family members (particularly grandparents), their perspectives concerning the knowledge of their elders or community members, their views about their agricultural, biological, and geographical education, and their understanding and feelings about various forms of science knowledge.

Semi-structured open-ended interviews were also conducted with teachers, while numerous informal conversations were held with the teachers of natural science classes and other teachers on school compounds, and in more casual settings on weekends. The teachers interviewed taught the classes that were observed in each school: these included the agriculture, biology, and geography teachers from Forest Secondary, the biology and geography teachers from Central Boys Secondary, and the agriculture and geography teachers at Uhuru Girls Secondary. In the interviews, the teachers were asked about their schooling and training in their subject areas, their motivation for becoming a teacher in a specific field, their thoughts about the Kenyan school system, and their approaches to indigenous natural science knowledge, local practices, and contextual information usage in and out of the classroom.

During interviews with students in the three sites, discussions of indigenous natural science concepts and practices were linked to specific topics or lessons that were presented in the classroom. For example, rural students would often include conversations concerning their grandparents' views or stories about farming in the Taita Hills and, in particular, the technologies they used to improve crop yields. As students recalled such conversations and interactions, specific aspects of the stories would be tacked to agricultural principles they learned in class or used at home, such as the use of pesticides and chemical fertilizers on small-scale and commercial farms. By introducing fresh curricular content into these exchanges, pupils were loosely tethered to the natural science material and concepts that perhaps seemed more familiar and simultaneously encouraged to situate the information gathered in formal and informal settings within their individual frameworks and perspectives.

Short Answer Questionnaires

A short-answer questionnaire to all rural and urban interview participants, including teachers, was also administered. The questionnaire contained six questions that addressed issues such as definitions of the environment and views of indigenous natural science knowledge. The answers provided were used to clarify perspectives of these issues and supplement the narratives of students and teachers. (See Appendix C for the questionnaire protocol.)

A Note about Language

It was necessary to address the practical issue of language difficulties that confronted the interview process. During the planning stages of the data collection phase, it was thought that students might express their understandings and knowledge of human-environment interactions and natural science concepts in their tribal vernacular (Kitaita in the Taita Hills and, possibly, Kikuyu, Kiluo, Kikamba, or another in Nairobi). However, once interviews were begun in each setting, it became apparent that this concern would not play a role in the interactions, although the reasons for this varied by student population at each site.

For rural students, information about the environment was communicated using English due to its usage in all aspects of natural science instruction (texts, lectures, and assessments). Despite their varied interactions with grandparents and community elders (who often only spoke Kitaita or Kiswahili), most of the rural students indicated that their Kitaita competence was insufficient for historical, personal, or technical discussions with these individuals. Furthermore, rural students implied that dialogue with elders took place in Kiswahili and rarely involved detailed understandings of human-environment interactions similar to what they learned in the classroom. Instead, most of these conversations consisted of recollections of the past or stories about local or traditional practices and folklore.

Urban students also attended classes taught in English and were inundated with English-language periodicals, newspapers, and satellite television broadcasts. Adolescents from Central Boys Secondary and Uhuru Girls Secondary had little contact with their grandparents and ethnic elders, and only a handful of the students that were interviewed were conversant in their ethnic language. Lastly, the conversations with urban pupils regarding natural science concepts referenced information that was

41

typically only discussed in science classes: for these students, natural science topics were school topics, and thus were best communicated in English.

Documents

Documents offer both historical and contextual information and knowledge that enhance the understandings gained through observations and interviews (Glesne & Peshkin, 1992). Bogdan and Bilklen (2003) note that, although the use of documents in qualitative research is more or less supplemental, researchers are increasingly using documents as their primary sources of data, in part by the influence of discourse theory in literary and cultural studies (e.g., Inokuchi & Nozaki, 2010). They contend that the use of documents in qualitative research should fall wihtin the naturalist, inductive mode of inquiry. At any rate, the state bureaucracy, schools, and mass media produce documents for specific kinds of consumption, and such documents can be seen (and so used) as "data rich in description" (Bogdan & Bilklen, 2003, p. 58).

For the present study, numerous documents were collected that addressed some of the many nuances and notable challenges facing natural science education and, more generally, the formal education system in Kenya. These included copies of the national secondary agriculture, biology, and geography syllabi and other documents generated and distributed to schools by the Ministry of Education (MOE). The analysis of such accounts and formal documents provided a glimpse of the issues that Kenyans themselves find pressing or alarming about the state of natural science education and the formal education system.

Other document sources included newspaper articles published in Kenya's two main daily newspapers, The Daily Nation and The East African Standard. Both were privately owned at the time of the data collection. The daily circulation estimations for the two papers were 200,000 and 75,000 respectively. The Daily Nation offered a Swahili language edition, *Taifa Leo*, which had an estimated circulation of 60,000 (International Research & Exchanges Board, 2008). Other newspapers included Coast Week (a Mombasa-based paper that focused on issues specific to coastal areas of the country), The Kenya Times (which was affiliated with the KANU political party), The East African (a business-oriented publication), and the Swahili newspaper *Kenya Leo* (CPU Media Trust, 2009).

Data Analysis

To clarify the processes used to analyze the data collected and formulate a discussion of how they address the research questions that are central to this volume, the guidelines prepared by the American Educational Research Association (AERA) in the Standards for Reporting on Empirical Social Science Research in AERA Publications (2006) were followed. All observational and conversational data collected in the field, including classroom and personal observations, and notes on informal discussions with teachers at schools and on weekends were transcribed from a personal notebook and journal into electronic document format using a word processing program. These data were categorized using two methods. First, classroom-based observations were transcribed and labeled according to the natural science subject that was observed, the grade level that was observed, and the date of the observation. For example, an entry from a class at Forest Secondary may have had the title "Geography 3W 5-18" (coding that as information recorded in a geography class for the Form Three white stream, taken on May 18th). A separate file was generated for each classroom observation regardless of the length of that observation. All transcriptions of classroom activities were stored on a laptop computer which was password protected.

Second, personal notations regarding interesting aspects of schooling and notes from informal conversations were categorized as "personal reflections" and were labeled and stored according to the date entered and the general topic noted. For example, extrapolated comments regarding the way pastoralists were represented in an agriculture class at Uhuru Girls Secondary were labeled as "PO 10-24 Pastoralists" (personal observation, October 24th, topic of the notation). All conversational confidants were assigned pseudonyms. Furthermore, if some facet of a classroom-based observation required additional deliberation, specific passages from the observational notebook would be bracketed ([ ]) and a personal observation file would be created that addressed the issue. All classroom-based and personal observations were electronically stored in master folders that were broken down according to the school and subject.

For individual and paired interviews, conversations were recorded using a Sony Clearvoice (model number TCM 150) voice recorder and supplemented with data collected using a separate notebook. All interview tapes and interview notations were assigned and labeled with random numbers, which were then matched to pseudonyms that had been created for all interview respondents. At the completion of each interview, individual tapes were blocked from erasure and were stored securely until transcribed. All interview data were organized according to the individual's pseudonym and the date the conversation occurred. Separate files were created for each interview session and were stored in folders on a laptop according to the school where the student attended or instructor taught.

In actuality, the analysis of all interview and observational data began during the process of transcription and organization in Kenya. As the Standards for Reporting on Empirical Social Science Research in AERA Publications (2006) states:

> [D]uring the initial stages of analysis, researchers may develop ways of segmenting the data (e.g., by person; by action, activity, event, or narrative; by time period) and sets of substantive categories or codes into which segments of data can be organized. (p. 37)

After exploring various features of the observational data and labeling personal observations according to general themes, broad patterns of behaviors and discourse were constructed that would then follow in subsequent observations and notations. The reading of the data did not only entail such rudimentary analysis, but also included important thematic analysis.

All documents in Microsoft Word format were initially read and tentatively coded using a code-key and text-color and highlighting techniques. Once all transcribed and observational data had been read, a preliminary list of themes that appeared relevant at that stage of the analysis was constructed. A thorough re-reading of all data also took place in order to establish individual codes that would be used to segment portions of the data to then be reassembled under the relevant theme or themes. To accomplish this task, NUD*IST (QSR NUD*IST version 4) software was used for qualitative data analysis.

For example, one significant theme that emerged during the first reading of the data was categorized as "indigenous knowledge-negative perspectives." This theme, as broad as it may be, was generated when a teacher or student responded to one of my questions (such as: What do you know about traditional or indigenous knowledge?) in a way that articulated their disfavor for such knowledge. During the coding of the data using the QSR software, numerous types of disfavor were separated into distinct categories, such as "seen as deficient" or "not applicable for use today." All data from rural and urban locations were organized according to macro themes and codes and labeled in this program according to the Microsoft Word document from which it originated, thereby allowing the origins of individual student responses and perspectives to be re-traced.

As the major themes began to develop, not only in simple terms of data support, but also in conceptual coherence with the overarching problem that was investigated, the academic literature was mined for books, articles, presentations, or other reports that addressed the specific themes or adjacent concepts that were constructed, whether in Kenya, Sub-Saharan Africa, Africa, or developing countries. In concert with the relevant academic debates and findings, the themes that were composed were then re-examined and theoretically developed to satisfy the original questions posed in this research and form the crux of the arguments concerning student and teacher perspectives of indigenous and schooled natural science knowledge, and the natural science education of Kenyan students.

Writing Up Multi-sited Ethnographic Study

Writing up a multi-sited ethnographic study brings the challenge similar to those raised in handling multi-case studies. Glesne and Peshkin (1992) suggest three ways to organize multi-case study: to organize the data to devote a separate chapter to each case; to identify major themes, concepts, and processes from each case and devote a separate chapter to each; and to do both to some extent. They state:

> On one hand, the cases kept intact might illuminate understandings and insights about the process . . . that would be lost if they were sliced up into corroborating data for general points. On the other hand, the general points . . . might be what represent the greatest potential contribution of the cases. (p. 164-165)

Glesne and Peshkin (1992) conclude that there is no agreement "that specifies what that contribution must be and what organizational procedure for writing thereby follows" (p. 165). That is, researchers must decide on their own strategy to present a multi-sited ethnographic study, and they may have to use an alternate strategy depending on their purpose, such as writing an article, short monograph, or volume.

It should be noted that multi-sited ethnographic data gathered for the present study were first analyzed, arranged, and written according to the emerging themes in a manner and style of comparing findings from the three sites. For example, a theme of instructional differences and similarities among the three sites were discussed comparatively and was followed by a discussion of another theme. However, it turned out that the theme-based chapters did not read well as ethnographic text. Then, the text was re-organized and re-arranged to present the findings school by school, the style of the present volume. The themes are dealt with in relation to the local, contextualized setting of each site. This decision was made in order to best present the complex data, understandings, and insights in a more ethnographic, reader-friendly manner and style.

NOTE

[1] As we maintain the importance of methodological reflection, or reflexivity, in an interconnected world—in particular as it pertains to ethnography—it is also important to acknowledge the notable contributions that participatory research designs (such as participatory action research, or PAR) have made in blurring the researcher-researched divide and establishing locally-defined approaches to inquiry and action. A thorough review of these methods and approaches are beyond the scope of this volume; however, we note that Reason and Bradbury (2006), Kapoor and Jordan (2009), and Walker, Fredericks, and Anderson (2013) (among many others) provide useful information and discussions pertaining to the history of PAR and the employment of participatory methods in various contexts.

KENYAN EDUCATION

The State, Schools, and Legacy of Colonialism

FORMAL EDUCATION IN KENYA

Education in Pre-Colonial and Colonial Kenya

For centuries before the widespread dominance of formal education in Kenya, indigenous African education existed to accomplish two main goals. First, indigenous education promoted the morals and practices that shaped the daily lives of specific ethnic groups. Second, this education aimed to transmit indigenous knowledge concerning humans and their relationship with the surrounding bio-physical environment from one generation to the next (Mungai, 2002). Despite arguments characterizing pre-colonial Africa as "unscientific" (Mabawonku, 2003), technological development in the areas of metal work and textile production that occurred in areas of what is now modern Kenya nearly 2000 years ago were equal to, or more advanced than, comparable technologies found in Europe at the time (Teng-Zeng, 2006). Thus, the indigenous knowledge generated and practiced before colonial domination was vital for the development of traditional African societies.

With the arrival of Christian missionaries in Kenya in the nineteenth century, Western-influenced educational practice supplanted the community-based, informal educational traditions that had, until that point, stood the test of time. While the infusion of educational arrangements rooted in Western cultures were not uncommon at the dawn of the colonial era in Africa (Lulat, 2005),[1] some aspects of this process were unique to Kenya, as discussed below.

Great Britain's colonial interests in the East African region were cemented with the official declaration of colonial rule in Kenya in 1902. With the crown colony governance system in place, the colonizers developed governmental, social, and economic institutions in Kenya that were descendents of the well-established institutional formations found in Britain at the time (Merryfield & Tlou, 1995). These institutional formations ultimately guided the development of Kenya's national school system, despite attempts during the colonial era to develop schools that served the interests of native Kenyans better, such as the Kikuyu Independent Schools Movement, which took place in the mid-1920s (Indire, 1982).[2]

The first schools established in colonial Kenya were concentrated around the economic and social centers, such as Nairobi, Nakuru, and Mombasa, and tailored exclusively for educating white European groups in Western-influenced academic subjects. For native Kenyans, so-called "village schools"[3] were built or located in areas adjacent to the colonial centers. The village schools aimed to train (mainly male) Kenyans for the labor niches that were needed by the white colonial land and business-owners; carpentry, masonry, and other crafts were emphasized over basic literacy or numeracy skills (Mungai, 2002). Furthermore, due to the uneven colonial influence across the country, the establishment of schools in remote areas was delayed. For example, white settlers colonized the lowland areas of Taita-Taveta District long before their interests in agricultural land and minerals led them to explore the upper reaches of the rugged Taita Hills (Spear, 1982). Consequently, Taita's schools and other colonial-influenced institutions were developed later than those located in other areas of the Coast Province, such as Mombasa and Malindi.[4]

During the 1940s and 1950s, modest gains were made in Kenya's education sector. For example, several acts of British Parliament passed in the years after World War II provided funds for both secondary educational development and the beginnings of university expansion.[5] Britain's attention to Kenya was also evident when, it 1961, it embarked on a reorganization of the colony's education system by scrapping its "triple four" structure[6] and opting for a system resembling the British "O" and "A" level two-tiered structure (Indire, 1982).

KENYAN EDUCATION AND DECOLONIZATION

When Kenya finally shed its colonial shackles in 1963, educational access for the population was still severely restricted; at the time, there were only ninety-five secondary schools nationwide for a population over eight million people (Lillis, 1985). Almost immediately, the leaders of the newly formed nation took decisive steps toward restructuring the education system, which in turn spawned several bureaucratic arrangements, such as the Ministry of Education (hereafter MOE) and the Kenya Institute of Education (hereafter KIE).

The new Kenyan government immediately prioritized the growth of the national school system in order to halt the dis-education of millions of newly independent Kenyan youth. Although the number of schools grew steadily during the 1970s and 1980s, enrollments in the nation's schools began to decline in the mid-1980s (Bradshaw & Fuller, 1996).[7] In response to this trend, aggressive reforms that targeted the ailing system were undertaken during the 1980s. One such reform, implemented by the administration of President Daniel arap Moi, included a complete restructuring program whereby the inherited 7-4-2-3 ("O" and "A" level) system was replaced with an 8-4-4 format for primary, secondary, and post-secondary education. Furthermore, campaigns such as the school milk program and Harambee school movement[8] bolstered the number of primary and secondary schools and students nationwide.

Another primary aim of the Kenyan government during this period was to use education to foster national unity and promote social and economic development. To do this, instruction and literacy in a common language—English—was viewed as a way to bring the country's many different ethnic groups together and link the new state to European-based economic and trade systems (Mungai, 2002). The fledgling Kenyan state, like other newly independent African states,[9] also took steps to connect the content of formal education to the national context by "Africanizing" or "indigenizing" the curriculum.

In the mid-1960s, indigenization of Kenya's curriculum involved the broad reconstruction of syllabi to reflect the country's diverse indigenous ways of knowing and promote social change and the empowerment of Kenyans. At that time, education policy makers viewed the reclamation of cultural identities rooted within the authentication of indigenous traditions as a way to decolonize the Western-dominated school curricula and make education more practical for Kenyans (Owuor, 2007). Yet, education was also viewed as a mediator between the diverse cultures of the fledgling state, a newly propagated national culture, and the global needs of the nation. Therefore, the commitment to indigenization was (arguably) superficial and the process failed to de-center educational elites who were products of Western schooling and valued Western conceptualizations of knowledge (Owour, 2007).

Kenya also attempted to Africanize the social studies curriculum in years following independence (e.g., Merryfield & Tlou, 1995). During the 1970s, the curricular focus of social studies shifted from a predominantly British worldview to "local" and "area" studies that were centered on the geographic region of East Africa. Through this process, the government also sought to integrate the viewpoints of different ethnic and religious groups into an African-centered education that would draw attention to Kenyans' African heritage and provide an improved focus on the community and nation. However, this bold curriculum never moved beyond the pilot stage and eventually "atrophied and died because of the . . . lack of interest from the education community" (Merryfield & Tlou, 1995, p. 264).

Conversely, other curricular reform efforts in Kenya were more closely aligned with the Western-influenced subjects and practices of the colonial regime. The complete curriculum revision that began in 1985 offered secondary students an array of disciplinary and practical options aimed to boost university preparedness, vocational competence, and employment opportunities (Kuhlman, 1992). Initiatives such as the School Mathematics of East Africa and the School Science Project both involved the transfer of "metropolitan curriculum influences" (from Great Britain) into the social and educational contexts of the newly independent country (Lillis & Lowe, 1987).[10]

Education in Contemporary Kenya

Since the move to the 8-4-4 configuration, Kenya has solidified its commitment to a three-tiered public school system of primary, secondary, and post-secondary institutions.[11] The secondary tier contains further stratification, including a small number of elite-class secondary schools (national schools), a broad middle class of secondary schools (provincial schools), and a common class of local secondary schools (district schools). The separation within the secondary tier that began almost immediately after independence has involved retaining the national schools' elite status (as colonial-era institutions) and incorporating the poorer, more local Harambee schools into the public school system (Mwiria, 1991).

Currently, fewer than twenty institutions are classified as national schools, and these are regarded as the highest quality public institutions in the country. By law, national schools are full-boarding and enroll students from each of Kenya's eight provinces. Provincial schools are numerous throughout the country and vary widely in their admission requirements, academic performance, and configuration. These schools may be restricted to all females or all males, and may also be full-boarding schools or mixed boarding and day-scholar schools. National education guidelines require provincial schools to enroll at least seventy-five percent of their students from inside the school's immediate district; the remaining twenty-five percent may come from other areas of the province or the country.[12] Lastly, schools designated as district schools are decidedly more local than their provincial counterparts. Descended from Harambee schools—community funded and run schools popular in rural areas in the 1970s and 1980s— they are primarily day-scholar institutions for local populations (Ndetei et al, 2007).[13]

In recent years, Kenyan schools in both rural and urban locations have struggled with increasing costs and booming enrollments. Under a directive issued by the MOE in 2001, all national schools are required to cap their tuition costs at 29,600 Kenyan shillings or Ksh (approximately 380 U.S. dollars), while full-boarding provincial schools and district schools are supposed to only charge 20,900 Ksh ($300) and 8,500 Ksh ($120), respectively. However, a recent investigation has found that a number of national schools are charging upwards of 50,000 Ksh ($715) while some district schools may charge between 14,000 Ksh. ($200) and 26,000 Ksh. ($370).[14] School officials claim such figures are the result of steadily increasing operating costs for schools and the need for expansion and development of institutions as national enrollments continue to climb (Ngare, 2007).

The Kenyan state has recently implemented a program that has had dramatic effects on school enrollments and, subsequently, teaching and learning at both the primary and secondary levels. Since 2003 and the initiation of a free primary education program, primary school enrollments are estimated to have increased over 500,000, with secondary populations up 50,000 and university numbers estimated to have increased nearly 10,000.[15] Similarly, enrollments in other institutions, including teacher training colleges, polytechnics, technical colleges, and institutions of science jumped over 30,000. As a result of these trends, student-teacher ratios in primary schools nationwide are estimated to top 45 to 1, while secondary ratios are officially reported at 20 to 1 (Kenya Central Bureau of Statistics, 2006).

Globalization and Education: The Kenyan Context(s)

Kenya's attempts at providing free primary and secondary education not only have been undertaken in response to the goals set at the World Education Forum in Dakar,

Senegal in April, 2000, but also have been viewed as political promises set forth during President Mwai Kibaki's election campaigns of 2002 and 2007. Although these initiatives are regarded as positive developments for promoting the role of basic education in the development of the country, the large-scale programs are also considered to offer more accessible insights into the significant educational disparities that exist in Kenya (Sifuna, 2005). These disparities, while evident since the time of Britain's colonization of Kenya, are strengthening in response to numerous domestic and international shifts in economics, social structures, and cultural factors. These shifts are often attributed to the multifaceted and complicated phenomenon ambiguously known as globalization.[16]

Globalization, according to Marginson (1999), is thought to include a number of interrelated and overlapping aspects, including the formation of strengthened economic hegemony located in the North and Far East; the growth of information technologies used for the transfer of knowledge and finances; the international movement of peoples due to economic pressures; and linguistic, cultural, and ideological convergence. Broadly, studies of globalization debate its effects on innumerable facets of modern societies, including public discourse and representations of "imperialism" and "modernization" (Kellner, 2000), organizational change in higher education (Vaira, 2004), and international representations of political violence (Bielsa & Hughes, 2009). Of greater interest to Kenya and its schools are studies that investigate globalization in the context of African countries, most notably in the areas of national and international development (Moss, 2007) and secondary education (Evoh, 2007).

In studies of education, it is argued that globalization and the new emphases on the global knowledge economy (in which, according to Castells [1998], ideas and information are as valuable as goods or commodities) are intensifying educational inequalities within individual African countries. Ayere, Odera, and Agak (2010) report how students in six Kenyan schools that were exclusively selected for Information Communication Technology (ICT) integration through the African Union's New Partnership for Africa's Development (NEPAD) outscored their non-NEPAD school counterparts on national examinations. Quist (2001) demonstrates that as urban areas of Ghana and Côte d'Ivoire have increasingly become sites of educational and cultural convergence (due in part to globalization), secondary education and students in rural areas are forced to move towards neocolonial influences emanating from the West (through Western-derived language and curricular policies). Although similar work has not been undertaken in Kenya, it is safe to state that the country shares contextual similarities with these West African countries as a result of its colonial past, rapidly developing but limited urban core, Western-influenced dress, cultural values, and norms espoused by the urban educated elite, and blossoming capacities for media and communications technologies (Quist, 2001, p. 305).[17]

As the country struggles to participate in the globalized economy, studies also look at specific manifestations of globalization in Kenya.[18] For example, in Kenya's manufacturing sector globalization has played a role in the earnings losses

51

by less-skilled workers and the widening inequalities in the earnings of skilled and unskilled workers (Manda & Sen, 2004). Globalization is also argued to produce negative consequences for Muslims in Kenya as border incursions by Somali refugees from the north lead to territorial disputes, restricted social provisioning, and notions of an uncertain citizenship (Gimode, 2004). Furthermore, globalization seems to have spawned a resurgence in ethnic nationalism, territorial citizenship, and violence in the rural and poor Tana River District (Kagwanja, 2003).

The uneven development of the country also increases the demand for an urban-based workforce that is educated to the post-secondary levels or beyond (Manda & Sen, 2004). Yet, even as these needs arise, the development of education services and resources in all areas of the country is not satisfying such demands (Sifuna, 2005). Therefore, as the effects of globalization serve as push and pull forces that influence the movement of Kenyans and the quality and quantity of educational opportunities nationwide, it is important that analyses interrogate the specific contexts of rural and urban schools to explore the particularities of specific subject matters ("natural sciences" in the case of this volume) in light of these changes. Such inquiries will help in (re)conceptualizing Kenyan science education, meeting the challenges of the nation's alarming environmental degradation and blatant educational disparities, and developing potential pathways for a sustainable future in Kenya (and beyond).

THE KENYAN STATE AND SCHOOLS

In order to contextualize natural science education in Kenya, it is necessary to outline the state agencies that are tied to the administration of schooling in Kenya, the development of curricula, the assessment of school knowledge at the secondary level, and their impact on daily practice in schools.

As discussed earlier, the history of formal education in Kenya is strongly rooted in the country's colonial past. In the economic and social centers of colonial Kenya, schools were developed for educating the white European minority. In areas adjacent to these centers, village schools taught native Kenyans vocational skills for employment by the European landowners. In some rural areas and remote districts, secondary schools were not even built until after independence (Mwiria, 1991). After the establishment of the Kenyan state in 1963, the system of schooling was built to resemble Great Britain's. In the years following independence, government bodies were established under the MOE to administer specific aspects of the national education system. Since then, despite the different educational experiences and opportunities of rural and urban Kenyans during the colonial era, the Kenyan education system has been highly standardized.

Currently, the MOE is one of the twenty ministries in the Kenyan government. The MOE's primary responsibilities are the provision and promotion of education and the formulation and facilitation of educational policy guidelines (Kenya Ministry of Education, 2008).[19] The ministry is involved in nearly all facets of education nationwide, including pre-primary and primary education, secondary education, teacher education, university education, special needs education, non-formal and adult education, and technical and vocational education and training. The MOE coordinates its efforts with numerous subsidiary bodies and institutes, including: the Kenya Teachers Service Commission, which is responsible for the training and posting of all public school teachers; the Kenya National Examinations Council (hereafter KNEC), which sets, conducts, and posts all nationally-administered primary and secondary tests, including the cumulative secondary exit examination, the Kenya Certificate of Secondary Education (hereafter KCSE) examination; and most important, in terms of natural science curriculum development, the KIE.

Despite large-scale reforms and a complete restructuring of the education system in the 1980s, these institutions continue to exert significant power over schools. Two of these bodies—the KIE and the KNEC—are extremely influential in terms of the daily practice of teaching and learning in the natural sciences in secondary schools, and, therefore, the actions and policies of these two agencies merit further discussion.

The Kenya Institute of Education (KIE)

The KIE was formally established in 1968; however, its origins trace to several education centers that began advising the MOE in the late 1950s regarding subject-specific standards and curricula development. Today, the KIE is responsible for all formal and non-formal curricula, as well as the formulation of subject-specific syllabi at the primary and secondary levels.[20] Furthermore, the KIE serves as the primary research center for education issues in the country and is the principal body in charge of preparing teaching and evaluation materials for syllabi support (KIE, 2009). Although the KIE exerts significant influence in all areas of curriculum development and implementation, its role in education is not limited to the assembly of prescriptive syllabi.

For example, the agency's influence also extends to the selection of the textbooks that are used in all subjects, including secondary agriculture, biology, and geography. The KIE is involved in the authoring, publishing, and evaluating course textbooks, teacher guides, and supplemental materials. In order for entities or individuals outside the KIE (such as private publishers in Kenya or multinational companies) to author textbooks, they must be legally incorporated and registered to conduct business in the country. Prospective texts are submitted to the Ministerial Textbook Vetting Committee, which is comprised senior of MOE officials (Rotich & Musakali, 2005).

After the reviews are completed by the Ministerial Textbook Vetting Committee and its subject-evaluation panels, a list of textbooks is approved by the MOE and KIE. As a rule, there can be no more than six titles offered for each subject, from which teachers can select one as the core text for their course. Yet, seldom are there more than three textbooks from various publishers that make the list for each subject and grade level (Rotich & Musakali, 2005). Frequently, teachers select one book as their core text, but also need to purchase (sometimes with their own funds) additional textbooks from the approved list to compensate for insufficient coverage of specific content areas in the core text. However, irrespective of the textbook that is used for a specific subject in a specific school, it is the national syllabus for that subject that is the single document guiding all teaching and learning throughout the academic year.

Given the scope and significance of its educational duties, the KIE's actions have been viewed as controversial. Due to its exclusive jurisdiction over the definition of what knowledge students must learn, how fast they must learn it, and the ways they must learn it, the concerns of educational stakeholders at various levels may not be heard or accommodated. In other words, there have been disconnects between the KIE and local schools.

For example, the School Mathematics of East Africa program, one of the failed initiatives, which was nationally mandated in 1978 and ultimately abandoned in 1981, focused on materials development for "modern mathematics" as well as in-service education for mathematics teachers. The initiative faced numerous problems during its several phases (Lillis, 1985). First, the program's external development made it inappropriate for poor public schools, low-status schools, and Harambee schools (all of which suffered from inadequate staffing and resources and an inability to master the concepts required for successful implementation). Furthermore, the aims of the project were in direct contrast with the highly formalized, teacher-centered, and authoritarian instructional styles that were used in Kenya at the time (Lillis, 1985, p. 91).

Another unilateral reform initiated by the KIE involved wide-spread curricular changes that were implemented in 2002 for all subjects at both the primary and secondary school levels. At that time, the Kenyan government initiated a four-year process of replacing the "old" secondary curriculum (drafted in 1995) with a newly revised secondary curriculum. The new documents included detailed listings of the topics that were to be covered in each secondary grade level. In addition, the specific content to be covered at each level was further dissected into sub-headings and included guidelines regarding the number of lessons to be spent on each heading or sub-heading. For example, the form three biology guidelines include the topic of ecology as a major subject heading and recommend that fifty-five lessons be devoted to covering the specific list of objectives (KIE, 2002). The new secondary curriculum included minor or significant alterations in each of the over twenty subjects to be taught in Kenyan secondary schools.[21] In the end, the prescriptive nature of this reform forced instructors to teach according to the "schedule" imposed by the new syllabi and left little room for subject exploration with supplemental or local resources.

In general, government attempts at comprehensive education reforms have been (and perhaps still are) unable to serve the needs of its people through curricular development, particularly in the areas of cultural values and the natural environment (see Kuhlman, 1992; Osler, 1993). More specifically, colonial and postcolonial education (and the curricular initiatives that have been implemented during this historical period), unlike pre-colonial indigenous education, has failed to give students a "firm foundation and deep roots in their own environment" (Maina, 2003, p. 13). What is needed, according to Maina (2003), is the establishment of locally-situated community schools and a relevant curriculum, put forth by agencies such as the KIE—which deconstructs the cultural barriers that have been erected between children and their community as a result of formal schooling.

Kenya National Examinations Council (KNEC)

Founded in 1980, the KNEC states that its core functions are:[22]

Development of both school and post-school examinations, registration of candidates, administration and processing of examinations, certification, researching into examinations and the curriculum, and equation of certificates from other examining boards. (KNEC, 2009)

In terms of secondary education, KNEC's most important duties are the development and administration of the KCSE examination. The KCSE exam is a cumulative, high-stakes exit examination that is administered to all form four students at the end of their secondary school career. The exam tests students' understanding of content from all four years of instruction in the five "core" subjects— biology, chemistry, math, Kiswahili, and English. Students are also assessed in their elective courses, such as agriculture (categorized under "applied sciences"), geography (categorized under "humanities"), or foreign languages. In an exam-oriented system, the performance of individual students, teachers, administrators, and schools is all judged by test scores—Kenya is no exception. In addition, the KCSE serves as the sole measure of a secondary student's academic achievement and potential and is used as the entrance exam for placement in Kenya's limited higher education sector.

To be sure, Kenyan secondary schools make concerted efforts to enhance student performance on the KCSE exam, which affect daily administration, teaching, and learning practices. For example, numerous motivational strategies can be employed by headmasters (principals) and teachers in order to improve student study habits and instructor and pupil motivation (Lynet, Kasandi, & Wamocha, 2008). Some of the strategies aiming to boost the academic enthusiasm of teachers and students may include the use of rewards (including food, extra break time, and trips), guidance and counseling, discipline, and fostering a positive school identity. Overall, highly motivated teachers who work with enthusiasm and interest enable students to perform better on the high-stakes KCSE (for further discussion of learning practices and performance of KCSE exam, see Lynet, Kasandi, & Wamocha, 2008). While it may be advantageous for some schools to uncover practical measures that can be employed by instructors in order to enhance student readiness and performance for this national exam, it has not been clear how issues of curricular content may factor into teacher and student motivation and KCSE exam results. Furthermore, research that analyzes the social implications of the high-stakes test itself is lacking.

In recent years, the KCSE exam has attracted negative attention and been the subject of controversy because of repeated scandals involving cheating, score fixing, and examination errors (Siringi & Menya, 2009). For example, in 2005, the Minister of Education, George Saitoti, ordered an investigation into inconsistencies involving three mislabeled questions on the mathematics test (Opondo, Orlale, & Muriuki, 2005). At the same time, the union representing teachers who graded KCSE examinations threatened to strike if the payments for their services were not increased (Nzioka & Kazungu, 2005). Two years later, there were reportedly scams involving the sale of counterfeit KCSE exam papers to parents who hoped to give their children an advantage prior to the commencement of testing (Otieno & Kangoro, 2007). Furthermore, the 2007 exam period was plagued by widespread rumors of exam leakage with reports that security personnel in charge of exam transportation and distribution had offered family and friends advanced previews of specific tests.[23]

What effects might this examination have on teaching and learning in the natural sciences in rural and urban secondary schools? Generally, the use of high-stakes national tests is argued to be inadequate and misguided for the further development of the Kenyan education system. Although the government has taken numerous institutional and legal steps since independence to improve its education system, development of the system in the postcolonial era has been hampered by numerous issues, including irrelevant curricula and the continued focus on high-stakes exams (Eshiwani, 1990). Pointing to the failure of several education initiatives due to a preoccupation with testing (among other factors),[24] Eshiwani argues:

It is now felt strongly that the general academic and certificate-oriented education that Kenya has had so far can no longer adequately meet the needs of a modernizing economy . . . (1990, p. 18)

Several studies implicate Kenya's emphasis on and employment of high-stakes tests such as the KCSE and the Kenya Certificate of Primary Education (hereafter KCPE) examinations in pedagogical difficulties faced by teachers, performance-related difficulties faced by students, and more general difficulties faced by the education system itself.[25] In an analysis of an unsuccessful curricular reform, Lillis (1985) notes that the opportunities for de-centered teaching styles and participatory learning in Kenya are limited by the "domination" of high-stake exams (the KCPE and KCSE) that are "dependent on authoritarian teacher-pupil relationships and the transmission of blocks of knowledge . . . to passively recipient learners" (p. 91). Students in underdeveloped and rural areas encounter added challenges when taking the KCPE and KCSE exams due to materials shortages at their schools. Yussufu (1989) asks how national examinations and assessments should be used when "there is a marked disparity of resources, and therefore opportunity, throughout schools offering candidates for examination" (p. 283).-

These studies questioning the use of the KCSE exam in Kenya raise important points; however, research that examines the effects of this high-stakes assessment on teaching and learning in the natural sciences is notably absent. Here, a general point raised by Connell (1993) about assessments can offer us some insights into the power of KCPE and KCSE examinations. He states:

[T]hey (assessments) shape the *form* of the curriculum as well as its more obvious *content*. An individualized, competitive assessment system shapes learning as the individual appropriation of reproducible items of knowledge and the individual cultivation of skills. (p. 32)

Connell is correct to assert the power assessment tools have to influence (and control) daily practice in schools. However, we must note that it remains unresolved whether Connell's point about the relations among assessment policy, curriculum content, and pedagogical approaches is consistent with the views of students and teachers regarding the knowledge that they think should be taught through natural science education.

Daily Practice of Teachers in Kenyan Schools

As we discuss above, the centrally-designed curriculum and high-stakes testing system in Kenya combine to produce substantial government control over the knowledge that is taught in natural science classes and the ways that student understandings of such knowledge are measured and assessed. These curricular and evaluative controls also impact teacher practice in natural science classrooms.[26] Public schools in Kenya are strikingly synchronized in terms of daily routine and instructional practice. Not only do students in all public secondary schools begin their long days of learning at nearly the same time each morning, but they also progress lock-step through centrally-defined syllabi for all coursework.[27]

Curriculum policies also have effects on the pedagogical approaches and classroom interactions between teachers and students in Kenyan schools—i.e., the predominance of teacher-centered recitation and repetition in Kenyan classrooms, as Pontefract and Hardman's (2005) study of twenty-seven instructors of mathematics, science, and English at the primary school level illuminates. While research can identify a number of issues and factors that contribute to the use of such instructional styles, including infrastructure and resource shortages and overcrowding in classrooms, the restrictive curriculum is argued to play a significant role in the development of classroom discourses. As Pontefract and Hardman (2005) state:

Overall, it appeared as if the classroom discourse was more of a collusion between teachers and pupils in order to create a semblance of curriculum coverage, knowledge and understanding... (p. 100)

It seems that curricular reforms should be introduced that replace the use of "chalk and talk, rote memorization, and corporal punishment" instructional methods with learner-centered approaches to teaching and learning (p. 101).

Kenya's rigid curriculum not only has adverse effects on teacher practice, but also is a significant factor contributing to the abandonment of the teaching profession by instructors of the sciences (where turn-over rates have been particularly acute). Science teachers who resign their positions in classrooms do so in favor of employment opportunities in other sectors. Indeed, in Wafubwa's (1991) study of an urban secondary school and a science-oriented parastatal (government-owned) organization, a number of the study's interview respondents, including eight teachers and eight ex-teachers of secondary science, viewed the national science curriculum as overbearing and too intense, given the amount of content that was prescribed for a single school year. For ex-teachers, the lure of higher pay and employment in more prestigious fields, such as engineering, agriculture, and pharmaceuticals, also contributed to their exodus from the science classroom. Overall, it appears that chronic hindrances to science instruction, including a broad science curriculum, severe time constraints, resource and materials shortages, and low pay are critical factors resulting in notably high turn-over rates for secondary science teachers. Without proper recognition and abatement of the unfavorable circumstances plaguing science classrooms by Kenya's education bureaucracy, the teaching profession will continue to bleed qualified science teachers and will be unable to attract talented and passionate graduates to the profession (for a further discussion of teaching in Kenya, see Wafubwa, 1991).

Sadly, these situations are not unique to Kenyan schools and instructors. In other African contexts, nationally-set syllabi are argued to have constraining effects on the practice of teaching and play a role in the low retention of teachers. For example, in several African countries, social studies curricula that stress democratic values (such as freedom of speech, fairness, and social justice) actually serve to limit the instructional approaches in classrooms and contribute to teacher burnout (Asimeng-Boahene, 2003). Where centrally-devised, rigid curricula blanket entire countries, political systems fail to include democratic principles, and national political climates are unsympathetic to critical analysis of social realities (as is the case in numerous African contexts), schoolteachers may feel that they are "not permitted to engage in a free analysis of major policies and established social habits" (p. 61).

As we noted previously, curricular amendments in Kenya previously entailed both broad changes to the national syllabi and alterations to specific subjects. Content-based reforms have also attempted to domesticate or nationalize curricula by including a regional focus and (although sparingly) paying increased attention to broader issues such as democracy, literacy, and inequality (Owuor, 2007). Yet, substantial frictions and challenges still exist in Kenyan education—notably the high degree of state control dissuading the establishment of a more progressive education, in terms of both curriculum and pedagogy. Kenyan public secondary schools across the country are treated in a nearly-uniform fashion by the MOE and KIE through the use of standard syllabi and a single, cumulative certification examination such as the KCSE. Pressures generated by overloaded syllabi and the strong emphasis on examination performance allow for significant government control of teaching and learning and affect instructional performance and teacher retention. Furthermore, tensions between Western-derived subject content and contextually-derived understandings also play out in the classrooms and staff rooms of Kenyan schools.

In the search for a natural science education that begins with needs, values, and insights of local people and communities, it is imperative to listen to the voices of students, teachers, and schools at grassroots levels. Bottom-up approaches to natural science education that deal with the tensions between indigenous knowledge and sustainable development have potential to lead a change on national levels both in Kenya and other national contexts that face similar challenges.

NOTES

[1] The influence and legacy of Europe's colonization on Africa's educational systems has been well documented by Lulat (2005), Zvobgo (1994), Mwiria (1991), and Johnson (1985), among others.

[2] Early in Britain's colonial reign, the era of "native paramountcy" aimed to include colonized Kenyans in the development process while also protecting the interests of the minority settlers. This era can be segmented into three phases: the first phase, from 1923-1928, was characterized by the spread of "bush" schools, which later became village or local elementary schools. The second phase was marked by the Kikuyu Independent Schools Movement, which was a reaction by this ethnic group to the poor quality and insufficient quantity of African schools. Although this phase lost momentum in the early 1930s as a result of the global economic downturn, Britain revamped educational development during the third phase of the "native paramountcy" era in response to Germany's aggression in Europe and the African colonial areas. However, despite the colonial power's stated intentions for increased participation by native Kenyans during the 1920s and 1930s, it was not until 1961 that the first Kenyan was chosen to hold the post of Minister of Education. For further discussion of education in colonial Kenya, see Indire (1982).

[3] So-called "village schools" were educational arrangements that varied from one or two room schools constructed of mud to partitioned "classrooms" in local churches or, in their most limited form, areas under trees (Mwiria, 1991). Colonial policies of racial segregation meant that any education that existed for native Kenyans was underfunded, limited in its academic scope, and restrictive in terms of enrollments or participation (Eshiwani, 1990).

[4] The Taita Hills, the location of the rural school studied in this dissertation, are located in Coast Province, which has been ranked as the second poorest province in the country, behind North Eastern (Society for International Development, 2004). While the coastal areas of the province, such as Mombasa, Malindi, and Kilifi, are moderately developed, the vast majority of the province is characterized by small villages and semi-arid landscapes.

[5] The Colonial Development and Welfare Acts of 1940 and 1945 both provided funds aimed at the economic and social development of Britain's dependencies. Funds from these acts were also used for the further development of a segregated educational system that catered to the white European minority settlers.

[6] The "triple four" structure included three years of both lower and upper primary, and three years of both lower and upper secondary. The structure that replaced this arrangement (the "O" and "A" structure) consisted of seven years of primary courses, four years of lower secondary courses, two years of upper secondary courses, and three years of university (Indire, 1982).

[7] Bradshaw and Fuller (1996) demonstrate that despite the use of discrete policy initiatives aimed at boosting school enrollments (such as lowering the cost of private education, offering food assistance at schools for attending children, and expanding secondary education opportunities in marginalized areas), school attendance declined in the 1980s as a result of diminished local demand for schooling and the poor quality of schools and instruction.

[8] *Harambee* is a Swahili term used in Kenya to mean a spirited coalescence of all Kenyans, translated as "let us all pull together." Harambee, or "self-help" schools, were established during the Harambee schools movement in communities that pooled financial and labor resources to build and operate a primary or secondary school. These efforts were organized around ethnicities or geographic location. Harambee schools eventually became district schools (Bradshaw, 1993). The school milk program

began in 1979 and offered free milk for primary school children nationwide, but has been criticized as diverting much needed funding from other aspects of education, such as equipment and teaching aides, workshops, and stationary (Amutabi, 2003).

9   Ogunniyi and Ogawa (2008) examine the context of post-apartheid South Africa and the potential difficulties for enacting a redesigned and "indigenized" curriculum, which called for greater usage of indigenous knowledge systems (IKS) in all areas of formal schooling.

10 The reforms that were implemented during the 1980s reflect the conflicts that exist between education that is more aligned with indigenous viewpoints (reflected in the attempts to "Africanize" the curriculum) and one that is aligned with Western-influenced knowledge and arrangements. Curriculum making in general always involves epistemological tensions (Nozaki 2006), including, in our view, the tension between indigenous and Western knowledge systems.

11 Public schools in Kenya are technically referred to as *government* schools by the MOE. However, in the interest of simplifying the descriptive language and presenting this common group of schools using terminology that may be more easily identifiable, in this volume, these schools are called *public schools*.

12 The three schools where the data were collected for the present volume were all classified as provincial schools.

13 A complete breakdown of secondary schools by type and geographic location in Kenya is unavailable. However, secondary school distribution, especially for provincial schools, is closely linked to population concentration. Accordingly, the densely populated cities of Nairobi, Mombasa, Nakuru, Eldoret, Kisumu, and their surrounding areas, contain high numbers of provincial secondary schools and fewer district schools. Conversely, residents in highly rural and remote areas are mainly serviced by district schools.

14 The tuition charged by similarly-classified institutions varies widely and can be viewed as a function of the location of the school. For example, the rurally-located provincial school in the present study charged approximately $315 per boarding student, whereas the two provincial schools located in Nairobi charged over $550 per student (as of 2005). Schools charging higher tuitions are able to secure higher quality educational materials and resources for their students.

15 The significant increases in post-secondary enrollments can be attributed to the influx of students at the primary level, among other factors, such as natural growth patterns. Yet, even as the Kenyan government reports increases in postsecondary participation through gross enrollment rates, participation in Kenya's limited higher education sector for rural inhabitants is lacking. While no government data are available regarding enrollments by district, it has been suggested that rural students experience more difficulties with higher education loan applications than their urban counterparts do. This result of general problems with the applications themselves, as well the extra costs incurred, in terms of financial resources and time away from the classroom, by rural students as they travelled to Nairobi to complete loan forms and follow up on applications (Ngolovoi, 2008). Although this volume does not specifically tackle the issue of rural versus urban higher education enrollments or educational trajectories, the suggestion of a rural-urban divide in the abilities of students to perform the tasks needed for higher education access should be acknowledged.

16 Although several of the characteristics of secondary schools highlighted in the present study can rightly be situated within larger discussions of globalization's effects on Kenyan development, national economic policies and influences, rural-urban flight, and even curricular development, this volume primarily focuses on the micro particularities of natural science education in rural and urban schools. In doing so, this volume echoes Hall and Tarrow's (2001) concerns, who ask if the emphasis on globalization serves to draw attention away from important developments in places (Kenya or elsewhere in developing regions) by situating its cultural, historical, and political contexts and trends within larger regions and characterizations that, paradoxically, swallow targeted and focused inquiries. Furthermore, Hall and Tarrow ask: Do researchers turn to globalization because they don't know what to say about the internal complexities of the societies they are studying? Therefore, instead of using languages of globalization instantly and exclusively (as would be suggested by Sobel, 2003), this volume begins with and retains a close examination of natural science education practices at the school and ministerial levels within Kenya, which, we believe, contributes to a more thorough

understanding of the milieu influencing students' and teachers' views and experiences in rural and urban sites in the era of globalization.

[17] Quist's (2001) work points out the widening gap between urban and rural areas and schools in these West African countries, and although similar trends are evident in Kenya, the rural-urban divide is not new. Globalization's mechanisms serve to enhance the rifts between socioeconomic groups in society, rifts that previously were widened, although perhaps through more opaque means. As pointed out earlier, the colonial regime concentrated wealth and resources in selected centers, which naturally led to improved educational development in some areas and not in others. Although thorough studies of knowledge stratification have not been conducted in Kenya, it would be unwise to ignore previous work that has been done in other countries regarding curricular avenues for stratification (e.g., Anyon, 1981). Although we could identify no studies that look at knowledge and educational stratification in Kenyan schools along the rural-urban divide, there have been a limited number of studies that address stratification in relation to other factors. Claudia Buchmann's (2000) quantitative analysis examines family structure, parental expectations, and the perceived returns to educational investment as factors affecting educational participation in Kenya. In addition, Sternberg et. al (2001) use a family's socioeconomic status as a factor relating to the relationship between academic and practical intelligence in a small village in Western Kenya. In other African contexts, there have been a very limited number of studies that investigate social class and knowledge issues. For example, Hoadly (2008) examines working class and middle class primary students in South Africa and how inequality is structured in schools there through pedagogical practices in literacy classes. In addition, Waters (2005) looks at issues of social class in adult education programs and the linkages of such programs to various social movements in South Africa. With Kenya's nationally prescribed and centralized curricula relying almost exclusively on Western-scientific subjects for content, it is reasonable to argue that similar limiting factors may be at play here as well. The study of specific syllabi (such as biology or chemistry) as possible instances of knowledge stratification and educational inequality should be explored further. We extend thanks to Lois Weis for her thoughts and suggestions regarding this issue.

[18] Although we acknowledge that the examination of globalization's effects in the Kenyan context are multiple and complex, we suggest that a thorough investigation of such effects would benefit from longitudinal data. The goal of this volume is not to provide such an examination, however. Yet, using the studies referred to in this section, we might suspect that globalization is indeed opening rifts in Kenya along the lines of economics and social class. We might also suspect that the resulting strains on the social cohesion of the country are having adverse effects on the relationships of Kenyans with indigenous knowledge systems. It is important to look at natural science education both in the context of Kenya's colonial history and in the current context of globalization.

[19] These responsibilities are found listed on the MOE's website (http://www.education.go.ke/), among other policy statements, such as the "vision," "mission," and "strategic objectives" of the ministry. Although this agency's stated goals include ensuring "equitable access, attendance, retention, attainment and achievement in education" for all Kenyans, the ministry's actual realization of such goals is unclear. Critical questions that can be raised regarding the effectiveness of the ministry's educational objectives are: Do the stated goals take place at the level of the school? Are such goals accomplished in all secondary schools, regardless of their designation (national, provincial, or district)? Are the views of teachers or students represented in official policy statements?

[20] In this volume, the term *curriculum*, when used in reference to secondary science education, will be taken to mean the entire body of (scientific) knowledge, natural science or otherwise, that is to be taught through the process of schooling. When discussing the organization of a specific natural science subject for secondary education, such as agriculture, the word *syllabus* will be used due to the term's prevalence in official documents and teacher dialogue. For example, the KIE biology content guidelines for forms one through four are referred to by teachers and the KIE as the biology *syllabus*, not the *curriculum*.

[21] Subjects that are offered at the secondary level include agriculture, Arabic, art and design, aviation technology, biology, business studies, chemistry, Christian religious education, computer studies, English, French, geography, German, Hindu religious studies, history and government, home science, Islamic religious studies, Kiswahili, mathematics, music, and physics (KNEC, 2006).

61

[22]   Prior to the establishment of the KNEC, test administration was conducted by the East African Examinations Council with the assistance of the MOE (Eshiwani, 1990).

[23]   Since the implementation of the No Child Left Behind Act in 2001 in the United States, several reports have documented testing scandals related to the testing measures related to this act (see Pascopella & Desoff, 2007; Popham, 2006).

[24]   Eshiwani's (1990) report notes the failures of the initiatives such as the New Primary Approach and the School Science Project due to several factors, among them being the system's use of high-stakes tests, the lack of technological inputs and skills required for the success of education initiatives, issues related to language of instruction, and ongoing problems concerning the relevance of the national curriculum.

[25]   The KCPE exam is another high-stakes, national examination for students exiting primary school. The test is the sole measure of a student's performance at the primary level and serves as the primary determinant of a student's future academic performance. Accordingly, this test is used by secondary institutions to select form one entry classes.

[26]   There are other individualized, systemic, and contextual factors that might affect the pedagogical approach of Kenyan teachers in natural science classrooms. These may include the education or training an individual instructor received, the policies concerning language of instruction, and cultural influences on pedagogy. While these factors are certainly worthy of further investigation, it is beyond the scope of this volume to fully include such an investigation.

[27]   According to a teacher at Forest Secondary, course content and the pace of instruction are so thoroughly prescribed, that nearly every class across the country will cover the same content areas within two or three days of each other. Such national uniformity of natural science instruction is the result of the centrally-defined and mandated syllabi.

FOREST SECONDARY SCHOOL

Schooling, Inequality, and Naural Science Education in Rural Kenya

Rising from the relatively featureless and expansive Tsavo plains are the Taita Hills, a unique and dramatic geologic feature isolated in the Taita-Taveta District of the Coast Province. Taita-Taveta District encompasses some 17,000 square kilometers (10,500 square miles) and stretches southeast from the arid and semi-arid lands of Makueni District (in Eastern Province) and Kajiado District (in Rift Valley Province) to the coastal plains of Kwale District. In the western and southern portions of the district lie the dusty border town of Taveta and unpopulated thorny bush-land leading to the Tanzanian border.

Located in the eastern portion of the district, the Taita Hills offer a sharp contrast to the thorny expanses of Kenya's southeastern plains. With lush (yet shrinking) patches of endemic forests and rainfall that is intermittent throughout the hills (and sometimes devastating in the upper elevations), the hills provide adequate natural resources for small-scale agricultural cultivation and light manufacturing. Individual homes, linked by well-worn footpaths and tarmac roads connecting local village centers, clutter the hillsides from the very lowest elevations all the way to the highest point in the district (and province) at 2,207 meters (7,244 feet). The geographically isolated Taita Hills, with sparse electrification, few roads (some of which are seasonally impassable), and a reliance on small-scale agriculture, provided an ideal setting for gathering rural perspectives on indigenous and school natural science knowledge and practices.

The area is inhabited mainly by people of the Taita tribe, an ethnic group of mixed ancestry who settled in the hills as late as the 16th century (Spear, 1982). The Taita people are estimated to have a population near 350,000 nationwide (Kenya Ministry of Planning and National Development, 2001). The language of the Taita (*Kidabida*) is Bantu in origin; therefore, the Taita share linguistic traditions with some of the larger ethnic groups in Kenya, such as the Kikuyu and Kamba, who inhabit the areas of central Kenya and parts of the Rift Valley. The Taita's predominant Christianity is the result of steady missionary influence throughout the lowland and highland areas of the hills since the late 1800s (Spear, 1982).

Economic activity in the Taita Hills centers on small-scale agricultural production on plots (*shambas*) that are terraced into the undulating landscape. These agricultural products are destined either for local sale and consumption, or export to urban centers and the tourist hotels on the coast to the north and south of Mombasa, nearly 160 kilometers (100 miles) away. Wage-labor, in the form of metal working, construction, and service employment, exists to a very limited extent in the town of Wundanyi, where the Kenyan government's district offices are located. Wundanyi also serves as the major launching point for rural development and extension work in the hills by international governmental and non-governmental organizations (NGOs) such as Plan International, The Danish International Development Agency (DANIDA), the United States Agency for International Development (USAID), and the Cooperative for Assistance and Relief Everywhere (CARE).

Throughout the hills and the lowlands of the district, primary schools are found tucked into ravines, on hillsides, or next to the few winding tarmac or maram (laterite) roads that race across the dry expanses of the Tsavo Plains. Secondary schools are more uncommon and are mainly located within reasonable distances from the main town centers of Voi, Mwatate, and Taveta in the lowland areas, and Wundanyi and Mgange in the hills.

Photo 1. View to the west of the terraced Taita Hills.

FOREST SECONDARY SCHOOL

Nestled high in the Taita Hills was Forest Secondary School, a small collection of tin-roofed mud and concrete buildings in close proximity to one of the main routes meandering through the hills. In 2006, there were 188 primary schools and thirty-nine secondary schools in the district (Kenyaweb, 2006).[1]

Forest Secondary was begun as a Harambee school in the early 1970s by a Christian church in order to accommodate the physical, intellectual, and spiritual needs of Taita Christians. The local community banded together to finance the entire school project and obtain land for the school. In 1974, the Kenyan government took over the administration of the school, making it a public provincial school. In 1980, due to increasing enrollments and demand for schools in the Taita Hills, Forest Secondary added a second Harambee stream to the existing public stream.[2] In 1992, the second stream was also acquired by the government, giving the secondary institution its current official designation as a two-stream provincial school.

For the 2005 school year, Forest Secondary enrolled approximately 320 pupils—a student body composed of a mixture of males and females and boarders or day-scholars. According to the school's headmaster, Mr. Mwadime, the ethnic composition of the student population was almost uniformly Taita. Students who did not have at least one Taita parent enrolled at the school because of the occupationally-driven relocation of their family (for example, a parent working in government might have been posted to the District's headquarters in Wundanyi, approximately ten kilometers away). The teaching staff, however, showed more variation in ethnicity, with five of the school's twelve teachers self-identifying as belonging to either the Taita or Taveta tribes, four identifying as Kikuyu, two as Kamba, and one as Luo. Teachers who came from outside the district (non-Taitas) were posted to Forest Secondary by the Teachers Service Commission (TSC).[3] At the time of data collection, one of these teachers had only been at the school two years, while another had taught at Forest Secondary for fourteen years.

Tuition fees varied depending on a student's status. The families of boarding students paid 23,000 Kenyan Shillings (KSh) ($315) per year while the cost for day scholars was 11,100 KSh ($152). These funds were funneled directly into the school budget, which was approximately five million KSh ($68,500) in 2004. The annual budget for the school included operating costs such as food for boarders and day scholars, utilities (electricity and water), supplies (stationary, textbooks, and notebooks for students), fuel (wood or kerosene), staffing (including non-teaching staff, secretarial and kitchen staff, and compound guards), school development and maintenance, and activity costs (such as travel costs for student athletes and coaches and funds for special events). Salaries for all teaching staff at Forest Secondary (as with all other public schools in Kenya) were paid by the Kenyan government, except for the salary of one individual, which was paid directly out of the tuition-dependent operating budget.

The physical layout of Forest Secondary was simple and relatively spacious. The school's compound was bordered by a combination of live fencing (hedges and thorny kei apple [*Dovyalis caffra*] bushes) and wire fencing. The front gate—a study iron door with spiked metal at the top to prevent individuals from climbing in or out—was guarded by a full-time watchman (*askari*). In the main compound, the administration block (containing the school's main office, headmaster, and headmistress offices, as well as the staff room) sat at the far end of two parallel blocks containing four classrooms each. Behind one of these blocks was the science laboratory, furnished with lab tables, stools, and scant supplies for chemistry or biology experiments. A small and outdated computer lab was also attached to one of the classroom blocks; students visited the lab after classes to play simple games and used basic word processing software for entertainment. Forest Secondary's new dining hall, dedicated in 2005, also served as a meeting space for parents and others affiliated with the school.

Boarding accommodations for the female students consisted of two very small dormitory buildings that were cramped with bunk beds and personal items. A double outdoor pit latrine was located close-by. These buildings were all positioned near the front of the compound and situated in an area that was unobstructed by trees and close to the guard station and dining hall. The dormitory facilities for male students—which were nearly identical to the girls'—were located on the other side of Forest Secondary's compound, where the property began to fall rapidly downward towards a small stream. Once boarding students reported to school in the beginning of the term or after official breaks, they were not allowed to exit the premises except for extraordinary circumstances (for example, the death of a parent or sibling).

Forest Secondary was organized like all other public secondary schools in Kenya: Forms One through Four roughly equated to grades nine through twelve in the United States. Since Forest Secondary was a two-stream school, each form was separated into two different classes, designated as white and red. All eight individual classes had their own classrooms. Therefore, students assigned to a specific class (for example, Form Two white) reported to the same room and sat at the same desk for the entire academic year. After time, these rooms became a second home for students; plastic bags with personal items and clothing adorned hinges on the windows, while shoes and sandals were stuffed under desks. The "lived in" condition of the classrooms was a product of the long academic days and the relentless class schedule at the school.

Days began very early in Kenya's secondary schools, and Forest Secondary was no exception. Boarding students were awake by 6:00 a.m., donned their school uniforms, and took their breakfast (usually bread and tea) by 6:30 a.m. Day scholars began arriving between 6:30 and 7:00 a.m. (for some, the walk up from villages at lower elevations took over an hour) and "private study" began shortly after 7:00 a.m. The private study period between 7:00 and 7:45 a.m. was used by teachers for additional instruction time if they fell behind in coverage of the syllabus (which happened often). Typically, all of Forest Secondary's students were in their classrooms at 7:00 a.m., regardless of a teacher's request.

Before the official start of the day at 8:10 a.m., teachers were in the staff room marking notebooks (to track student progress in individual classes), preparing lessons, reading the daily newspaper, or just socializing over a cup of tea (*chai*). The room lacked sufficient desks and chairs for the entire staff to sit, so some teachers found alternate spaces to do work (such as in the computer or science labs), or they simply shared desk space. Classes lasted fifty minutes and ran from 8:10 a.m. until 4:00 p.m. Students and staff were given a ten minute break for tea each morning and a lunch recess that lasted sixty minutes, during which students were served their meals in shifts according to their grade level (pupils in Form Four ate first). Most of the faculty ate quietly in the staff room.

At the end of the day, students participating in athletics and clubs practiced or met from 4:10 p.m. until 5:30 p.m. or later. Other students continued with their studies (sometimes under the guidance of a teacher who stayed late) or socialized. Day scholars began their walk home around 5:45 p.m., while boarding students reported for their evening meal at 6:00 p.m. After dinner, boarding students returned to their classrooms for "evening preps," where they wrote notes or completed assignments given by their teachers until 9:00 p.m., when they retired to their dorms.

In accordance with the national education guidelines, Forest Secondary offered classes in the five subject areas that were mandatory for all four years of secondary school—biology, chemistry, math, Kiswahili, and English. The other courses offered at the school were agriculture, geography, business studies/commerce, history, Christian Religious Education (CRE), and social education and ethics. In Forms Three (11th grade) and Four (12th grade), students were allowed to select electives from these additional courses to tailor their education according to their interests.

Throughout the day, teachers crisscrossed the small compound for their lessons, bringing with them the materials they needed for instruction. Most of the instructors at the school taught five or six lessons per day on average, and some cleared thirty lessons in a week (this did not include morning or evening preps).[4] Due to the lack of financial resources at Forest Secondary, nearly all of the teachers had lessons in more than one subject. For example, Mr. Mutua, in his second year at the school, provided instruction in geography and biology, while Mr. Macharia doubled up in math and business studies/commerce. Assessments in all courses came in the form of bi-annual tests (known as continuous assessment tests, or CATS) that were set by teachers at Forest Secondary and used to measure the pace of instruction and coverage of the national syllabus for each course. Homework and other assignments were recorded in notebooks (provided by the school) and were checked periodically by teachers. At the end of Form Four, students sat for the national Kenya Certificate of Secondary Education (KCSE) exam, a cumulative test that determined student placement in the country's higher education sector.

Overall, the location of Forest Secondary in a highly productive agricultural area with nearby forests and other natural resources provided an ideal setting for teaching and learning in the natural sciences. However, the school's meager physical and financial resources obstructed students' and teachers' abilities to utilize these settings and opportunities in such educational efforts. The prescriptive agriculture, biology, and geography syllabi and overwhelming pressure of the KCSE examination further influenced instruction in the natural sciences.

Given the severe constraints and detached nature associated with formal natural science instruction, the applicability of indigenous understandings of natural science concepts seemed particularly critical for rural populations. Yet, these students' proximity to practitioners of indigenous types of natural science knowledge (such as extended family members and community elders) and rural lifestyles had limited influence on their perspectives about such types of knowledge. As discussed below, there were a number of reasons—including conditions of existence and school resources—for this limited influence.

Educational Resources and the Natural Science Education at Forest Secondary School

At Forest Secondary, teaching and learning in the natural sciences were adversely affected by the school's remote location and failing infrastructure. In each of the classrooms, missing window panes allowed for various distractions to occur during the course of instruction; insects, noises, and the occasional bird flowed freely into the rooms from time to time. Furthermore, the onset of the short rains in the Taita Hills brought temperatures that were described by most Kenyans as "very cold;" daily highs between eleven and fifteen Celsius (mid and upper fifties Fahrenheit), a strong breeze, and dampness combined to produce conditions that made it difficult for students to engage in their courses. Observations from a Form Three agriculture class reflected the difficulties students faced in classrooms with little insulation. A field note from the class read:

> Today at school it is very cold; the students are actually having trouble staying warm throughout the day. The classroom is a touch warmer than the staff room, but not by much. The wind is blowing in here (the classroom) pretty good. Students are rocking back and forth with their hands covered up and some with hats on. It is genuinely chilly in here; the students seem to be paying attention, but really are not "into" the class as much as in past classes. Especially as he talks about 'servicing cows' and other specific details about cow mating; this should be fodder for giggles and snickers. Not today though. They look too cold to be sharp.

The porosity of the school's buildings also allowed plenty of noise, both from within and outside the school compound, to reach levels that made it difficult to hear the teacher. O'Hern's field note captured the atmosphere in one classroom during an exceptionally noisy afternoon. As it read:

> It is a particularly cold day today, and since the classes are so open, it is not only cold, but noisy. There is an athletic field just near the school and another school from the area (about fifteen minutes away) is having its field day today. So the entire secondary school is cheering and yelling at runners and other students participating in athletic games. That noise carries into this classroom very easily, because the Form 2 room is toward the front of the school. So, students by the windows seem a bit distracted during the beginning of the lesson and at times when the cheers from the field reach high levels.

These and other observations from Forest Secondary showed signs of an educational setting that frequently faced environmentally-based interruptions and obstacles. A more concentrated and efficient instruction, while impossible to eliminate all the impediments, could have been alleviated with improvements to the physical structure of the school.

Students also had limited access to the fundamental materials that were required for mastering the content mandated by the national syllabi, including textbooks and laboratory supplies. In order to provide notebooks and textbooks for its pupils, Forest Secondary used funds garnered from student tuition to purchase the necessary materials. However, these funds were not enough to provide each student with the textbooks required for each course. Furthermore, families in this area were typically unable to bear the additional costs of textbooks for their dependents. What resulted was a chronic shortage of course textbooks, a condition that seriously hampered the educational prospects of students at Forest Secondary.

For example, in a Form Two geography lesson, Mr. Mutua was given the task of distributing fifteen new textbooks to a class that contained approximately twenty-seven students.[5] In order to accomplish this, he picked students he thought were "active" or performing satisfactorily in the course. The remaining students were instructed to borrow the texts from the other students when they needed to read for class or complete assignments. Such events, while telling of the immense challenges rural schools faced when trying to equip their students with adequate educational resources, also pointed to the difficult choices teachers had to make in order to proceed with the everyday tasks of instruction in the natural sciences.

Students at Forest Secondary not only lacked textbooks for their natural science courses, but also had little access to supplemental resources that could enhance both their familiarity with specific science content and their overall education. The school's library, which was housed in a small multi-purpose room at the edge of the compound, consisted of a small collection of outdated volumes that were not useful as reference materials and was strewn with disabled chairs and desks from classrooms. Students rarely used this space for research or studies; instead, it functioned as an overflow area for pupils who were waiting to use one of the institution's few dated computers in the adjacent laboratory.

Moreover, youth at the school had little or no contact with periodicals and other media that might have complemented the formal content of their courses. Daily newspapers, while typically available in the village centers and *matatu* stages (public transportation hubs) of the Taita Hills, were cost-prohibitive for daily purchase by most residents. At Forest Secondary, a single newspaper was occasionally brought to school by a faculty member. This copy bounced from teacher to teacher throughout the day. During three months of observations and interactions at Forest Secondary, students were never seen to be reading a daily newspaper on or around the school compound. Furthermore, televisions were a rarity in the Taita Hills due to their cost, the lack of rural electrification, and the poor reception of transmission relays.

While all of these impediments were indeed significant, they were compounded by a highly-structured educational milieu, where course content was rigidly prescribed by a central bureaucracy that employed high-stakes exit testing as the sole means of student assessment. These conditions had a profound effect on the teaching and learning that took place in natural science classes. These same conditions also reinforced teachers' and students' adherence to the primacy of school science and contribute to the relegation of indigenous kinds of natural science knowledge as less important.

Curricula, Testing, and Teaching in the Natural Sciences at Forest Secondary School

At Forest Secondary, there were many factors that affected the way natural science education (and, more generally, schooling) was carried out each day. In agriculture, biology, and geography classrooms, the possibility for enthusiastic and effective instruction was compromised by myriad considerations, such as the overwhelming task of traversing the overloaded and prescriptive natural science syllabi in the time allotted by the school day and academic year.

As we noted in Chapter Three, the syllabus for each of the three natural science subjects was defined by the Kenya Institute of Education (KIE) and was organized to the point of breaking course material into major headings and subheadings, including the number of lessons to be spent on each topic. The information that rural students worked to digest in their natural science courses included topics such as microbiology, geology, land formation, and livestock health. Furthermore, the objectives of the agriculture, biology, and geography courses also promoted social goals associated with the study of a particular subject.[6] The national syllabi also instructed teachers to adopt geographically-specific approaches (by using local examples of flora and fauna) to the teaching of subjects in order to ground or link school science content to their immediate surroundings.

Despite the inclusion of "general objectives" or more socially-oriented goals, the rigidly defined content of Kenya's secondary natural science courses left teachers little room to improvise in their teaching or extrapolate on a given topic. For Mr. Mwakisha, Mr. Mwachofi, and Mr. Mutua, each day was filled with class after class of expeditious content coverage and timekeeping in order to ensure completion of the course syllabus by the end of the school year. Given the external pressure of the national syllabus, these teachers adopted instructional approaches that allowed for maximum information transmission and content coverage.

In informal conversations and interviews regarding the agriculture, biology, and geography syllabi, these three teachers refrained from becoming overly critical of the core information and skills that the KIE sought to develop in Kenya's secondary students. Each of these instructors did, however, share the view that there were flaws in specific areas of content in the current syllabi. These flaws were elucidated by Mr. Mwakisha, Forest Secondary's agriculture instructor, when he described the attention given to environmental concerns (such as pollution) in the agriculture syllabus as "deficient" and "lacking." Although he acknowledged the difficulties in preparing an agricultural course of study for all public secondary students across the country, he also pointed out gaps in the coverage of important issues that transcended local or regional particularities. According to him, the revised national syllabus in agriculture (which was released in 2002) failed to highlight issues that were pertinent to the environmental realities faced by Kenyans. Mr. Mwakisha conveyed his opinions during an after-school conversation with O'Hern as follows:

O'Hern: So, in 2002, the syllabus they released only had some small sections on environmental issues and pollution?

Mr. Mwakisha: Yes, and the former one was even worse. It had nothing like pollution, nothing like agroforestry or tree planting; there wasn't much.

O: Do you think those topics are relevant?

Mr. Mwakisha: Yeah, to me it's relevant because now, you see, the forest cover in Kenya, in our country, is now diminishing, so the only form of forestry we can talk about is in the agroforestry part. We must encourage them (students) to think about these things.

While there had been incremental changes to the agricultural knowledge found in the formal syllabus, this teacher believed that the current state of the environment and increasing ecological decline required added attention by curriculum developers. This desire, for a more relevant and proactive natural science education, especially in geographic areas that were more susceptible to natural resource degradation, was unlikely to be met by state educational policy makers. Therefore, regardless of teacher intentions or desires, instruction in the natural sciences at Forest Secondary reflected the enormous burden of covering the national syllabus.

Complicating instruction in agriculture, biology, and geography was the attention given to the ever-present Form Four exit examination, the KCSE. As students progressed from Form One to Form Four, student performance on the KCSE became the primary focus of all instruction in natural science classes. As such, this cumulative test had a substantial effect on the methods instructors used to teach natural science content. With an eye on the KCSE exam requirements, teachers at Forest Secondary used KIE-approved texts as their guides as they held class sessions that were primarily teacher- and text-centered and devoid of student-teacher interactions.

Instruction in agriculture, biology, and geography classes varied little from instructor to instructor or grade level to grade level. Class sessions usually began with the teacher briefly mentioning the last portion of information that was covered during the previous class or note-taking period. This abbreviated review was followed by teacher-centered instruction that very often involved page-by-page coverage of the approved text for the course, including the re-creation of text-based diagrams by the instructor (on the blackboard) and students (in their notebooks). Teachers prepared for their lessons by consulting their books and moved from topic to topic according to the format of chapters and sections. During lessons, student behavior often reflected the daunting educational tasks that confront pupils in public secondary schools: With substantial amounts of information to capture and digest, students remained reserved during lessons and their attentiveness fluctuated according to the specific material being covered in each subject.

However, even though teachers approached their classes in a methodical manner, the significant pressure instructors felt to cover their course content required a relentless pace of instruction. In natural science courses at Forest Secondary, benchmarks were established for the purposes of gauging progression through the syllabus. If instructors deemed that a class was moving too slowly, they would press their students in the hope of making up lost time. The feeling of "being behind" seemed to be shared by every teacher on staff at Forest Secondary and was clearly articulated to geography and agriculture classes on several occasions. An observational note on a geography class read as follows:

> In the beginning of geography class today, Mr. Mutua notifies the students that they are very behind in the syllabus. So, in order to make up some material, he wants them in class tomorrow by 7:00 a.m.; they groan. He also tells them he wishes to give a lesson on Saturday, but they will arrange that tomorrow. This announcement is common in classes these days.

Similarly, agriculture classes were conducted with the pressure to proceed swiftly. An observational note on an agricultural class read as follows:

> As Mr. Mwakisha finishes this topic, he wants them to look back in their notes from the material covered over the last few weeks and ask questions. He tells them to share their notes and if there's something that they are unsure about, they can come to see him alone or in groups. He makes this offer because, as he tells them, "in class, we must move very fast from now on."

As the school's natural science teachers led their students through the course textbook or their notes on a particular topic, they occasionally broke to draw a diagram or add emphasis using an example. At times, students were instructed to take notes on important bits of information; otherwise, they were pulled through the lesson using a process referred to as "verbal leashing." This entailed the use of similar or identical verbal prompts and hanging phrases that were consistently asked by teachers and answered in unison by students, whether they were paying attention to the lesson or not. For teachers, this activity seemed habitual and usually followed segments where they covered a significant amount of information or where the content appeared technical or dense. Observations in biology and geography classes captured the instructional atmosphere where these interchanges took place. For example, a field note on a biology class read:

> Students . . . [seem] a bit distracted currently. Yet, they are mechanistically answering his repetitive questions: "Are we together?" They answer: "Yes." They also are completing his half-finished sentences, a common characteristic of these teachers. For example, he says: "The parasites will live in a..." "Host." And he'll repeat the question or phrase again.

The habitual way to teach a content was prevalent in geography lessons. As a filed note on a geography class read:

There is a lot of repetition in the class today. Students answer questions almost as if they are not sure of what is going on or what the teacher is asking them. He asks them: "Do you all see the grids?" They all answer together (although at a low volume): "Yes." A few of the students in the rear of the room…are not paying attention at that time, but they answer nonetheless. This type of activity, the question and answer, mechanical back and forth exchanges, go on throughout the period. He poses a question, or completes a word half way, and they finish the word or sentence or answer "Yes" to a question. Most of the class answers in this way; some students don't say anything at all.

Instructor-pupil interactions such as these above were common methods of teaching in the school—consistent with the findings of several studies identifying the teacher-led recitation and repetitive answer patterns as the dominant discourse patterns in Kenyan primary schools (Cleghorn, Merritt, & Abagi, 1989; Pontefract & Hardman, 2005). Like the primary school teachers highlighted in these studies, secondary instructors at this school used these methods to ensure some level of participation from students in the class instead of actually challenging the students to answer questions regarding the course content. In addition, these types of exchanges might have been attributed to cultural norms governing adolescent-elder interactions. However, it was more likely that the step-by-step character of these instructional periods resulted from habitualization of such teaching methods and the prescriptive nature of the natural science syllabi.

Rural teachers struggled to maintain pace with the national syllabi and prepare their students for the KCSE. For students, the lack of material resources that could bolster their natural science education, including access to textbooks and supplemental information from outside sources, created added difficulties. In a lush and ecologically-rich area such as the Taita Hills, it was possible that practical exercises and hands-on educational endeavors could have closed the gap between what students learned in their fast-paced classes with meager resources, and what they ought to have been learning, as prescribed by the Ministry of Education. Yet, this was not the case at Forest Secondary.

Forest Secondary's natural sciences teachers identified the lack of practical learning opportunities for students as an aspect of instruction that could have been improved upon. Despite the frequency of students from the area (especially the day scholars) interacting with livelihood activities that were directly related to environmental conditions and practical knowledge, these instructors still sought expanded occasions for hands-on learning and participation for their pupils. In a conversation with Mr. Mwakisha, he was particularly critical of the way the agriculture syllabus was drawn and the constraints teachers faced in the presentation of the mandated material. For him, these conditions de-emphasized hands-on experience and resulted in teaching that was too abstract for his students. As he stated during the interview:

Mr. Mwakisha: I think what would have been better for us is to put more emphasis on what the subject can do, practically, maybe even for the examination to also look at what they do. If it is growing cabbages, they can tell you: Grow it. Like the project they have at the end of Form Four. If, from the lower levels (Forms One through Three), we can have some form of a mini whereby at least they can try and show what they can do, then that would be good. Then they can constantly draw on their experience.

Asked if those types of exercises, or knowing by doing, helped the students to learn, Mr. Mwakisha answered, "Yes, for something you do physically, you do not forget it easily." He continued to state, "it sticks better other than [to] just leave it at theory."

Mr. Mwachofi, the biology teacher at Forest Secondary who originally trained as an agriculture instructor, agreed with his colleague's assessment of the importance of practical education. He maintained that most, if not all, of his students had never seen the agricultural machinery that was taught in the syllabus, such as combine harvesters, tractors, or even disk ploughs. The lack of everyday experience with such items could be compensated for with some form of hands-on education, he reasoned, but he was skeptical about the availability of such opportunities for the institution's adolescents. During our discussion of the syllabus, Mr. Mwachofi stated:

If at least they have the opportunity to attend one agricultural show, they can see several items on various types of plants, animals, and management practices that can stick into their head, unlike when they see diagram in a book. So it is better to be taking them out. But you see, the other issue is resources. So sometimes you push them so hard, but they are unable to pay the fees. You ask the headmaster (for funds to support a trip), and he says the school doesn't have money, and then it is an optional subject, so they prefer to take the students from geography other than agriculture.

The flourishing natural environment surrounding this rural school was therefore underutilized for formal educational purposes.

Overall, the rigidity of the natural science syllabi led to overwhelming time constraints for Forest Secondary's instructors and a blistering pace in natural science lessons. Despite these conditions, the teachers at Forest Secondary did their best to push and pull their pupils through the mandated lessons and units without the benefits of tapping into the school's natural surroundings or relying on adequate educational materials for their entire student population. Furthermore, the broad natural science-related experiences that many of these rural students had while growing up seem to have been forgotten, given the technical content of the agriculture, biology, and geography syllabi and the limited definition of science knowledge that was tested on the KCSE.

During the course of interviews with students and teachers at the school, it became clear that teaching and learning in the natural sciences took place without the assistance of the environmentally-related contextual knowledge that resided in the practices and traditions of the local community. This was evident by the finite associations students made between indigenous kinds of natural science knowledge and specific roles or usages for such kinds of knowledge, such as medicinal applications or the mythical processes included in folklore. Forest Secondary's instructors, for their part, could not infuse indigenous kinds of knowledge into their teachings, and saw limited applicability of such epistemologies in the context of the formal curriculum and the KCSE requirements. Despite these perspectives regarding such kinds of knowledge, students and teachers did not completely dismiss the indigenous understandings and ways of their ancestors during interviews.

Students, Teachers, and Indigenous Natural Science Knowledge at Forest Secondary School

For visitors to the Taita Hills, a cursory examination of the topographic features and vegetation of the region revealed a significant reliance on small-scale agricultural production and sale in local markets for household income generation. In this setting, young and old worked the family *shamba* (small agricultural plot) side by side in order to maintain the family's cash resources and keep food on the *jiko* (charcoal cook-stove). Many students at Forest Secondary shared these common experiences as Taita adolescents growing up in the terraced hills; some continued to be actively involved with agricultural activities at home on weekends and on school breaks. Similarly, non-Taita students had links to extended family members in the Taita region and often spent their youth planting and harvesting in the family's *shamba*, albeit in a different geographic region of the country. Taken as a group, the rural pupils of Forest Secondary had substantial familiarity with the daily responsibilities and activities involved in agricultural production and livestock rearing.

Individual students learned about natural science principles and environmental concepts from their parents, grandparents, or other extended family members in their ethnic language or in Kiswahili, depending on the ethnicity of their family and where they were raised. However, once they began their primary and secondary education, information about the environment was almost exclusively communicated using English due to its use in all aspects of natural science instruction (texts, lectures, and assessments). Most of the rural students at the school (whether they were ethnic Taitas or not) indicated that their Kitaita competence was insufficient for technical discussions of natural science issues with their grandparents or other elders. Furthermore, pupils implied that dialogue with older relatives took place in Kiswahili and did not focus on in-depth understandings of human-environment interactions, but instead consisted of stories and folklore about local practices or traditions.

In discussions of natural science knowledge and practices with selected students at Forest Secondary, their narratives seemed to weigh the sophistication of the knowledge of Taita elders in relation to the natural science principles that were imparted through the formal education system. Maghanga, a bright and articulate Form Two student at Forest Secondary, clearly embraced the information and content he learned at school. Maghanga was a dedicated farmer who recounted many occasions upon which he would be asked to help his grandparents to clear or plant their *shamba*, which neighbored his home (located nearly three hours, by foot, away). As the eldest of five children, he had numerous responsibilities around the family compound but had also broken away from the agricultural work at home (he was the first individual in his immediate family to reach secondary school). As he worked to master the natural science concepts that were included in the secondary syllabi, he was able to reflect on the nature of his extended family's knowledge of natural systems. The following exchange took place in an interview held in the school's science laboratory:

O'Hern: When your parents and grandparents were teaching you those things about soils, was it different than what you were learning in school?

Maghanga: I can say there is a difference. Because they are not; they are not enabled to go deep to the matter pertaining soil (gestures with his hand in a cutting, downward motion). So, in this we are at least going deep in educating on soils.

O: What do you mean by that?

Maghanga: They could not explain any; they could not give the better reasons for things. It (their knowledge) was not fully there. It was not fully digging in. What we are learning here in school, it is very detailed; it is deep knowledge.

Maghanga went further in his analysis of localized knowledge and practices when he linked his ideas about the specificity of such information to the reality that the practitioners of such ways had not been formally educated and that, in some ways, this rendered them incapable of fully analyzing or understanding the natural science phenomena that were taking place around them. He stated that "those people [the older generations of Taita], they don't know; they don't have the knowledge of these things [concepts and systems of knowledge found in formal schooling]. So, when you come to this secondary school, you were now able to understand better."

The fixing of indigenous natural science knowledge to a lack of education but not to the resolution of specific, contextually situated problems or circumstances per se was abundantly clear in the answers given to the short questions that were answered by each of the interviewees. In response to the prompt "Tell me what you know or think about indigenous or traditional knowledge about the environment," students provided the following descriptions: "The traditional knowledge was different from present knowledge because during olden days people didn't go to school. They got their knowledge from clan elders while nowadays children were taught by teachers." "In those days people had very little knowledge about the environment or the children were taught informal education by their mothers and grandparents but nowadays children go to school and learn formal education." "What I think about indigenous knowledge is that it is less expensive than today's knowledge and this is because if you have to undergo knowledge now you have to pay school fees at school but traditional knowledge is free of charge because we obtain it from our parents or older people."

The analysis of indigenous knowledge represented by students' written comments and by Maghanga's spoken comments reflects a perspective that situates indigenous kinds of knowledge as unequivocally different from and inferior to the bodies of natural science knowledge that were transmitted through formal instruction. For Maghanga, types of indigenous agricultural, biological, or geographical knowledge were less technical and not as detailed as the knowledge of these subjects that he learned in school. When conversing about their interactions with natural science concepts, both in and out of the classroom, other rural students expanded upon this notion, indicating that indigenous bodies of knowledge and methods were not practical for tackling contemporary issues relating to the environment or the development of the country.

For example, Jackie, a tall and athletic Form Three boarding student who was raised near the school, remembered the opportunities she had to converse with her maternal grandmother, who was forced to live with Jackie's family after an illness. The conversations, she recalled, addressed the physical changes that occurred in the Taita Hills over a period of decades and also touched upon localized farming techniques that were no longer in practice. Although her grandmother expressed concern over the pollution produced by modern agricultural methods, Jackie was resolute in her support for such methods and products. In an interview, her grandmother's thoughts about changes in agricultural technology was discussed as follows:

Jackie: My grandmother told me that during the past the people did not use fertilizers, but they just used simple methods.

O'Hern: What methods are those?

Jackie: Maybe they just used to make fertilizers and pesticides. They made some manures and used some herbs for pesticides. There were some plants; maybe they can smash them, apply some water, and use them, but they did not affect the environment very much.

O: What do you think about those old ways? Was it better back then or is it better now?

Jackie: According to her, we pollute and it was better during their time. She says it was better back then. I think now it is better; the current technology. Because it is more effective when compared with the one from the past.

Another student at the school shares Jackie's assessment of indigenous technologies and methods. Anne, a Form Two student who was among the top ten students in her class, identified herself as a student from western Kenya whose deceased mother was a Taita and father was Luhya. When it came time for her to select a secondary school to attend, she chose Forest Secondary because of its proximity to her maternal grandparents' home. On school breaks and holidays, Anne left the school compound and spent time with her grandparents, both of whom were too old to farm anymore.

Anne indicated that over the previous three years, she consistently helped her grandparents and other neighbors with agricultural work and livestock maintenance. She enjoyed being outside and contributing to the productivity of her family's *shamba*. In speaking with her grandparents about their experiences living and farming a small plot on the Taita Hills, she heard stories about how things were in the past, including methods of farming, crop yields, and climatic conditions. In her estimation, modern cultivating techniques and crops combined to make agriculture and life in the rural area better than in the past. She pointed to shifts in agricultural produce—from plants such as cassava and arrow root to more "modern" ones like green peppers and zucchini—as signs of progress and development. Furthermore, even though Anne's grandparents spoke fondly of the past, they also shared their granddaughter's assessment and agreed that agricultural diversity and production were presently better than in years past.

The remarks of Anne and her schoolmates illustrated student perspectives of indigenous and "modern," or school-based, natural science knowledge and practices. In interviews and informal conversations, students assigned a higher value to the types of information they learned through their textbooks and in their classes. Even though school science knowledge was preferred by these rural students, they did not fully reject indigenous systems of knowledge either. Their protection of indigenous knowledge system might have resulted from the associations they made between such kinds of knowledge and certain individuals or beliefs.

In this rural school, students intertwined indigenous natural science knowledge with agricultural or medicinal practices, environmental folklore, and beliefs to create narratives of their grandparents, whether maternal or paternal. As students spoke of specific traditions and beliefs, the narratives became somewhat guarded or protected; despite the intellectual distance these pupils had from indigenous frames of reference and the implausibility of traditional beliefs, there was a tangible reluctance to completely dismiss the stories and lore that had been passed down to them.

The resistance to upend indigenous bodies of knowledge and stories concerning the environment was seldom articulated by students, however. Instead, the pupils at Forest Secondary often characterized indigenous knowledge and the stories, beliefs, and practices associated with it as antiquated, lacking in technical sophistication, and unusable. Predictably, the school-going youth in this rural area viewed the natural science knowledge they learned in their agriculture, biology, and geography classes as superior and more suitable for usage by modern Kenyans. Similarly, Mr. Mutua, the school's geography teacher, thought that Western-influenced bodies of knowledge and problem-solving approaches were the key ingredients needed for Kenya's development.

Although Mr. Mutua was not an ethnic Taita and did not grow up in or near the Taita Hills, he identified with the rural lifestyle and livelihood activities of the area. As a boy in the semi-arid Kitui District, he spent long days during his school breaks working in the family *shamba* and helping with other household chores. Once he finished primary school, he attended an all-male boarding institution in the province's largest town and continued his flight from his rural home when he attended university in Nairobi. During his progression through the formal education system, Mr. Mutua had infrequent interactions with his grandparents and ethnic elders and, consequently, lost familiarity with the practices and rituals of his rural family members. When he discussed the stories and beliefs that were expressed by students and others in the Taita Hills, Mr. Mutua voiced skepticism at the applicability of such frameworks and doubted the possibility of merging indigenous knowledge systems and principles with the superior technical, "scientific" knowledge embodied in the curriculum. A discussion between O'Hern and Mr. Mutua took place as follows:

O'Hern: I've asked some students about traditional knowledge and they have some remarkable stories about the bringing of rain and other things like that. Have you ever noticed students thinking about those stories or talking about what their grandparents said?

Mr. Mutua: Okay, the culture is there. But now they have to accept the reality, because you see the modern science addresses reality. So even if the myth is there, like in the rains, you just associate something with the coming of rain. If a certain tree flowers this year and it rains, next year it flowers and it rains, they associate the flowering of that tree with rainfall, which is true. But now, here we come and we say: Which are these types of rainfall? How are they formed? There is the scientific aspect. So they have to accept (the scientific explanation) despite that myth. So they keep it aside, because it can't be infused into science.

O: Do you think it's disturbing to see those myths, those stories, and those practices not being followed now?

Mr. Mutua: Okay, I will say that, somehow, merging the culture, especially the deep culture, with the modernity is not possible. It is not possible because of the environment. We are exposed to the curriculum which does not take care of the myths. So, somehow, naturally, you have to drift away from those things.

For Mr. Mutua, the infusion of Western bodies of knowledge and cultural influences into modern Kenya was not only inevitable, but also desirable. In his view, the ways of the past had somehow failed to make life better for Africa's inhabitants through a lack of specific and technical information and the misguided emphasis on lineage and cultural continuity. As he talked of Africa's lagging economy, the lack of sound environmental management, and the pervasive underdevelopment that plagued the continent, he situated the knowledge and approaches of "outsiders" as the pathway to prosperity for Kenyans. As he shared his views during one conversation:

Mr. Mutua: You see, now there is some Westernization in Africa.

O'Hern: Is it good or bad?

Mr. Mutua: It is good. Okay, if we go to aspects of economy, it is the Western ways of conserving the environment that are really working. And then it is from that kind of way of life that the economy can grow and somehow uplift the living standards of the natives and therefore, we eradicate some of the problems that we are facing. So, somehow, we don't have a choice.

O: It's sort of moving in that direction?

Mr. Mutua: Yeah, because these things have been practiced and they have been seen to work. Even the donor projects; there are some donors who come and sponsor projects on soil conservation and then we are there just looking at people coming to our home country and showing us how to conserve our own land. You see, it's a big lesson and there's some kind of a challenge. People are coming from outside (laughs), and they are coming to your home area and they are telling you, 'This is the right thing to do,' and you've been there, but you don't have that initiative.

O: So the elders, they weren't able to provide that information? The outsiders had to come?

Mr. Mutua: They can't. They lack the information. You see, somehow we have lagged behind in terms of civilization. That is the state of affairs; we've lagged behind. So for them, for our grandparents, it was to conserve the culture and to see continuity in the lineage. In fact, their pride was how many kids does my son have? How many children do I have? Which is not the case in the life that we are living in. There has to be a balance between numbers and resources. So, they did not have that information; somehow, we were not keen on the environment. We just lived there; and you know, at times there were no numbers, there were not many people. And now the improvement of health services and such things, numbers are increasing exponentially, compared to the resources. So, we need that information from the Western sources.

For Mr. Mutua, indigenous bodies of knowledge and practices and the legends that grew from them lacked scientific backing and therefore led to the mismanagement of natural resources and misguided priorities, both of which hindered Kenya's economic and social development. What was needed, according to Mr. Mutua, was difficult—the accommodation of Western bodies of knowledge and frameworks without the abandonment of ethnic heritages. He stated, "I would say that maybe we should not forget completely our indigenous things; our origin. But now, if we are really becoming modern, we have to adopt the Western way of life."

Teachers at this rural school, understandably, favored the Western, technical information that was propagated through the natural science syllabi. Indeed, this was the framework and these were the concepts that they were not only educated in, but that they taught each day. They almost instantly regarded the natural science knowledge of community experience and the natural science content of the school as oppositional. However, through these teachers' narratives, it was also clear that they faced difficulties in reconciling the lives of their rural students with the natural science syllabi that they had to follow.

Many of the rural students that attended this secondary school grew up in an agriculturally-intensive setting laden with human-environment interactions and wildlife, and yet, teachers had limited opportunities to utilize pupils' pre-existing natural science knowledge in class to bridge the content of the syllabus with their life experiences. Through conversations with three teachers, it was evident that Mr. Mwakisha, Mr. Mwachofi, and Mr. Mutua agreed on the usefulness of locally-available examples and contextualized experiences to illustrate specific points in class. However, in discussions concerning the actual integration of natural science-oriented indigenous kinds of knowledge and practices into classroom settings, these individuals found it difficult to move beyond conceptions of such integration that involved more than just the use of local examples.

For example, contextual information was occasionally integrated into agriculture lessons by Mr. Mwakisha, a local Taita who was raised within an hour's walk of the school. As an adolescent, he farmed his family's *shamba* with his parents (neither of whom had completed primary school) and his eight siblings. His paternal grandparents, who were also farmers, lived in close proximity to his family's compound, an arrangement that was typical for the Taita area. Mr. Mwakisha was not formally trained in agricultural sciences in secondary school and admitted that, as a youth, he was not attracted to studying the subject: "By the time I finished high school, you used to look for opportunities to work, so I wouldn't say I had some special interest in agriculture as such." However, after enrolling in an animal health course at a postsecondary training institute in Central Province, he became increasingly interested in all aspects of agricultural science and eventually pursued his teaching credentials in the subject.

In class, he used examples that centered on the predominant livelihood activity of the region—small-scale agricultural production and sale in local markets. For the students enrolled in agriculture at Forest Secondary, Mr. Mwakisha's lectures and note dictation occasionally broke for an abbreviated discussion of common farming techniques or agricultural products that included locally-specific references. This instructor relied on his first-hand agricultural experience to aid in his teaching and indicated that these resources were "within me," and as such, he often gave students examples that were directly tied to their shared practical experiences in the Taita Hills. When non-Taita students were unfamiliar with local agricultural products or methods, he brought specimens to class or performed short demonstrations in an effort to bolster their understanding of specific topics.

However, Mr. Mwakisha's use of local examples—whether they entailed plant or animal specimens or discussions of farming methods or techniques— typically did not incorporate indigenous ways of knowing or understanding the environment, let alone the customs or the beliefs that were entangled with such understandings. He concluded that integrating such contextual information into agricultural lessons was problematic and, ultimately, undesirable. Despite his recollection of indigenous bodies of knowledge and practices pertaining to agriculture and medicine, he rarely referenced such information due to its limited usage in contemporary agricultural production, both within and beyond the Taita Hills. Furthermore, Mr. Mwakisha indicated that the lack of traditional references produced an uncertainty regarding the usefulness and applicability of indigenous knowledge and contextual, localized practices. In a conversation, the applicability of traditional practices was discussed in the following way:

O'Hern: What traditional practices and beliefs do you use in your teaching?

Mr. Mwakisha: Now, in treating livestock, we still have some, like some plants that we may crush and give to the animal, and they work, but they have been overtaken by modern medicine. Because, maybe they have grown out of using them, and they may not be having the technology on how they are supposed to be used.

O: Okay, so you may try to talk about those ways, but are the students going home and using those (practices/methods)?

Mr. Mwakisha: No, not really. You go by what has been tested and what maybe you have seen working. And if you see some medicines from the agrovet[7] working well, and they are cheaper and have local availability, they will be used.

In Mr. Mwakisha's estimation—one that perhaps was rooted in his advanced training in animal health and livestock maintenance—measuring the usefulness of local or indigenous systems of knowledge involved testable observations in order to see what "worked" or was effective. For him, traditional practices and beliefs, which were transferred from generation to generation through oral and applied means, did not meet the contemporary standards of empiricism and testability that underlay many of the concepts included in Kenya's natural science syllabi. The information provided by this instructor (as well as Mr. Mwachofi and Mr. Mutua) revealed that, while local examples were periodically utilized to contextualize formal science content, indigenous understandings and conceptions of natural sciences were normally skirted in the classroom.

The reasons for this avoidance, as we outline above, were multiple and complex. Natural science education at Forest Secondary (and elsewhere, as we will reveal) was affected by the tight state control over school science knowledge. Teachers and students at the school struggled to keep up with the relentless pace of the natural science syllabi prescribed by the Kenyan government. In response to the external pressure of the national syllabi and KCSE examination, the natural science instructors at Forest Secondary School adopted teacher-centered instructional approaches that varied according to their individual teaching styles but allowed for maximum information transmission and content coverage. These practices discouraged the use or acknowledgement of indigenous knowledge in agriculture, biology, and geography instruction.

Schooling in these subjects was not responsive to student life or reflective of student experience either. Development in the rugged Taita Hills had progressed at a meandering pace and physical environments had suffered. The lowlands of the district faced difficulties from overgrazing, drought, intensive agriculture, and population pressure. Residents relied heavily on small-scale agricultural production for income generation and household food supplies and adolescents were given noteworthy responsibilities in daily and seasonal agricultural and livestock activities. In this region, technical content related to agricultural practices and concerns of the modern (mechanized) agricultural sector, which permeated the secondary agricultural syllabus, were not applicable to the daily experiences of rural students.

SUMMARY AND DISCUSSION

In the Taita Hills, indigenous knowledge was not an intangible concept that mystified community members, teachers, and students. Instead, numerous residents of the area articulated the practices, information, and beliefs that characterized their local natural science knowledge. The varying familiarity with past practices often led to varying levels of usage, yet simple reflection on "what works and what doesn't work" appeared to be a stronger determinant of natural science-related practices. For Taita's farmers, achieving their desired outcomes meant using the cheapest and easiest methods, irrespective of whether those methods were rooted in indigenous knowledge or Western science.

Natural science education at Forest Secondary School was adversely affected by a number of resource-related issues as well. The situation created by the school's limited financial resources led to a chronic shortage of textbooks, scant laboratory supplies, library materials, and computer facilities and an inability to improve the school's failing infrastructure.[8] In addition, the school's remote location resulted in limited interactions with supplemental materials, such as newspapers and television broadcasts, and few opportunities for educational interactions outside the classroom with parks, governmental or non-governmental organizations, or industry. The educational environment resulting from such resource issues limited the potential for linking indigenous natural science knowledge with the school science knowledge that students interacted with in classrooms on a daily basis.

In contexts where the heavy hand of the state and resource issues plague science instruction, as they did in this rural school, it is imperative to interrogate natural science education from perspectives—critical and postcolonial—that emphasize the potential for transformative education for sustainable development. At Forest Secondary, the emphasis placed on school science led to a more restricted natural science education for students as they became further divorced from the knowledge and experiences that existed outside the classroom walls. Indeed, the high value students placed on school science not only decontextualizes their education, but, as Paulo Freire's work leads us to point out, it also integrates them into an oppressive knowledge system that is dominated by state controlled curriculum, texts, and tests. Furthermore, Connell's writing reminds us that practical knowledge is subjugated and that the practitioners of nonacademic knowledge are considered second class in societies where curricular and evaluative controls dominate, as they do in Kenya. Yet, rural students, by virtue of the geographic areas they inhabit, their ethnicity, and their socioeconomic status, are already considered second class, regardless of the knowledge they prize.[9]

The voices of students and teachers also suggest that the disconnection between school science and indigenous knowledge results from their devaluation of the latter. Although students and teachers at the school had consistent contact with community elders and family members who still remembered or used indigenous natural science knowledge, they favored and prioritized school science knowledge over indigenous knowledge. In their view, indigenous knowledge was linked to underdevelopment, folk stories, and unsophisticated understandings of the environment. The traditions and practices that were thought to produce indigenous knowledge, while still guarded by selected elders, were ultimately viewed by youth as outdated and inapplicable given the contemporary realities of life in rural Kenya. Mr. Mutua, the school's young geography teacher, summed up the views of students in regards to indigenous knowledge when he said, "Nowadays, somehow they (students) are emancipated." However, one may wonder if students from this rural location were truly emancipated. Does adherence to school science equate to freedom, or sustainable development, or the attainment of social justice or equality in the Kenyan context?

The complex nature of these students' and teachers' views of indigenous knowledge may have been a product of their educational environment and continuing interactions with such knowledge and practitioners. While this could have been the case in the rural location, urban students undoubtedly had different educational experiences and interactions with school science and, therefore, potentially dissimilar views concerning indigenous natural science knowledge.

NOTES

1 It should be noted that the internet site *Kenyaweb.com* no longer exists in the capacity that it did in 2006. At that time, the website contained lists of primary and secondary schools that were searchable by district. Currently, the domain Kenyaweb.com is owned and operated by a company that provides internet service for Kenyans. A comparable database on Kenyan government websites and non-governmental sources does not contain a current listing of the primary and secondary schools in Taita-Taveta District. Therefore, although this citation's verification is impossible now, the school statistics for the district are included here, as it gives a sense of the widespread existence of primary schools and the fewer numbers of secondary schools in the mostly poor district.

2 The term "stream" refers to the number of individual classes that exist at a certain grade level in a Kenyan school. For example, if a secondary school has four individual classes of students in each of the Forms One through Four, it is designated as a "four stream secondary school."

3 The Teachers Service Commission (TSC) is a semi-autonomous government entity, separate from the Ministry of Education, created in 1967 by Parliamentary Act 212. The TSC is charged with the registration, recruitment, deployment, transfer, monitoring and remuneration of all primary and postprimary teachers in the country at government institutions. The TSC also plays a role in the registration and accreditation of teachers who are employed at private institutions.

4 The average teaching load for secondary teachers nationally is 18 lessons per week (Siringi, 2009).

5 The numbers of students in Forest's classes varied from week to week and depended on the number of pupils who had been "sent home" to collect school fees. Students may wait up to three weeks for their families to raise the funds necessary for them to continue the school year; during this time, they were disallowed from attending any tutorials or preps and were responsible for all course material upon their return.

6 A more complete assessment of the social goals associated with the study of the natural sciences is provided in Chapter Four.

7 Agrovets are local agricultural chemical wholesalers that double as livestock veterinarians. They often have storefronts in village centers and larger towns.

8 Throughout this volume, our mention of computers is intended to simply catalog the existence of (or lack thereof) functioning computer hardware in the three target secondary schools. While we acknowledge the complex relationships between and among computer technology, information and

communication technology (ICT), education policies, pressures, and practice, and development in Africa, these issues have been explored in considerable detail elsewhere (e.g., Ayere, Odera, & Agak, 2010; Chinsembu & Kasanda, 2012; Ewusi-Mensah, 2012; LaFond, 2004; Langmia, 2006). Our objective is not to discount the importance of disentangling these issues, but to use the presence of computers to demonstrate disparities in educational resources that exist between rural and urban schools and among urban schools themselves.

9 A thorough evaluation of the social class issues that underlie the rural-urban education divide in Kenya is beyond the reach of this volume. Investigations that address these issues specifically in Kenya are lacking; however, substantial work has been done in similar postcolonial African contexts (e.g., Mjelde & Daly, 2012; Umar, 2005). In addition, post-Apartheid South Africa has been the setting for numerous studies focusing on social class and education in rural, suburban, and urban environments (e.g., Dolby, 2002; Hoadley, 2007; McKinney, 2013).

CHAPTER 6

CENTRAL BOYS SECONDARY SCHOOL

National Curriculum and Natural Science Education in Urban Kenya

Situated on the edge of the Great Rift Valley at 5,400 thousand feet above sea level, Nairobi is in many ways a place of transition and change for Kenyans. Geographically, Nairobi is in close proximity to the thorny bush-land of Kenya's central plains and the lush agricultural land of the northern Rift Valley highlands. The area's historical inhabitants, the Maasai tribe, referred to the lands as *ewaso nyirobi*, which is translated as "cool waters" due to the confluence of the Nairobi River and its northern tributaries (Gatheru, 2005). Nairobi's unique location offers residents reliable access to abundant agricultural products grown in Western and Central Provinces and provides visitors opportunities for nearby game viewing and other ecotourism activities.

Kenyans have seen Nairobi grow from a simple town at a railroad junction to the commercial and cultural hub of East and Southeastern Africa. In and around the city, there is an impressive international presence with dozens of international governmental and nongovernmental organizations maintaining offices there, including the world headquarters for the United Nations Environment Programme (UNEP), among others. In addition, many European and Asian countries have official missions in Nairobi, with some using their Kenyan offices as the hub for regional and continental diplomatic activities.

Nairobi also has tremendous cultural diversity; individuals from most (if not all) of Kenya's estimated seventy distinct ethnic groups live or work in or around Nairobi's central business district or its sprawling suburban areas and slums. Kenyans of Indian and Middle Eastern descent have strong representations in the city's business community, and in recent years the numbers of people from the Horn of Africa, particularly Ethiopians and Somalis, have swelled as political strife and ethnic conflict has persisted in that region. The greater Nairobi area also hosts a sizable expatriate community and the number of international residents continues to grow as the city becomes increasingly important for regional trade, diplomacy, and communications.

Yet amid the contemporary and modern feel of Nairobi is the abject poverty and desolation that characterizes many of Sub-Saharan Africa's rapidly growing urban areas. The city and its suburban and slum areas lie within Nairobi Province, the smallest of the country's seven administrative provinces at 696 square kilometers (432 square miles). During the past decade, it is estimated that the population of Nairobi Province jumped an alarming twenty-five percent to reach nearly four million people. As more and more people pile into the area, shoddy housing developments and an expanse of slums have been erected to accommodate the growth. Africa's largest slum, Kibera, is home to an estimated one million people and lies just six kilometers (3.75 miles) from Nairobi's skyscrapers, movie theaters, and trendy restaurants.[1] Accompanying such rampant growth has been the intensification of the HIV/AIDS pandemic in low-income areas and a dramatic increase in the amount of violent crime and drug use. These and other demographic and cultural transitions continue to spur Nairobi's chaotic and frenzied atmosphere.

The capital is where the wealthiest and most influential Kenyans reside, are employed, and attend movies, restaurants, and nightclubs—all within close proximity to the deprivation of the surrounding slums. There are exclusive private and selected government (public) schools that cater to this segment of Kenyan society. There are also schools for members of Kenya's middle class, and students attending such schools have parents or other caregivers who are employed in managerial or professional positions and who are able to afford the relatively expensive tuitions charged by the institutions. They live in single-family homes on the outskirts of town or in tasteful apartments in generally safe areas.

Photo 2. The Globe Cinema roundabout matatu stage, Nairobi.

CENTRAL BOYS SECONDARY SCHOOL

Central Boys Secondary School, safely described as a school for Kenya's middle class, was located in a hilly area approximately eight kilometers (five miles) from Nairobi's central business district. When the school was established in 1969, this area was sparsely populated and contained very few businesses or industrial properties. At the time of research, the land surrounding the school was rapidly growing into a commercial destination, with a number of newly constructed high-rise office buildings and several offices for international non-governmental organizations located near the compound. The institution was designated as a full-boarding, four-stream provincial school with 783 male students, some hailing from districts as far away as Kwale in Coast Province, approximately 400 kilometers (250 miles) away. Most of the school's students were drawn from the highly populated Nairobi Province, thereby giving the school an ethnically diverse student population (due to the diverse population of the greater capital region). Similarly, staff members also represented numerous areas of the country, including western Kenya, Central Province, Rift Valley Province, and the coast. There were thirty-seven full-time teachers at Central Boys Secondary teaching an average of twenty-two lessons per week.

The school's annual tuition of 36,000 KSh ($520) per student covered the costs for instruction and residence at the school and also included books for each class. The operating budget for the 2004 school year was nearly thirty million KSh (approximately $430,000), which encompassed all expenses incurred by the running of the school except for teacher salaries. Given these figures, Central Boys Secondary spent approximately 39,000 KSh ($550) per pupil per year—a figure that was nearly identical to the per pupil expenditure at the all-female urban school discussed in this volume, Uhuru Girls Secondary (see Chapter Six).

Although the school did not outwardly appear to be limited by its financial resources, Central Boys Secondary was limited in terms of its physical and spatial resources. The school's layout provided enough space on campus to accommodate an athletic field and soccer pitch; however, the academic buildings that constituted the essence of the school were arranged in a dense grouping toward the front of the compound. The administrative offices and small staff room sat adjacent to one another in the main building, with the three science laboratories and a variety of small staff offices situated nearby. The classroom block was a three-story structure with eighteen classrooms and a handful of small, stuffy offices for teachers. The classrooms, with cracked concrete floors, yellow walls, and pale blue-green desks arranged in tight rows, appeared slightly decrepit. Overcrowding in classrooms was a part of schooling at this institution: some streams in Forms One and Two had individual classes that exceeded forty-five students in a single room.

Students at Central Boys Secondary began their academic days very early: The male pupils were awake by 5:00 a.m. and in the breakfast hall by 6:00 a.m. Morning preps were held in individual classrooms at 7:00 a.m. and were occasionally guided by teachers if extra instructional time was necessary. Typically, teachers left work for the boys to complete during their evening and morning prep sessions. The school day started at 8:10 a.m. when a student rang a small hand bell on the walkway bordering the main courtyard and the classroom block.

Like the other schools included in this study, teachers and subjects came and went from classroom to classroom as each class unit remained in its own room.

Lessons continued throughout the day in segments of forty minutes and paused for two breaks: one fifteen-minute recess in the midmorning for tea, and another, longer hiatus for lunch. During the brief five-minute respite between lessons, boys raced about, visiting individual teachers in their offices or merely stretching their legs and socializing. During the day, students from Forms Three and Four moved from class to class, depending on the schedule of elective subjects they had selected. Elective courses provided the opportunity for boys to tailor their educations to their interests while also allowing them to mix with age-mates from different streams.

Teachers at the school averaged three to four lessons per day, which produced a weekly teaching load of about twenty-two per instructor. The school's financial resources and staff size allowed most of the instructors to lead courses in their primary areas of specialty only, with their courses often spread across the various grade levels and streams. Throughout the day, teachers moved to individual classrooms and usually spent free time in their offices or in smaller rooms that catered to specific subjects. For example, three biology teachers often commiserated in the biology laboratory storage room, which also functioned as a makeshift office with three desks. In general, teachers had a limited presence on the school compound as a result of the dispersed work areas available for them.

After classes ended at 3:00 p.m., the school compound came alive with the energy and movement of hundreds of young men. Students assembled into clubs or groups or work on extracurricular activities such as performances or projects. Athletic teams headed to the field for practice or scrimmages. Others simply passed some of the free time socializing or working on their academic assignments independently. By 4:00 p.m., nearly all of the school's pupils were engaged in some sort of organized club or academic activity, rendering the walkways and common areas of the school empty. All activities were suspended at 6:00 p.m., when the boys sat for dinner. After the evening meal, students performed evening preps in their classrooms and were allowed back into their dormitories two hours ahead of "lights out" at 10:15 p.m.

In general, the spaces reserved for learning and living on the compound of Central Boys Secondary appeared congested and in a state of disrepair. Although the students at this school did not enjoy the spacious accommodations that their female peers did at Uhuru Girls Secondary, it appeared that instruction in the natural sciences was not affected by cramped classrooms or dilapidated chairs or staircases. Pupils at this institution enjoyed sufficient materials and resources that were directly related to their learning in the natural sciences. These resources are discussed in the next section.

Educational Resources and the Natural Science Education at Central Boys Secondary School

The educational atmosphere projected to visitors was that of a teaching staff and administrative personnel that were dedicated to maintaining a high degree of professionalism when interacting with parents, students, and each other. In addition, a cursory tour of the school revealed an institution that was equipped very well with the materials necessary for instruction in the natural and physical sciences. O'Hern's field note described the school's atmosphere as follows:

> Central Boys appears to be a very busy and lively school with plenty of resources for students...[T]he headmaster [is] in his office, which has a boardroom feel to it and is filled with books that appear to be academic texts and reference materials. [T]he laboratory facilities...are very nice; each laboratory station has working sinks and gas outlets and in the storage rooms there are ample chemicals and hardware for lab exercises. The library is somewhat small, but still holds plenty of materials for the students to draw on if needed.[2]

At Central Boys Secondary, the core educational facilities were in good working order and some, such as the chemistry and physics laboratories, were outfitted very well. All of the laboratory facilities were stocked with chemicals and instruments and functioned properly. Classrooms, while cramped, each had plenty of writing space for instructors and contained maps or poster diagrams of plants or flowers. While the school's library was limited in size, it did contain a selection of targeted resources that could be referenced by students. Furthermore, the provision of learning materials, including textbooks, was not an issue at Central Boys Secondary, as the school supplied each pupil with the texts and notebooks needed for every course.

The school's students also took advantage of additional resources and supplies that were available for them. In several classes, pupils used two different textbooks for a given subject in order to cross-reference information provided by the instructor or found in the official course text. Moreover, students used a variety of writing instruments to organize natural science information in their own notebooks. In class, many students often had multiple pens and pencils out at one time, usually consisting of different colors, and switched from one color to another as they coded their notes according to the teacher's lecture.

The school's young men also interfaced with natural science information during their time away from the school compound by visiting libraries and utilizing television broadcasts and print media. During school closures for holidays and other events, some of the school's pupils continued to gain exposure to information sources through their proximity to other facilities such as the Kenya National Library or the World Agroforestry Centre. Others took advantage of their family's ability to afford and power a television to watch science-related programs or news stories. David, a Form Four student, referenced the availability and usefulness of public resources when he and O'Hern discussed the natural science information he connected with outside the classroom. He expressed his interactions with these resources in this way:

> O'Hern: If you want to get additional information about the environment, where do you go?

David: Basically, I really depend on books. I like (the) Kenya Library- the one just there on Ngong Road. I just take the *matatu* (public minibus) from town. They have a very wide (and) extensive part on agriculture there. It has quite a good range of books and you can really learn a lot. I don't really depend on taking all the books but I can sit and read them because it is a nice place.

The proximity of Central Boys Secondary to Nairobi and its abundant industrial facilities, non-governmental organizations, and governmental ministries offered the school tremendous opportunities for field study. In fact, the institution seized such opportunities by funding field trips for several class levels and subjects. For instance, during three months in late 2005, trips were taken to the world headquarters of the United Nations Environment Programme and Nairobi National Park (both of which were located on the outskirts of the city). All costs associated with these trips were borne by the school, with the exception of the nominal admission fee charged to Kenyan residents at Nairobi National Park. The school also reserved a sizable allocation of travel funds for Form Four students to embark on a significant field trip each year that took them to environmentally- and sustainability-related facilities and provided tangible examples related to the content of their natural science courses. Mr. Otieno, one of the school's geography teachers, discussed the availability of hands-on learning exercises in the natural sciences for boys at the school. During an interview, as he put it:

Sometimes, we will work here and we go out to check on vegetation just around the compound, because it is available. But, every year, the final class— the Form Fours—goes out on a trip. This year they went to Misinga Dam, which is in Eastern Province, where there is electricity being generated. Last year, the class went to the Rift Valley and they saw geothermal power projects there. And of course, they interacted with the environment as they went on those trips.

With ample financial resources, Central Boys Secondary provided its students with the educational materials they needed for their natural science classes. Yet, natural science education at this school was not immune to the curricular and testing pressures that challenged teachers and students at Forest Secondary and Uhuru Girls Secondary. It is clear that the prescribed content of biology and geography courses and the overwhelming burden of the KCSE examination also affected instructional activities at this school.

Curriculum, Testing, and Teaching in the Natural Sciences at Central Boys Secondary School

In geography and biology classes at Central Boys Secondary, teachers worked hard to traverse the demanding course syllabi in cramped and crowded classrooms. Like all of the other rural and urban teachers highlighted in this book, the practices of the natural science instructors at this school were, in the end, defined by requirements of the national syllabus. The voluminous information prescribed for each subject required that teachers introduce concepts and provide definitions and facts that were left to be memorized by students in classrooms after school hours or in the quiet of the dormitory at night. After students worked through long classes of dictation and content transmission for nearly four years, they were then required to recall such information in preparation for the KCSE examination.

At Central Boys Secondary, discussions of the KCSE occurred intermittently throughout the Form Two and Form Three classes. The Form Four boys, however, were required to constantly revisit and revise three year's worth of natural science content. The teachers at this institution focused their KCSE preparations on maximizing the number of points, or "marks," students could potentially be awarded on subject-specific sections of the exam. For example, Mrs. Omollo reiterated the need for her Form Four geography students to be cognizant of the potential point totals for each question. A field note from one class read:

> Mrs. Omollo is covering topics they learned in Form One. Last class, she gave them [her students] some work to do… [S]he is disappointed with the work they have done for her. She tells them this during class and says: 'You need to get eighteen out of twenty-five marks on these, and many of you are not.'…As class goes on, she is really pushing them. They are answering questions and using the map to give answers, but they are not getting them right. After one student replies with an answer, she corrects him: 'No. That is incomplete. You will get zero marks for that answer.' She gives them the correct answers and then explains everything on the board.

Likewise, Mr. Okech micromanaged his students' preparations for the biology section of the KCSE. In one lesson with the Form Four students, he focused on the point value while going question by question on a mock exam with his students. A field note captured the drill as follows:

> While going over the questions, Mr. Okech tells them [his students] what they [individual questions] are worth and how to make sure they get full credit for the questions by answering them completely. 'How many marks is this question?' he asks. While revising the mock tests, he is really focusing on how to wring out every mark from each question. He says, 'Answering like that will only get you half of the credit. You need to expand on that.'

Overall, the instructors at Central Boys Secondary demonstrated a genuine concern for the performance of all their students at all levels and embraced the school's motto—"strive to excel"—as they taught the natural curriculum. However, their attention to the academic preparedness of the Form Four students was particularly acute toward the end of the school year. As they prepared their pupils for the grueling exit examination, they were occasionally disappointed in the performance of their students during the review period. In a conversation with Mrs. Omollo about the KCSE, she discussed the enormity of the comprehensive exam and the responsibility teachers had for the preparedness of their students. The conversation about the exam continued for a while. As a filed note read:

> Most of what she says about it [the KCSE] is negative. First, she complains about the difficulty of testing the cumulative geographical knowledge of students in one examination. "You are testing on four years of content in two-and-a-half hours."… [She] discusses how boys can be good students all throughout school, but when it comes to the exam, they can flop. And if they flop on the KCSE, that's it. She also explains that she reaches out to those students that she feels need the help. She is passionate about helping out the students that are lacking: "What are we supposed to do? Let them die their own death? No." She is really adamant about how the teachers converge on students that need to be 'uplifted.'

Mrs. Omollo also voiced concern over the inequity inherent in a system that employed a nationally administered, high-stakes, and cumulative examination as the single measure for student advancement to post-secondary education. She felt that because of the vast differences in educational resources between rural and urban schools, it was nearly impossible for rural students to score as well as their urban counterparts. "Imagine," she stated, "that students here (in Nairobi) and students there (in rural areas) have to sit for the same exam." This comment offered another example of the tremendous systemically-generated stresses (i.e., national syllabi and a cumulative examination) that were exerted on both students and teachers at the secondary level in the Kenyan education system.

The concern that the natural science teachers at Central Boys Secondary showed for the academic success and general wellbeing of their students helped to create an educational atmosphere that appeared to be intense, focused, and highly goal-oriented. Their attention to individual questions, point totals, and the fate of their students reflected the enormity of the KCSE exit examination and the challenge of preparing their students for the test. For students at this institution, it was advantageous that the school had access to sufficient educational resources, both on the school compound and off-campus in the greater Nairobi area. Yet, regardless of the high expectations of teachers and their intentions to use all available educational materials for comprehensive instruction in the natural sciences, teaching and learning carried on much like it did in Forest Secondary: Their attempts at decentered teaching were often upended by the need for expeditious content coverage and exam preparation.

Yet, teachers at this urban institution attempted to encourage participation by students when they could, which created a setting that shifted the authority from the teacher and allowed for peer-to-peer and pupil-teacher questioning and critique. In a Form Four geography lesson, Mrs. Omollo's instructional approach typified the frequent involvement of students in the construction of examples during natural science classes. A field note from one of her classes depicted her approach as follows:

Once she gets into the lesson, she asks questions of the class. For some of the questions she asks, they [students] answer in unison, and for others they raise their hands. At one point, a student is asked to go to the board and draw a diagram of some sort of folding or faulting. He is also asked to explain it. The student takes a stance almost like he is teaching the class. He explains what he diagramed very thoroughly and is very confident. When he is done, Mrs. Omollo asks, 'Do we agree with him?' The students answer in the affirmative and then ask specific questions about the example.

During lessons in biology and geography, teachers asked questions and challenged the boys to contribute and the students, in general, obliged by raising their hands and responding in ways that reflected their academic commitment and confidence.

The participatory teacher-student interactions in natural science classes could certainly be attributed to a number of factors, such as the motivation of individual teachers or content enjoyment and perceived importance by students. In addition, the fact that Mr. Otieno, Mr. Okech, and Mrs. Omollo had been educated at the secondary and tertiary levels in Nairobi meant that these individuals had undergone rigorous academic training with access to sufficient educational resources and information capabilities. Armed with quality school-based experiences and access to multiple information sources, these instructors employed a broadened instructional repertoire and used national and international examples as they provided illustrations that resonated with pupils. Mr. Otieno's teaching in a Form Three geography lesson reflected how instructors approached course content using these methods. As a field note read:

Mr. Otieno gives them examples of tree species found in the tropical hardwood forests, and all of the examples come from Kenya, South Africa, and West Africa. He also mentions the Amazon Basin and Southeast Asian forests as well, and tries to draw parallels between the ecology of those areas and some areas of Kenya. He indicates that in the next class he will give them specific examples of forests here in Kenya and what their distinguishing characteristics are.

At Central Boys Secondary, targeted instruction and participatory discussions of content took place between teachers and pupils. However, like many other Kenyan secondary teachers, instructors at the school were forced to default to lectures and note dictation to cover course material in a more prompt manner. When the school's natural science teachers lectured at length, they, like their colleagues at the other schools in this study, dictated specific passages to students or reproduced diagrams that were found in the course text. In Form Two biology classes and Form Three geography lessons, the instructors engaged in this type of instruction. For example, in one of the biology classes, the lesson took place as follows:

Towards the end of the class, he (Mr. Okech) says to them: 'I think you should put down something.' He then rolls on for about ten minutes of straight note taking, repeating every sentence and more or less defining everything he talked about for the past twenty minutes. Sentence after sentence, he repeats himself and makes sure the students have entered what he has said in their notebooks.

Similarly, according to a field note, one of the geography classes ran as follows:

Mr. Otieno gives them straight definitions today. Each student has his notebook open, and Mr. Otieno goes definition by definition, adding at some points where he wants them to put a comma. For example, he says: "Agroforestry; underline agroforestry (pause); agroforestry is the practice of..."; "...are found in tropical areas, comma, and can have the following species..." He walks them through each of the definitions and there is no student input in this class whatsoever. Students have their heads down the entire period and they look up occasionally as he puts a term or two on the board.

The noteworthy variations existed in instructional practice on the part of Mr. Okech, Mr. Otieno, and Mrs. Omollo. Such variations might simply have been a condition of teaching in the curricular and evaluative atmosphere that characterized secondary schools in Kenya.

Central Boys Secondary's ample financial resources, coupled with its commitment to providing valuable educational endeavors through field trips and fieldwork, gave students an enhanced education in the natural sciences. Dedicated biology and geography teachers used the school's accessible educational supplies to arm students with the information they needed for the grueling KCSE examination. However, regardless of the time teachers spent on the practical aspects of the natural sciences or the usefulness that school-sponsored trips might offer in granting pupils exposure to targeted, real-world examples of scientific concepts, most of the students at the school had no real frame of reference for such issues or concepts because they rarely (if ever) ventured out of the greater Nairobi area. Field studies, for the boys at Central Boys Secondary, meant limited interactions with environments that existed within a reasonable distance from the school, but still nearby to the urban locations with which they were familiar.

In many ways, the urban students at this institution had little or no access to the contextualized natural science knowledge that existed beyond the school curriculum. Similarly, the pupils at this school were unable to envision the applicability of their fragmented natural science knowledge to real-world issues that Kenyans faced in both rural and urban areas each day. Their inability to ground school natural science knowledge was primarily the result of their physical and intellectual distance from the natural science-related knowledge, livelihoods, or practices of individuals in rural areas, including their own extended families, distant relatives, and members of their ethnic groups.

If pupils at this school had few formal and informal interactions with rurally-generated knowledge and practices, including indigenous bodies of natural science knowledge, how would they discuss such bodies of knowledge and the individuals or groups who still utilized it? During discussions and interviews with students and teachers about indigenous knowledge, it was evident that students' lack of experience with such practices and bodies of knowledge had a profound effect on their viewpoints.

Central Boys Students and Indigenous Bodies of Natural Science Knowledge

The young men who attended Central Boys Secondary were highly urbanized and connected to Kenya and Nairobi's popular culture. In informal conversations with students, they related an attraction to contemporary hip-hop music and artists as well as movies and other elements of popular entertainment. Some of the school's students also chose to accessorize their uniforms and footwear with subtle logos and signs that signified their familiarity with contemporary sports personalities or their taste in music. Furthermore, students often infused *sheng* (a Nairobi-bred slang-based dialect that mixes Kiswahili and English) into their conversations when they congregated in small groups after classes ended or on weekends. Demonstrating an appreciation of contemporary music and popular culture or infusing a distinctly urban dialect into informal conversations did not necessarily disassociate young, urban, Kenyan males from rurally-produced and rooted knowledge and practices. However, it appeared that life in the capital and infrequent visits with extended family distanced these youth from indigenous bodies of natural science knowledge.

During individual and group interviews at the school, students offered their viewpoints of indigenous bodies of natural science knowledge and practices. The school's pupils always conveyed respectful attitudes toward their grandparents and ethnic or community elders; however, they also discussed the knowledge and practices of these individuals of older generations in unfavorable ways. Their views of indigenous bodies of knowledge centered on two predominant themes: the ways that indigenous knowledge arose or was generated, and the fundamental differences between curricular natural science knowledge and indigenous knowledge and the general inapplicability of the latter.

Students at this school conveyed the notion that indigenous knowledge was constructed through hands-on activities and practical applications (such as farming or traditional healing) and, therefore, was only useful under circumstances—geographic and historical—similar to which it was created. These young men affixed indigenous bodies of natural science knowledge to simplified agricultural practices and manual work that was rooted in rural lifestyles and livelihoods. The comments of a Form Two student, David, reflected the perspective that such kinds of knowledge were generated internally (by individuals or specific groups) and transmitted from generation to generation not through the use of texts, but by oral means.

David's personal experiences were unique among his urban peers at Central Boys Secondary. As a young primary school student he lived in the rural town of Namanga, which sits at the border of Kenya and Tanzania, approximately 175 kilometers (110 miles) south of Nairobi. David referred to himself as a "half-caste" because his mother was Kikuyu and his father was Maasai. His family moved from Namagna to their current home in a traditionally Kikuyu area immediately north of Nairobi just before he entered standard five (Fifth Grade). Although David had been removed from his first rural home for over six years, he vividly remembered his early education and interactions with his paternal Maasai grandparents and extended family.

Despite the fact that his family resided in a highly populated area, David's father still managed to cultivate a very small *shamba* on the property and kept two cows that he brought from his home area because, as David put it, "my Dad really loves taking care of those cows." David's history of spending significant time in a rural area and his close ties to agricultural practices (as limited as they were) was a rarity among the urban students at Central Boys Secondary. As he talked about indigenous bodies of natural science knowledge, David reflected on memories of his time with his grandparents in Namanga and invoked their oral traditions concerning interactions with the natural environment. Ultimately, David felt that the lack of formal education for members of his extended family was the defining factor that shaped their environmental understanding. The source of indigenous knowledge was discussed in the following conversation:

> O'Hern: If you think about your grandparents, where did they get most of their knowledge about the environment from?

> David: Most of the knowledge, they just got it from themselves. Like my grandfather has lived for so many years, so he has got to know when the rains come, when it's time to plant, when it's time to harvest, the right time of everything to take place. So, actually I cannot say that they got their knowledge from books, because they are illiterate; my grandfather cannot read. So, I think they just get the knowledge from the past experiences that they had. Like, when I go to their place, there are some kinds of plants, roots, leaves they use for treating different kinds of diseases. This knowledge is not really given to them through books or maybe learning in class, but from past experiences from past people who have taught them, their grandmothers, and the knowledge is just passed on to the community.

According to this view, certain kinds of indigenous natural science knowledge were exclusive to specific groups (in this case, the Maasai) and limited to individuals who engaged in some sort of practice (whether it was agriculture or medicine). Books and other texts, therefore, were reserved for the technical knowledge that was taught in schools.

The second theme that recurred in interviews with students was the view that "old" (indigenous) knowledge was not only fundamentally different and less technical than "new" (curricular) knowledge, but that old knowledge was also a relic of the past when life was "simple" and primitive. In conversation after conversation, students declared that the "new" natural science knowledge found in schools was more applicable for modern Kenyans than the unsophisticated "old" knowledge that was harbored by their grandparents and elders and rooted in rural areas. For these urban youth, indigenous bodies of knowledge were better suited for "simpler times" and a more "simple life" than the ones they led. The comments of a bright and talkative Form Three student named Paul reflected the polarized views students had of "old" and "new" natural science knowledge.

Paul was born in Nairobi but had lived in a number of urban areas in Nairobi and Central Provinces due to the nature of his father's work. He attended several primary schools in the greater Nairobi area and at one point was a boarding student at an institution located in Nakuru (approximately 155 kilometers [ninety-six miles] northwest of the capital). At the time of data collection, his family resided on the outskirts of Nairobi in a highly populated area where there were no opportunities for agricultural activity. Both of Paul's grandmothers lived "up-country" on moderate parcels of land that were farmed by hired laborers.

Paul, unlike most of the other urban youth encountered in this study, enjoyed leaving the comfortable surroundings of his urban home on school breaks to travel north of the city and visit his paternal grandmother. During his time away from Central Secondary, he opted to forgo "moving around" (socializing) with his friends and watching television to help his aging grandmother with some of the work around her home and *shamba*. In primary school, this interest in hands-on activity and his enthusiasm for environmental protection led him to be recognized nationally for his knowledge of environmental issues and concerns in Kenya as well as his dedication to environmental stewardship.

Paul appreciated environmental concerns and understood the role that rural livelihoods and urbanization played in the degradation of natural resources in Kenya. When discussing indigenous bodies of natural science knowledge, his experiences in the biology and geography classrooms at Central Boys Secondary helped shape his views concerning the nature and origins of such epistemologies. About this body of knowledge, the interview with Paul took place as follows:

O'Hern: Do you think there is a difference in the knowledge about the environment that your grandmother has and the knowledge that you get about the environment here in school?

Paul: I think there is some difference. Her knowledge is more practical. Here, it's more about you knowing it, but you have not done it, because we don't know the culture of those rural places here. So, it's more of knowing it than doing it. So there is some difference.

O'Hern: Do you think the difference is very great?

Paul: Now I think there is a big difference, because I get to learn some things that they weren't knowing in the past. Like, during my grandmother's time, they did not know anything about the ozone layer affecting global warming, and all that. So, now we learn the present hazards to the environment, so I prefer to know these things now, because these are the things that affect us and they will affect us in the future. But back then, they didn't need to know about those things because the industries were very few, so the environment was very clean. The life was more simple.

O'Hern: Do you think it is important to keep talking to your grandparents about the knowledge that they have about the environment?

Paul: Yeah, because it gets to show me how much us Africans have changed. I listen to what she says, and I compare it to now. From that, I have learned that there have been very many changes in some small years. Ok, about the environment, if maybe I was put in her shoes, I would be very sad about the environment because there was less pollution then and they used to think about the soils and the environment in general, but not at the moment. There's not so much care now.

For Paul, older Kenyans had little need for detailed or technical natural science information due to the nature of past environmental issues and the history of underdevelopment in many areas of the country. Life for his grandparents and elders progressed in a linear fashion, with indigenous bodies of natural science knowledge providing the basic information and practical guidance needed to maintain life in a "simple" state.

The linkages between "old," indigenous knowledge and past lifestyles characterized as "primitive" were made even more clearly by Gideon, a Form Three student who reflected on sporadic visits to his family's rural home-place and communicated a sense of separation from the residents and ways found there. Like many of the school's pupils, Gideon was born and raised amid the dusty and bustling urban and suburban landscapes that characterize Nairobi and its sprawling surroundings. His home, which was located in a densely populated area within a five-minute bus ride from the school, contained three small rooms and had, as he put it, "no room for *shamba*."

Gideon's parents both came from western Kenya and lived in Nairobi for a number of years before Gideon and his siblings were born. After his mother's death in 1998, his father relocated his two younger siblings to live with extended family in western Kenya while he and Gideon moved into their present home. Every year, Gideon visited his siblings, aunts and uncles, and paternal grandmother during the Christmas holiday. There, he had the opportunity to help with daily activities on the family compound. It was during these yearly trips "upcountry" that he spent time with his grandmother and listened to her stories and advice about farming and living in rural Kenya. When he talked about these interactions, Gideon associated the natural science knowledge of his elders with a distant period of time when living conditions were, in his view, inferior to what was currently found in his rural "home-place." During an interview, he spoke of traditional knowledge and practices as follows:

O'Hern: When your grandmother tells you stories about things in the environment there, what do you think of them?

Gideon: Okay, in my view, those were the dark days. All of those things are not applicable now. They even talk of when they used to wear only hides and skins, and they never slept on blankets; they slept on banana leaves. The conditions were harsh and things were different.

Using language that was slightly more pointed than his classmates, Gideon distilled the information and practices of his ethnic elders into a characterization of rural life before the advent of modern building practices or textiles. In the eyes of this young man, indigenous natural science knowledge and the practices and customs linked to it represented underdevelopment and poverty. Most of the knowledge that guided his ancestors during those periods of time, with the exception of indigenous medicinal remedies, was "not applicable now."

Gideon's friend and age-mate, a tall and slender young man named Jackson, also linked indigenous bodies of natural science knowledge to a depiction of rural life that was "simple" and lacked the benefits of modern technologies. Jackson's parents were born and raised in Nyanza Province, located in the extreme southwest corner of Kenya, and they still had brothers, sisters, and parents who lived on the outskirts of a medium-sized city there. Jackson, however, had spent his entire life in Nairobi and attended primary school near his home in the city's eastern suburbs. He described the area as "very urbanized" and indicated that although there was not sufficient room to farm, his family kept a small kitchen-garden behind their house.

Unlike Gideon, Jackson did not visit his rural relatives with any frequency. Although his parents embarked on yearly trips to their home-place, the trip to western Kenya did not appeal to him. During the few trips he took to the area, he was not required to engage in agricultural work or household chores because his grandparents employed casual laborers to work their *shamba* and care for livestock. Instead, his memories of those trips included playing sports with his cousins and taking adventures in a nearby forest. As a result of Jackson's urban residence and his lack of participation in the typical livelihood activities of rural Kenyans, his practical understanding of small-scale farming was limited. With little hands-on experience and infrequent interactions with his rurally-based extended family and elders, Jackson's perspectives of indigenous bodies of natural science knowledge were restricted to the ways they could complement or bolster "modern," school-based natural science knowledge. These views were elaborated during an interview at the school. As Jackson conversed with O'Hern:

O'Hern: What do you think about traditional knowledge about the environment; is it important?

Jackson: The way I take it, if we can combine it with the modern technology, I believe it can actually achieve a common goal. Common goal, like for example, even in terms of medicine, it actually might achieve a lot. You know, we got technology from a lot of time actually, from there at home. It has been inherited, so actually you might say, if it's mixed properly with the modern technology, you can achieve something good.

O'Hern: Do you find that the modern ways and technologies are becoming more dominant than the traditional ways that you are talking about?

Jackson: Yeah, it's actually turning out like that, unfortunately. Some of the good things which are traditional are dying away, but actually some of the good things are also coming up. The modern ways are better sometimes, I may say. They're easier. Supposing even in cooking, it is better now these days. The gas we use is actually more friendly to the environment than using fire wood. So, in some ways, those modern ways are better.

Jackson's comments not only articulated a rift between indigenous and school natural science knowledge, but also make larger connections between types of knowledge and technological advances or products. Jackson's (and Paul's) remarks addressed the social and environmental benefits spawned from "modern" knowledge and ways, but also hinted that new approaches and understandings of the natural world might not be enough for Kenyans. For Jackson, the merging of indigenous natural science knowledge and modern science knowledge offered ways to achieve "a common goal"—whether that was improved levels of development or greater overall health for Kenyans. Similarly, Paul suggested that modern knowledge and technical understandings of the natural world were not taking care of Kenya's environment or protecting against further ecological damage. Therefore, despite students' clear and united denunciation of indigenous natural science's role for modern Kenyans, these particular pupils offered a subtle narrative that, in the end, softened their critique of these ways and provided possible opportunities for future consideration of indigenous knowledge.

Challenges Faced with Central Boys Teachers and Indigenous Bodies of Natural Science Knowledge

One of the school's geography teachers, Mr. Otieno, discussed the challenges teachers face when trying to infuse locally-applicable examples into natural science instruction. Throughout the course of Mr. Otieno's education, he spent considerable time in both rural and urban communities. He attended primary school in a rural location on the outskirts of Kisumu, but was schooled at the secondary and university levels in Nairobi. Before assuming his teaching responsibilities at Central Boys Secondary, Mr. Otieno taught geography and English literature at two smaller, non-boarding secondary schools located near his family's rural home-place in western Kenya. After returning to Nairobi and taking the teaching position at the school, he became involved with environmental initiatives and projects with his students. In class, he stressed the importance of fieldwork and the practical applications of natural science concepts.

When conversing about his students' interactions with indigenous bodies of natural science knowledge, Mr. Otieno drew on his experiences in rural and urban schools. In his view, it was difficult to incorporate such perspectives into urban school settings and, if attempted, such efforts would be met with resistance from a cosmopolitan student population. When interviewed, he explained these hindrances as follows:

O'Hern: If you mention traditional knowledge about the environment or things like that, what do they (students) think about that?

Mr. Otieno: Now, traditional knowledge is very important. Especially now in the rural areas, they're even taught, in the first two years, something about learning the indigenous languages and those traditions. So those people there have it. Unfortunately in the urban areas and the urban centers, there is very little of that. Now, in this place, you cannot use those local things, those indigenous languages and those ways in the class.

O'Hern: Do you find that students from Nairobi have some idea of what the concept of traditional knowledge is? Would they know what you were talking about if you asked them?

Mr. Otieno: Yes, but they tend to brush it away. You know they are in a cosmopolitan place, so they are all mixed up. So, once in awhile, yes, you will go to it (traditional knowledge), but there's just an attitude that, no, that's not for us.

Mr. Otieno's remarks on the difficulties associated with using indigenous kinds of knowledge in class implicated the weak ties his students had with the rural lifestyles that their parents and grandparents once knew. As the students' conversations demonstrated, most of the young men at the school had few, if any, interactions with their rurally-based extended family. Furthermore, only a handful of the pupils were able to speak their ethnic vernacular with any level of proficiency. This resulted from the lack of instruction in tribal dialects at the primary level, as Mr. Otieno pointed out, and also was a product of the irregular usage of tribal languages in the homes of these urban students. The cumulative effect of these circumstances was a significant disconnect between urban students and their individual ethnic heritage, including languages, customs, traditional beliefs, and indigenous bodies of knowledge.

In a country with such noteworthy ethnic and socioeconomic diversity, the process of schooling could serve to de-emphasize differences and break derogatory associations or stereotypes regarding fellow citizens. However, opportunities to address the detachment between urban students and their rural counterparts were missed. For example, a Form Three geography lesson with Mrs. Omollo revealed the way that rurally-based knowledge and rural inhabitants were represented in urban classrooms, whether on purpose or inadvertently. Her discussion regarding various agricultural practices and subsistence farmers, while not overtly derogatory or inflammatory, lacked the balance that may have derailed students' construction of rural bodies of knowledge and practices as backwards, un-enterprising, and contributing to the underdevelopment of Kenya. A field note from the class read:

In class, Mrs. Omollo first establishes the different kinds of farming, and then looks at the advantages and disadvantages of subsistence farming. There isn't much time spent on the advantages of subsistence farming, and she notes that it 'encourages low standards of living and hinders any form of economic development.'... Later in the class, she talks about some of the technologies that plantation farmers use as opposed to 'peasant farmers,' such as fertilizers and pesticides... Any small-scale farmers that can be seen around are referred to [by Mrs. Omollo] as peasant farmers and it is more or less taught that they don't use these modern ways to produce good yields.

The in-class portrayal of peasant farmers (and small-scale agricultural producers) pointed toward the tendency of the school's instructors and students to lump all rural residents into a single group that clung to indigenous bodies of natural science knowledge and was incapable of contributing to the economic development of their regions or Kenya as a whole. Because many of the pupils at the school had little, if any, interaction with individuals or institutions outside of Nairobi, such representations were easily cast by figures of authority (teachers and administrators) and left unchallenged by the school's adolescents. While exposure to these characterizations surely contributed to views of rural backwardness and the uselessness of indigenous science knowledge, the students at Central Boys Secondary also used rural linkages with agriculture and manual labor as negative epithets in social situations. Mr. Otieno described how his male students used rural symbols (such as the family farm, or *shamba*) to ridicule each other and, in the process, position themselves and their knowledge as superior to the knowledge and practices of their rural counterparts. During one interview, these interactions were discussed in the following way:

O'Hern: Do the students have a good understanding of certain topics before you address them?

Mr. Otieno: Well, in agriculture, you find that few are in touch here, because most of them are in this urban setting. So, in fact, there is negativity. You talk about agriculture and that has to do with the garden; that's called *shamba*. So, if someone is inclined or comes from that background where there's *shambas*, or gardens, they are called *mshamba*. So, you bring in such a topic and get that maybe just one or two (students) have that background. Like in the Form Three class, there is a boy they call *mshamba*; there's a negative attitude.

O: How do you mean? There's a negative attitude towards farming?

Mr. Otieno: Yes, towards farming, because they look at it as something backward, as opposed to urbanization and civilization. So the rest think, ah, we are civilized, we are above agriculture.

O: Are they actually saying negative things in class, or do you just get that feeling from the students?

Mr. Otieno: No, you'll get them reacting. Let's say you bring an issue like agriculture; it's a topic that's always been fused in geography. So, you ask something and they all turn and say, we don't know, but this guy knows, because he stays in the garden. Yeah, him, *mshamba*, a rural guy. So, they sort of stigmatize farmers. You know, one of the things about schooling, apart from the education, is it's a vehicle to jobs. You want to see at the end of your education (that) you'll get a job. So in most cases, students ask: What pays more? It is the white collar jobs, not the *shamba*. Of course it will be paying, but again, agriculture has got to do with lots of manual work. It is manual with hands because we don't have machines here (in Kenya). So, there's that negative stigmatization because you ask: Which way are you taking? The way for manual work? But you want to be computer literate, you want to be scientific, high tech, civilized, and stuff like that. So there is where the catch comes, the stigmatization.

Given the nature of the interactions at Central Boys Secondary regarding indigenous knowledge and rural Kenyans, it was understandable that urban youth responded negatively to inquiries about indigenous bodies of natural science knowledge. The viewpoints on indigenous natural science knowledge that were expressed by urban students were reinforced by classroom discussions that did not address the benefits of indigenous knowledge and attitudes that linked it to rurally-based lifestyles deemed backwards or counterproductive.

SUMMARY AND DISCUSSION

Embracing the possible role indigenous natural science knowledge can play in "achieving a common goal" or protecting the environment would potentially involve some level of cooperation with the processes involved in formal science education in Kenya. Yet, in a system where a centralized set of natural science syllabi blankets over three thousand secondary schools, such cooperation seems conceptually unacceptable and logistically impossible. Even if secondary institutions in the country marginally accommodate the instruction and assessment of indigenous bodies of natural science knowledge, other obstacles exist, such as teacher positions on indigenous knowledge and urban attitudes towards what are commonly thought to be rurally-situated practices and traditions.

At Central Boys Secondary, like Forest Secondary in the Taita Hills, biology and geography teachers traversed overloaded national syllabi using pedagogical approaches that were predominantly teacher-centered and lecture-based. The course content prescribed in the natural sciences required that teachers present concepts in ways that were thick in definitions and segmented information and thin in descriptions, explanations, or examples. In doing so, teachers at this school also focused students' attention on the KCSE examination and the ways they could maximize their performance on the cumulative test.

Although the physical amenities found at Central Boys Secondary may not match the ones found at other urban-based secondary schools (such as Uhuru Girls Secondary, which is discussed in the next chapter), the young men at this institution were given sufficient resources for their study of biology and geography. Working and reliable laboratory facilities, a small but functional library and computer lab, and school-provided texts combined to give students the educational equipment needed for their natural science studies. Unlike their rural counterparts, students at Central

Boys Secondary participated in off-campus educational trips to organizations and facilities specifically related to the content of their natural science courses. Furthermore, the institution's highly urbanized student population was able to interface with science information during school breaks because of their access to public libraries, television broadcasts, and print media.

The natural science education provided at this school was highly streamlined by instructors and prepared Central's pupils for success on the biology and geography KCSE sections by focusing on the professional and managerial aspects of these disciplines. This was evidenced not only in the ways that the teachers and students described "manual" (i.e., agricultural) work in and out of the classroom, but also by the fact that Central Boys Secondary did not even offer agriculture as an elective subject for study. Agriculture and the practices associated with it (such as agricultural methods or indigenous knowledge) were viewed as unsuitable for contemporary instruction and usage. Teachers at the school did not incorporate local or indigenous knowledge into their natural science lessons and students concluded that such information was fundamentally different from the science information and techniques that they worked to master in their biology and geography lessons.

The dichotomization of indigenous knowledge and school science at this school must be underscored here. Time and time again, students used terms like "old" and "simple" as they rejected indigenous bodies of knowledge in favor of the "new" and "more practical" science knowledge embodied in the national curriculum. In conversations, they tended to associate indigenous knowledge with a "primitive" state of underdevelopment that was best left in the distant past. Furthermore, characterizations of rural residents, who were classified as the modern practitioners of such antiquated ways, were used as derogatory epithets or punch-lines of jokes. The geography teacher at Central Boys Secondary also de-prioritized indigenous knowledge, acquiescing to his students' attitudes that indigenous kinds of knowledge were not for them.

One may wonder if indigenous bodies of knowledge are not for these urban students, then for whom are they for. The socially backward? The nomads, peasant farmers, and ethnic groups deemed cultural relics? In an educational setting such as the one at Central Boys Secondary, where state influences dictated the mastery of segmented and abstracted knowledge, the formal natural science curriculum served to stratify and separate groups in Kenyan society. R. W. Connell reminds us that in such environments, academic knowledge becomes the prized knowledge, consumed by the elite and educated classes, while vocational and practical (indigenous) knowledge is reserved for those occupying the lowest rungs on the ladder of society. If these urban males communicated distaste for indigenous bodies of knowledge and the practices associated with rural lifestyles and livelihoods, would a similar population of urban females share some, if not all, of these perspectives? In the next chapter, we discuss the natural science education of pupils at the third and final school examined in this volume, Uhuru Girls Secondary.

NOTES

[1]   Estimates for the population of Kibera vary widely. The 2009 Kenyan Census indicated that Kibera's population was near 175,000 residents, whereas efforts like the Map Kibera Project estimate a population closer to 250,000 (Maron, 2010).

[2]   In our descriptions of schools and education in rural and urban Kenya, we use the term "resources" to depict a multitude of objects, services, and environments, all of which are associated with teaching and learning in the natural sciences in Kenya. Although the bifurcation of resources into separate categories—most importantly "Western" and "non-Western" resources—might serve some purpose, it is important not to forget that schools themselves are Western-rooted institutions and formal schooling a Western-derived construct. We suggest that schools, teachers, and students incorporate and utilize all resources (Western, non-Western, or otherwise) in contemporary natural science education.

UHURU GIRLS SECONDARY SCHOOL

*Gender, Natural Science Knowledge, and Education
for Sustainable Development*

During the early years of Kenyan statehood, schools like Central Boys Secondary—male-only institutions catering to specific social and economic classes—were common in the handful of large towns and cities that were scattered across the country. Although female adolescents were legally capable of attending school throughout the state's early years (but discouraged or not allowed by family to do so), it was not until the mid-to-late 1970s that girls began enrolling in educational institutions in greater numbers (Sifuna, 2006). Continued improvements in female access to education and educational facilities led to the establishment of respectable secondary schools for female students. In more recent years, the push for gender equality in education, including access, participation, and the availability of gender-sensitive environments, processes, and outcomes (Amunga, Musasia, & Julius, 2010) in Kenya and elsewhere was strengthened through the Millennium Development Goals and Education For All initiatives.

Indeed, since the beginning of the millennium, Kenya's school enrollments in general, and primary and secondary education in particular, have constantly been on the rise. According to the data collected by the Institute of Statistics of UNESCO, the gross enrollment ratios (GER, hereafter) of primary education for girls were 89.6% in 1995 and 112.0% in 2009, which have been just slightly lower than that of boys' (91.1% in 1995 and 114.6% in 2009).[1] The net primary enrolment rates (NER, hereafter), have been almost equal between two sexes or slightly higher for girls (NER for girls was 56.7% in 1998 and 83.2% in 2009, while for boys 56.1% in 1998 and 82.3% in 2009; see also Table 1) (World Bank, 2012). We should note, however, for primary school enrollments, aggregated national-level statistics obscure regional variations that are related to population densities, dominant livelihood activities, and tribal customs.

Table 1. NER and GER for Kenyan Primary Education*

		1995	1998	2000	2005	2009
NER	Male %	No data	56.1	64.2	75.0	82.3
	Female %	No data	56.7	66.0	75.5	83.2
GER	Male %	91.1	93.6	95.6	109.6	114.6
	Female %	89.6	91.8	94.5	105.3	112.0

Table 2. NER and GER for Kenyan Secondary Education*

		1995	1999	2000	2005	2009
NER	Male %	No data	No data	33.5	40.5	51.6
	Female %	No data	No data	33.0	41.1	48.4
GER	Male %	No data	39.3	40.2	48.8	63.2
	Female %	No data	37.6	38.2	46.5	57.1

Table 3. GER for Kenyan Tertiary Education*

		1995	2000	2005	2009
GER	Male %	No data	3.6	3.7	4.7
	Female %	No data	1.9	2.2	3.3

*The Tables 1, 2, and 3 present the data accessed on June 5, 2013, through World Bank's Edstats < http://web.worldbank.org/WBSITE/EXTERNAL/TOPICS/EXTEDUCATION/ EXTDATASTATISTICS/

At the secondary level, GERs of secondary education for girls and boys have been almost equal in recent years. For example, the GERs for girls were 37.6% in 1999 and 57.1% in 2009, while those for boys were 39.3% in 1999 and 63.2% in 2009. The NERs for secondary education for girls were 33.0% in 2000 and 48.4% in 2009, while those for boys were 33.5% in 2000 and 51.6% in 2009 (see also Table 1 of Appendix A) (World Bank, 2012). Although these enrollment numbers have been steadily increasing with almost no gender gaps, the numbers suggest several problems. Comparing the primary education GERs and NERs with those of secondary education suggests that a large portion of students do not—or cannot— continue their education after the primary level and that those who left schools are not likely to return to resume their education.[2]

At the level of postsecondary education, the major problem is perhaps low enrollment rates for both boys and girls. While a persistent gender gap exists in favor of boys, the gap is not wide (see also Table 2). Some researchers, however, argue that the trend of female underrepresentation has continued in higher education in Kenya. For example, in 2007 only thirty-seven percent of enrollments in public universities were women and, across the entire postsecondary sector (which includes private universities, vocational schools, and technical colleges) the percentage dropped to only twenty-two (Onsongo, 2009).[3]

Setting these points aside, there have been marginal gender gaps at the levels of primary and secondary education in terms of enrollment numbers, and because of this one may suggest that Kenya is more successful in providing education for women than many sub-Saharan African countries (Mareng, 2010). Yet, despite the attention gender equality in schooling has received, disparities have continued to exist at many levels of schooling in Kenya to date—in particular, at the level of secondary and postsecondary education. Reasons for discrepancies between male and female participation align with the factors hindering participation at the primary level, but are also exacerbated by the fees and costs associated with secondary schooling.

Even if female students can circumvent or persevere through the severe bottlenecks that exist at each stage of schooling in Kenya and graduate from a post-secondary institution, they may also encounter gender-based inequality in the workplace and beyond. Mabarika, Payton, Kvasny, and Amadi (2007) note that women employed in the booming information and communication technologies (ICT) sector often are relegated to clerical and data-entry positions which are lacking in pay and status and offer few opportunities for promotion. These authors also report that structural barriers, such as the reluctance of ICT firms to hire women into managerial positions (irrespective of their training or credentials), strengthen the notion that the technology professions are more suitable for males than females. In addition, Kimani and Maina (2010) uncover political, cultural, structural, and judicial obstacles that disenfranchise women seeking property rights or inheritances.

In this context of women's education and labor participation in Kenya, one may wonder what kinds of views young female students express when they portray indigenous knowledge. Is it gender-neutral knowledge, or is it women's knowledge or "grandma's knowledge"? Such portrayals would play a critical part in the erecting of social and economic barriers and the occurrence of physical abuse against women in contemporary Kenya and elsewhere. Given today's rapid growth and changes in the fields of science, technologies, and environments, it is imperative to explore intersections of gender dynamics, indigenous bodies of knowledge, and natural science education, as they are told young women in school.

It seems that gender inequalities in Kenya involve complex social processes. Here, it is critical to examine the ways social and gender orders are maintained through the knowledge represented in school curricula as well as manner in which such knowledge is taught in classrooms. In particular, given today's rapid growth and changes in the fields of science, technologies, and environments, it is important to explore intersections of gender dynamics, indigenous bodies of knowledge, and natural science education.

UHURU GIRLS SECONDARY SCHOOL

On the fringe of Nairobi's central business district (CBD), but gated from the hustle and bustle of cars and pedestrians, was Uhuru Girls Secondary. In its history, Uhuru Girls Secondary, founded in 1954, began as a primary school for both boys and girls on the grounds of a hospital that served colonists in the early part of the 1900s. As enrollments and interest in the school grew, secondary grades, which later became the primary focus of the institution, were added. After independence, the number of white colonial students decreased steadily and native Kenyans began to fill their seats. In 1970, the institution became an all-girls school focusing on (according to the school mission) "providing quality education, developing talent and self-discipline, for holistic growth of every student through mutual interaction between the management and the school community."

At the time of data collection for the present study, the school was an institution that had endured and adapted to political, economic, and social changes over the past fifty years and that possessed a spacious academic complex with a majestic administrative building that dated to the colonial era. With the national statistics of lower rates of participation and completion than males at the secondary level and smaller enrollment number in higher education when compared to their male counterparts, educational trajectories for the students at Uhuru Girls Secondary School appeared limited. However, this all-girls school offered excellent facilities and instruction in the natural sciences (and other subjects) and challenged its students to master the official content of national syllabi and outscore other schools—male, female, or mixed gender—on the national KCSE exam.

The administrative building at the school was a stately colonial structure with a garden courtyard and hallways leading out to enclosed rooms and covered landscaped paths that snaked across the compound. At one end of the courtyard, the main offices were equipped with computers and a waiting area for visitors. At the other end, the staff room was a cavernous space with over twelve desks in the main area. Teachers also utilized smaller offices that were located in various places around the sprawling campus. Individual classrooms sprouted from the main hallway at various intervals, reflecting the suitability of the design for the structure's original role as a hospital ward. At the end of the main hall were a large auditorium and a small lunch area for teachers.

Most of Uhuru Girls Secondary's classrooms were located outside of the main building in smaller structures located sporadically on the campus. Meandering walkways connected classrooms with the chemistry, biology, and home science laboratories, and linked the labs with more spacious areas, where the school's recently constructed library and main dining hall were found. Beyond these buildings was the main dormitory, whose four floors housed all of the school's students in crowded but neat rooms that accommodated eight to twelve girls. Uhuru Girls Secondary also had a small block of three-room houses that were available for teaching staff and their families at a reasonable cost, and separate houses for both the deputy headmistress (assistant principal) and headmistress (principal) of the school. The school grounds also contained maintenance facilities and a deceptively large agricultural plot, complete with a limited number of livestock.

The school was classified as a full-boarding provincial school containing four streams with an enrollment of approximately 630 female students. The majority of the school's girls came from the Nairobi area; however, many also hailed from provinces and districts across the country. Because of the size and ethnic composition of the greater Nairobi area, the student population at Uhuru Girls Secondary was a diverse one, with many of Kenya's major and minor ethnic groups represented. Ethnic diversity also existed among the administrative staff and 44 permanent teachers, although to a lesser extent; of the 14 staff members that were regularly contacted, all but three self identified as being members of the Kikuyu or Kamba tribes (of the remaining, two were from the Meru tribe and one was Luhya).

Tuition at Uhuru Girls Secondary was 35,000 KSh ($500) with an additional 6,000 KSh ($85) charged for extra fees and projects. These figures did not include textbooks. Students at the school were responsible for the purchase of all textbooks themselves, a cost that could reach upwards of 7,000 KSh ($100). With higher tuition came a larger operating budget: 2004's budget of 24.2 million KSh ($345,000) was used for non-teaching staff salaries, food for the students, utilities, services (such as guards and maintenance workers), and supplies (notebooks for students, laboratory equipment, etc.). Contributions from alumni and fund drives added surplus monies to the institution's coffers and allowed for the financing of small beautification and construction projects and other on-site activities.

Over the past three decades, Uhuru Girls Secondary distinguished itself as a selective institution among public provincial schools and private secondary schools alike. One way they accomplished this was by steadily raising the minimum Kenya Certificate of Primary Education (KCPE) exam score that candidates had to achieve in order to be considered for enrollment at the school. For example, in 2006, students scoring lower than 380 marks (out of 500) were not considered for enrollment, whereas the cut-off score was 350 in years past. The prestige associated with more stringent acceptance standards limited the available pool of applicants to a specific stratum of students who attended well-equipped and well-staffed primary schools.

Uhuru Girls Secondary offered classes in the five mandated subjects (biology, chemistry, math, Kiswahili, and English) and also the "common" social and physical sciences such as history, Christian Religious Education, geography, agriculture, physics, and chemistry. Uhuru Girls Secondary also offered its students language classes in German and French in addition to art, music, home science, computer, and others, for a total of 19 course offerings. Like most secondary schools in Kenya, student progress was measured through the use of the bi-annual Continuous Assessment Tests (CATS), which were developed and administered by the teaching staff at the institution.

On school mornings, students were dressed and in the dining hall for their morning meal by 6:15 a.m. Immediately following breakfast, the school's girls moved to various classrooms for morning preps with teachers or for independent study. The school day officially began at 8:20 a.m. with the first class. Like the students at Forest Secondary, pupils in individual streams had their own rooms to call home. Different teachers came and went from their rooms each day and for the students in Forms Three and Four there was considerable mixing between the individual classes due to the number of electives offered at the school. This constant blending of students seemed to foster a strong sense of cohesion among grade-mates at Uhuru Girls Secondary. At the end of each forty-minute lesson, a loud bell located just outside the main office rang and the paths and hallways gradually filled with students changing rooms, seeking out teachers for academic assistance, or briefly socializing.

Throughout the day, teachers arrived in the staff room after their lessons and often consulted the master schedule before sitting at their desks. Instructors at Uhuru Girls Secondary had upwards of twenty lessons per week, depending on their field and "rank" in their respective departments.[4] Because of the size of the teaching staff, teachers had a fair amount of free time for planning, grading, or even leaving the premises to run quick errands in town. At the end of the day, the girls at the school attended club meetings, athletics practice, or sought help with their studies from teachers or other classmates. Dinner was served at 6:00 p.m., and afterwards students attended evening preps in their classrooms or found quiet spaces to do private work. By 9:30 p.m., all of the students were in the dormitory ahead of "lights out" at 10:30 p.m. In general, the students at Uhuru Girls Secondary enjoyed a schooling experience that provided them access to abundant educational resources, coupled with a school compound containing expansive physical dimensions and a historically-rich ambiance. In a physical setting such as this one, instruction in the natural sciences flourished, as we will describe below.

Educational Resources and the Natural Science Education at Uhuru Girls Secondary School

The interactions with teachers and students at this urban school began much in the same way as they had at Central Boys Secondary and Forest Secondary and in the Taita Hills: once contact had been established with the school, teachers and administrators were informally courted in the staff room and corridors in order to identify the individual instructors to be observed and interviewed. The focus of the observations was the nature of instruction in the natural sciences and the actions and words of students and teachers during the course of daily teaching and learning.

The transition from the rural location to urban Nairobi revealed significant disparities that existed between rural and urban schools in Kenya. However, despite the recognition of vast differences between the schools that were studied, the educational environment available to the students of Uhuru Girls Secondary (the first urban school visited) was still alarming when compared with their rural counterparts. O'Hern noted these differences in a field note:

> The physical structures are markedly different [than the ones at Forest Secondary]; the school has an aura of a palace, with a big pool, stately gardens, and a beautiful courtyard. The offices are very modern and nice, with computers and a nice waiting room . . . [T]he condition of the classrooms [is noticeable]; the desks are in much better shape than at the rural school. The chalk boards are actually chalk boards and not a black compound painted on the walls. Windows to the courtyard are positioned up high so students really can't look out and daydream or be distracted. Overall, the set up is much more conducive to learning and instruction.

The physical infrastructure of the school was only one component that allowed pupils to receive a thorough education in the natural sciences. As we mentioned previously, the provision of certain educational supplies, such as reference materials and laboratory equipment, was tied directly to tuition that the school received. This allowed Uhuru Girls Secondary to outfit its laboratories and library with functional hardware and relevant resources. Furthermore, while course textbooks were required to be purchased by the families of students, it appeared that such costs were, in fact, absorbed by families as every pupil that was observed possessed the required course textbooks. Inside the classrooms, supplemental instructional and reference resources also bolstered the possibilities for effective natural science instruction. As a field note from a Form Three agriculture class depicted:

In class, there is a student who asks if the nut from some weed is edible. This gets a laugh out of her classmates, but Mrs. Kibet actually comes back and shows her a picture of the plant individually and asks her if it could be eaten. What's great is that they have a color photo album with pictures of all different types of plants and weeds in the class; they have this weed in there. The book is over on a shelf and a student went to get it when the question came up.

Consistent access to course textbooks, reference materials, and superior facilities all combined to give students at this school a strong foundation for the mastery of sanctioned natural science knowledge. Newspapers and other media sources offered yet another layer of information that was readily available for these urban students. The school recently added a two-story library facility which included a lounge area where students browsed Kenya's English and Swahili language daily newspapers. The school's proximity to downtown Nairobi enabled it to receive strong signals from the three major television networks and other channels, thus allowing students the opportunity to view news broadcasts and science-related programs produced both domestically and internationally. In one interview, two Form Four students, Rose and Beatrice, described their reliance on media sources for additional information regarding the environment in the following way:

O'Hern: Where do you think you get most of your information about environmental issues and environmental processes from?

Rose: I get it from the papers, then the knowledge I have, I expand on it with the help of my teachers.

O: If you want more information, beyond what you get from the newspapers or your teachers, where do you go?

Beatrice: To the computer lab here at school or when I am home I watch NTV or Sky News.[5]

115

It should be noted that the mere availability of media resources to students at Uhuru Girls Secondary did not necessarily translate into substantial utilization of supplemental information for the acquisition of natural science knowledge. Yet, the environment many of these girls lived in may have led to a higher degree of comfort with such sources of information. For urban students and their families, consistent access to print media and television broadcasts was merely a part of life. Newspaper sellers dotted each street corner and clamored at every public transport stop in and around Nairobi, selling the daily prints for thirty-five KSh (approximately fifty cents). In addition, the school's pupils were accustomed to being bombarded by print and television media, advertisements, radio news, and other information sources. Their experience in the city, in turn, heightened their access to diverse types of knowledge on a spectrum of issues.

At Uhuru Girls Secondary, students and teachers drew on course textbooks and other targeted reference materials in their pursuit to cover the natural science content of the agriculture, biology, and geography syllabi. In addition to newspapers and television programming, pupils at the school took advantage of Nairobi's internet access, which offered sporadic interactions with supplemental scientific information. The capital's developed infrastructure and abundant secondary schools also provided a fertile landscape for participation in sponsored co-curricular activities and heightened school-to-school interactions. Furthermore, a number of governmental and non-governmental agencies located in the capital addressed scientific and social issues through educational programs and challenged students to use the arts to supplement their learning and express their academic and personal interests.

For example, the common areas and hallways of the school were continuously plastered with advertisements for various student-led competitions and promotions that addressed specific themes or issues. After browsing a number of bulletin boards in the main portion of the compound, a letter was observed that invited the school to solicit artistic performances and pieces from the students regarding anti-drug themes and to encourage their submission into a contest. The school was formally invited to participate in the event, which was sponsored by a Nairobi-area "students against drugs" association. Other printed materials and documents were also displayed, including posters that provided information on rape, drug use, pollution and air quality, and HIV/AIDS. Many of the advertisements and pamphlets appeared to be generated by various organizations and government agencies and were displayed in the corridors and around the offices.

It was apparent that students at Uhuru Girls Secondary were strongly encouraged to participate in clubs, study groups, and other associations (some of which existed outside of the school). At the end of the school day, there was a brief period of on-campus movement and activity, followed by little (if any) loitering or free-time. Nearly all of the girls at the school engaged in some activity, whether it was a classroom-based prep, language club, religious group, or sport. The assortment of events and options at this institution allowed its students to build more comprehensive understandings of the world around them.

The pupils at Uhuru Girls Secondary benefitted from the physical and monetary resources of their school and their proximity to Kenya's social, cultural, and economic nucleus. Their ability to use multiple information pathways resulted in tangible advantages for their natural science education, and ultimately helped them in their quest for scant university places and professional employment.[6] However, students at this institution, like their rural counterparts, were also required to engage school science knowledge through unyielding syllabi that focused on segmented bits of reproducible information that was devoid of contextual or local applicability. Furthermore, even though the natural science instructors at this school drew upon supplemental materials, their practice was indelibly shaped by prescriptive content guidelines and the cumulative KCSE examination.

Curriculum, Testing, and Teaching in the Natural Sciences at Uhuru Girls Secondary School

The instructors at Uhuru Girls Secondary, like their rural counterparts, continually battled the arduous task of covering the prescribed syllabi for their subjects. Teachers at this school occasionally complained about having to "make up ground" on the voluminous information included in the syllabus. For the most part, the pace and import of each class was dictated by where each class "was" relative to where "they should be," according to the national syllabus.

One of the most distinctive characteristics of the natural science teachers at Uhuru Secondary was the way they trained their students' eyes on the ultimate measure of their secondary education—the cumulative KCSE examination. The content of agriculture, biology, and geography lessons was often tacked to specific questions or sections of the KCSE, and the work of these teachers reflected their commitment to having the students at Uhuru Girls Secondary score well on the exit exam.

This single-goal oriented approach to teaching was assuredly not unique to these instructors; indeed, teachers in every subject made mention of the KCSE exam in all three secondary institutions that are discussed in this volume. However, continual focus on the examination by the natural science teachers at Uhuru Girls Secondary occurred earlier and more frequently than at either Forest Secondary in the Taita Hills or Central Boys Secondary in Nairobi. For example, Mrs. Kibet mentioned the exam to her Form Two agriculture students. As a field note described the incident:

> [E]ven at this early stage [Form Two], the girls are being prepped for the KCSE. The teacher tells them to look at the book's diagram and then tells them that on the KCSE, they can be given a diagram like the one they were looking at.

The power of this looming test was surprising. Two years in advance of these students sitting for the KCSE, Mrs. Kibet felt that it was important to prepare and coach them.

It is prudent to note that although observations at this school portray teachers casting a spotlight upon the KCSE at all times, there may have been an additional factor at play here. Perceptions of an urgent focus on the test were perhaps skewed due to the timing of observations in the rural and urban settings; comprehensive review sessions and exam preparations were the primary task for Form Four students, nationwide, during the final three months of the academic year, precisely the time of the interactions with Uhuru Girls Secondary (and Central Boys Secondary). Therefore, the seemingly premature mention of the high-stakes KCSE to students just beginning their secondary school career may have been the consequence of an institution-wide (and, indeed, a system-wide) concern for the senior students who were on the precipice of beginning the nearly month-long test.

Regardless of this caveat, however, secondary institutions in Nairobi (and across Kenya) had substantial interest in the exam performance of their students. For teachers and administrators, the KCSE was linked to institutional reputation and the financial well-being of their schools. Consequently, individual schools (at all tiers for public schools and in the private sector) leveraged themselves against neighboring institutions by becoming more selective in their admissions and demanding increased school fees as their Form Four students scored higher and moved into prized positions in colleges and universities, both in Kenya and abroad. In urban settings, where a greater number of residents were able to afford the inflating costs of secondary education, the interplay of test scores, school reputation, and school fees seemed more palpable than in rural areas.

Yet, even in an educational system that dictated content in lock-step fashion and measured student accomplishments using a single, high-stakes test, teachers at this school remained upbeat and devoted significant time and effort to their students and their work. The high degree of professionalism and seriousness that they displayed was evidenced by the time they spent before and after classes preparing lessons and grading papers in the staff room or their individual offices. The seemingly strong work ethic of the natural science teachers and their heightened attention to academic matters reflected their own schooling experiences in semi-prestigious secondary and post-secondary institutions.

The teachers that were observed had each spent significant time in Nairobi, with one (Form Two and Three biology teacher Mrs. Irungu) having been born and raised in the immediate proximity of the city. Two of the instructors (geography teacher Mrs. Ngilu and Mrs. Irungu) attended boarding secondary schools in Nairobi and the third (agriculture teacher Mrs. Kibet) was schooled in a highly selective boarding school near her family's "home area" of Eldoret. For these instructors, rigorous schooling prepared them for successful entrance into competitive teacher education programs located in Nairobi, where all three completed their teacher training. Such educative experiences gave them access to superior instruction and resources at both the secondary and post-secondary levels and allowed them to interact with the information technologies and capabilities available in Nairobi. The educational histories of these teachers contributed to the heightened sense of enthusiasm and diligence as they worked to cover the prescribed syllabi.

With an ethnically diverse student body and staff room, highly trained staff and administrators, nicely appointed school facilities, and a cosmopolitan setting surrounding the institution, the processes of teaching and learning in the sciences seemed charged and energetic and proceeded with few distractions. In class, instructional time was often interactive, with a substantial number of question and answer exchanges between instructors and students. The observations recorded in a Form Three geography period reflected the participatory nature of teaching and learning in this institution. As one of the fieldnotes read:

> To begin class, Mrs. Ngilu reviews what was covered in the last class and is asking particular students individual questions while walking around the class listening to their answers. She stands at the back of the room and just listens and asks follow up questions. For the first bit of class, she sort of just walks around the class without any agenda; she is simply conversing with the students about the content. This gives the students a chance to actively participate in the building and reviewing of the lesson.

The instructional approaches of the school's natural science teachers appeared to promote less intense classroom environments, where teacher-student rapport was constructive and students confidently contributed to the lessons. In a Form Three agriculture class, the interplay between Mrs. Kibet and her students characterized the tendency of these three teachers to maintain focused class periods while allowing for slight diversions from the unyielding syllabi. As a field note depicted it:

> Mrs. Kibet draws a detailed diagram and explanation of the pollination of rice and goes slowly through it and then asks: 'Is it okay? Have I gone too fast?' ...[T]his is a bit better than the typical 'Are we together?' question, which students are programmed to say 'Yes' to automatically, regardless if they are with the teacher or not. There is a point when the students are kind of just lacking in participation and are answering incorrectly, so she asks: 'Should I prepare a quiz?' They all say 'No' with a light laugh and some chatter. There is a rapport in this class between them and her... Mrs. Kibet is pretty no-nonsense, and very relaxed, but she definitely wants to make sure everyone is paying attention and does so by asking questions and having discussions.

Episodes, such as the one captured above, conveyed an aura of dynamic science instruction that differed dramatically from the teaching and learning in the rural school. However, the abilities of Uhuru Secondary's teachers to engage their students during natural science instruction were also restricted at times.

The professionals teaching at this school employed instructional practices that alternated between fostering student participation and didactic approaches that served to transmit segmented information. During classes where the teacher used the latter approach, natural science lessons often mirrored those at Forest

Secondary. Pupils at the school, like their rural counterparts, drifted in and out of attentiveness and engagement with course content as they endured compressed instructional time and a rigid syllabus. Student engagement was quelled when the agriculture, biology, and geography instructors used lecture formats to cover material in a controlled and measured fashion. When the natural science teachers lectured at length, they directed students to write specific passages or construct diagrams that were lifted directly from the course text or other notes. This type of teaching occurred in each subject and at all levels from time to time, and occasionally consumed entire class periods. The observations from a Form Two biology class depicted these teacher-centered interactions. For example, one day the following event took place:

> Mrs. Irungu gives them definitions and reads them over and over until everyone copies them down. Then she moves on to another term or definition and does the same. When she gives them notes, all their heads are down and writing. Some of the girls have their books open and are checking things as they go along. She also takes the time to draw a diagram on the board, straight from the book, and requires the girls to draw it . . . [T]he book's diagram is the one [Mrs. Irungu] is drawing, except in her reproduction it becomes somewhat convoluted. But she insists that they draw it, and even at one point begins to walk around and check notebooks.

The variations in instructional practice did not appear to be tied to any specific topics or themes within a subject. Instead, Mrs. Ngilu, Mrs. Kibet, and Mrs. Irungu struggled to balance, on one hand, teaching that made students more comfortable and engaged and, on the other hand, teaching that effectively covered the prescribed course content. As the teachers at this school alternated between the two types of instructional approaches, they also tapped the school's financial resources and location to break the monotony of teacher- and text-centered lessons that were sprinkled with brief periods of student-teacher interactions.

Educative experiences were not only defined by the availability of educational materials at school and by what took place in classrooms and laboratories, but were also catalyzed by opportunities to engage in co-curricular activities and to explore educational settings outside the boundaries of the school. At Uhuru Girls Secondary, students were offered numerous avenues to engage in hands-on learning activities and pursue creative interests linked to the natural and social sciences. The fact that students at this institution had greater access to field-based or hands-on educational opportunities and resources was not surprising; geographic proximity to Nairobi and the surrounding environments gave the school's pupils several occasions for valuable and impressive educative experiences that were simply not an option for many students in other areas of the country. For example, Mrs. Kibet's Form Two, Three, and Four agricultural students were given the opportunity to take a field trip to Sunnyville Farms, a major dairy production facility located on the outskirts of Nairobi. This outing provided immediate and detailed information that was then fused with content included in classroom work. As one of the fieldnotes recording this pedagogical process read:

> [The staff at the dairy] takes [the group] through the plant where all the products are packaged and assembled for shipping and explains the entire process, from individual farmers collecting milk, to offloading and testing, to processing (depending on the product to be made), to quality assurance, packaging, storing, and shipping. Mrs. Kibet put together a small set of questions that she gave out on the bus ride home which asks specific questions about what they saw in relation to concepts they were studying. The girls huddle together in seats and across the aisle and talk about the answers.

This trip also offered a glimpse into the ways that urban students interacted with livestock and other farm-based animals. For example, when the group first approached a pen containing dairy cows, the students began to call to them, as if they were domesticated animals, so they could pet them. Additionally, when the group was able to interact with and pet a small number of calves, they reacted with giddiness and laughter at the texture of the calves' tongues. These interactions and behaviors reflected their inexperience with some of the basic components of small-scale agricultural production and rural lifestyles in Kenya.

At Uhuru Girls Secondary, abundant educational resources, coupled with teacher attempts to produce and maintain student-centered instruction, provided middle- and upper-class urban students with a comprehensive natural science education. Although the comfortable and engaging instructional styles of the school's natural science teachers fostered student participation, these teachers intermittently used top-down approaches and long lecture sessions to traverse large portions of content from the syllabus. In many respects, the educational atmosphere that Mrs. Ngilu, Mrs. Kibet, and Mrs. Irungu sought to promote was trumped by the rigid timetables of the agriculture, biology, and geography syllabi and the natural science knowledge bound to the prescribed curriculum. This overwhelming burden exposed the reality of teaching and learning in secondary science classrooms in Kenya: All instruction had to eventually attend to the official science knowledge defined by the syllabus and tested on the KCSE.

As we described in the Chapter Four, rural teachers and students offered compelling perspectives on indigenous bodies of natural science knowledge and epistemological frameworks. Such indigenous knowledge about agriculture, biology, and geography were not included in the national syllabi for these subjects and were only sporadically discussed in rural science lessons. While the urban teachers and students at Uhuru Girls Secondary, like their rural counterparts at Forest Secondary, could articulate descriptions and examples of such "alternative" systems of science knowledge, their interactions with these epistemologies seemed to have ended with these views. In interviews with urban natural science teachers and students about indigenous bodies of science knowledge, respondents fortified schooled science knowledge and offered intriguing characterizations of indigenous bodies of knowledge, practices, and the individuals who still utilized them.

Students, Teachers, and Indigenous Science Knowledge at
Uhuru Girls Secondary School

It is important to note two spatial limitations that existed for urban students at this school. First, mandatory boarding requirements at the institution limited the opportunities for students to venture into Nairobi and interact with educational opportunities offered through cultural events and social activities. Second, the highly urbanized student population had restricted relationships with extended family members and natural settings located outside the greater Nairobi area. As a result, the school (and educational resources located within) was the nucleus of natural science knowledge for these pupils. With the institution, the formal curriculum, and instructors playing such prominent roles in the development of students' understanding of agricultural, biological, and geographical concepts, it crucial to discuss teachers' and students' views of indigenous science knowledge and the rituals, practices, and individuals that are closely linked to them.

During interviews with Mrs. Kibet (teaching agriculture) and Mrs. Ngilu (teaching geography), they did not associate indigenous bodies of natural science knowledge with the students they taught. Instead, they linked the concepts to rural locations and inhabitants. For Mrs. Kibet, these linkages were intricately tied to her experiences as a teacher. Before assuming her teaching duties at Uhuru Girls Secondary, she taught for ten years at a mixed boarding and day-scholar provincial school near her home in Eldoret. During her ten years at Uhuru Girls Secondary, she traveled back to her home area during school breaks and holidays and would participate in agricultural activities while there. In general, Mrs. Kibet appeared very knowledgeable about the farming practices she taught and often used supplemental resources (books and other information) in her teaching. She seemed to push her students hard in class, continually challenging them to think about the content and problem solve, while also referencing old tests in order to give her pupils examples of the KCSE questions. Having taught in both rural and urban areas, Mrs. Kibet also had an acute understanding of the dichotomous nature of the Kenyan education system.

In an interview concerning indigenous types of science knowledge, Mrs. Kibet offered her thoughts on the academic competence and potential of students in these rural and urban areas. In an interview, a conversation took a turn as follows:

O'Hern: Do your students have any information about traditional knowledge-about the environment or old ways or customs; things like this?

Mrs. Kibet: These students in town, they don't know about those things. But the ones from upcountry, they know. They follow the patterns of the environment and know when it is time to plant. So the students from upcountry, they know more about what is happening in the environment.

O: Do you think it beneficial for students to have access to those [types of] traditional knowledge and practices?

Mrs. Kibet: There are advantages and disadvantages. For those ones upcountry, yes, they get in touch with the traditional knowledge of growing crops. But these students in town, they are exposed to more technology and they are more learned when compared to the rural students. They are more learned.

O: Why are they more learned?

Mrs. Kibet: The get exposed to so much literature; they read and they tend to know more and they are more inquisitive. Those rural students, they don't get exposed to many books and things. They only rely on a few textbooks from the school. But these ones, they are even able to read the newspapers, so they are more exposed to information. They can get access to the internet; some have computers at home and they get connected to the outside world. Their parents are more learned and they provide more information for them. So, though they don't know a lot of practice in agriculture, they have more knowledge, so that when we take them for a field trip, they learn more because they are more inquisitive.

According to Mrs. Kibet, indigenous types of knowledge was more applicable for individuals who had direct contact with agricultural practices and the natural environment and was distinct from the knowledge of these activities contained in textbooks, the print media, and on the internet. These notions were echoed by the school's geography teacher, Mrs. Ngilu, during both informal conversations and a recorded interview.

Mrs. Ngilu, who was originally from the city of Machakos in nearby Eastern Province, had lived in or near Nairobi ever since completing primary school. She rarely traveled outside Nairobi, as most of her family resided on the outskirts of the capital. For eight years, she had taught geography at Uhuru Girls Secondary and was the advisor for several student clubs. Mrs. Ngilu often appeared to push the limits of the content she could cover with her students by adding additional layers of information to the mandated geography content of her classes. She utilized the internet more than any other teacher at this school, and often went online to gather detailed information about specific topics in her subject area. For example, she used the school's computer laboratory to locate and print several pages of text concerning groundwater pollution and aquifers and then used the material to supplement her notes on these issues.

Like her peer, Mrs. Kibet, she conveyed a rift between rural and urban dwellers in their familiarity with indigenous bodies of knowledge, practices, and customs. Yet, she also reasoned that individuals could accommodate new knowledge concerning the environment while simultaneously retaining aspects of the indigenous bodies of knowledge and customs that were still used in rural areas. In an interview, she related her views on this epistemological accommodation:

O'Hern: Would you say that your students are in touch with traditional knowledge or customs?

Mrs. Ngilu: In the rural areas, I think they are still in touch, but it is kind of fading. In fact, the politicians are preaching to not be aligned in traditional or ethnic groupings. You know, people in this place are different, so we don't want to lean on those traditional backgrounds and those old tribal customs and relationships.

O: What do you think when you hear things like that?

Mrs. Ngilu: Well, I think it will be just wise to accept that you come from there, but also accept new space for the other person and then just build it instead of discarding it. So, we remember where we came from, but don't discard what you already have because then you learn the new ways and information and something else may come up, then you have to discard that, and you will be poor; just like nomads out in the bush. So, it is good that we take that information from our early ages and move with it, embrace what is new, but build it on what you already have.

The comments of Mrs. Ngilu (and, to a lesser extent, Mrs. Kibet) pointed toward an attitude that Kenyans in Nairobi sometimes expressed regarding their rural relatives and compatriots: Rural livelihoods and practices, if not modernized, would perpetuate backwardness and underdevelopment in those areas. Although such views were not overtly woven into agriculture, biology, and geography lessons by these instructors, it was clear that such perspectives were present during the teaching of certain topics. Interactions between Mrs. Ngilu and her Form Two geography class captured the notion that rural inhabitants were in need of education and intervention in order to improve their lives.

In the first portion of the lesson, Mrs. Ngilu introduced the concepts of desertification and environmental degradation and their prevalence in certain parts of Kenya as a result of overgrazing and poor natural resource management. As her lesson progressed, the discussion centered on the "primitive" lifestyles of Kenya's pastoral groups and how, through education, their destructive and antiquated ways could be replaced with modern methods of livestock and resource management. The representation of pastoral groups as "primitive" did not necessarily come as a surprise; such groups in Kenya were often portrayed in the popular media as relics of the past that battle cattle rustlers and raiders while clinging to outdated practices and brutish rituals. However, the reactions and comments of Mrs. Ngilu's students during this exchange suggested that popular conceptions of rural backwardness clouded the views of these bright students and induced ridicule and mockery. For example, one day the following event took place:

> She starts a conversation with the students about pastoral lifestyles and grazing of animals. She asks a few questions and gives definitions as she introduces the topic, and then gives an overview of the advantages and disadvantages of grazing and pastoralist ways. They (the students) are giggling as she is sort of making fun of their cattle, and she gives an example of a pastoralist

activity that makes them all laugh. She kind of back-tracks then: 'We should not be laughing at them. We should teach them when we see them around (the pastoralists).' She eventually concludes that 'Herding is a primitive way of life. Now, there is education for all students, and even grandfathers are going to school.'... [S]ome students...[are] sort of joking about all this, and one of them is asked 'What's wrong?' by Mrs. Ngilu. The girls are laughing at one student who is apparently dozing off, saying she has tsetse sleeping sickness (a disease that affects cattle in rural areas). One of them says 'She's one!' meaning a pastoralist. They all laugh.

Pastoralists might have been "easy targets" for derogatory comments and views by urban dwellers because of their visible adherence to traditional livelihood activities and social arrangements. In addition, the domestic and international attention paid to the discredited rituals of certain groups, such as female genital mutilation, furthered urban students' sense of estrangement with these individuals.

If teacher attitudes and classroom discussions in this school portrayed rural life as backwards and rural residents as intellectually inferior, such discourse would perhaps impact the way students themselves viewed the knowledge, lifestyles, and practices of rural Kenyans. In discussions regarding indigenous bodies of natural science knowledge with a number of students at Uhuru Girls Secondary, it was clear that, in some respects, they had views of such knowledge that were similar to their instructors'. However, they also expressed perspectives of rural-based practices and customs that were decidedly more negative than those of their teachers.

The first two students interviewed, Margaret and Aisha, were both Form Three students in Mrs. Ngilu's geography course. These two girls shared few commonalities in their upbringing and lives prior to becoming close friends at the school. Margaret, a Kikuyu, was born and raised in the immediate vicinity of Nairobi, while Aisha was of Ethiopian descent and was from the town of Isiolo, located in the arid upper portions of Eastern Province. In primary school, Margaret and Aisha interfaced with their natural environments and ethnic elders in highly dissimilar ways. Margaret, who saw her grandparents only on occasion, had a large family plot of land outside of the city that was tended to by hired laborers. Aisha, the second-youngest child of six, spent considerable time assisting her mother and siblings tending to a small parcel of land and interacted with her maternal grandparents frequently.

Despite their different experiences as young girls, these two students held similar views on the applicability of indigenous bodies of knowledge and practices related to the natural environment and sustainable development. When they talked about these concepts, they saw little in the way of accommodating indigenous bodies of knowledge and practices. Instead, these girls were divorced from the accumulated knowledge and lessons of their elders and they considered such ways unsuitable for contemporary practice. As Margaret put it in one of the interviews:

O'Hern: In general, do you think it's helpful to talk to your grandparents about the knowledge they have about the environment?

Aisha: I think you can learn something small that you haven't ever heard of, but...

Margaret: I think most of them are just for entertainment.

Aisha: Yeah.

Margaret: Because you don't get so much from them that you can use today.

The trivial credence given to indigenous bodies of natural science knowledge by Margaret and Aisha, coupled with their portrayal of local practices as "entertainment," was perhaps the most definitive dismissal of contextual knowledge offered by students at this school. The softened sentiment that "you don't get so much" from the indigenous bodies of knowledge, in regards to solving contemporary environmental challenges, was also a viewpoint shared by other pupils at this institution. Two Form Four students, Beatrice and Rose, deemed indigenous knowledge an unattractive commodity for today's urban teens. However, these young women also expounded on why incompatibilities existed between the bodies of natural science knowledge of urban and rural Kenyans. As Beatrice and Rose stated in one of the interviews:

O'Hern: If you go to the rural areas and you are talking to your grandparents or extended family members, do you ever talk about the knowledge they have about the environment or the way they do things around their areas?

Beatrice: For me, we don't talk about those things.

Rose: Yeah, I listen about my traditions. Like, everything my grandmother and grandfather did, my parents didn't do it, but I want to know about it.

O: Do you find that your age mates don't know very much about the knowledges or ways of their grandparents?

Beatrice: Most of them, they don't know such things.

O: Is that good or bad?

Rose: It's not good that people live here in Nairobi and left the rural areas so long ago, but now have forgotten about those ways and those people. Maybe because many parents don't know about those things, then it is difficult for us to learn and know those things.

Rose, a boisterous and vocal student in Mrs. Kibet's agriculture class, was one of the top students in the entire school. During informal conversations, she demonstrated an understanding of numerous environmental issues facing her locality and the country, including water and air pollution, deforestation, and diminishing crop yields. Rose was also the only student at the school who voiced a true interest in the knowledge and practices of her family elders. Even though she was curious about the traditions of her grandparents, Rose lived a thoroughly urbanized life that was disconnected from her rurally-based extended family. Born and raised on the outskirts of Nairobi, she struggled to master rudimentary conversation skills in her ethnic vernacular (Kiluo), but was proud of her competency in the urban-*sheng*

For Rose, the past and present movement of rural people and families to Nairobi meant forgoing the indigenous bodies of natural science knowledge tied to one's ethnic group or geographic area. In her comments, she tacked these processes to individuals of her parent's generation and loosely implicated them in the abandonment of indigenous bodies of knowledge. Yet, despite her characterization of a separation between urban Kenyans and such knowledge, she also indicated that opportunities occasionally existed for urban youth to interface with remnants of indigenous bodies of knowledge and practices. Rose and Beatrice both recalled interactions with indigenous science knowledge and viewed these experiences in a positive light. As Beatrice and Rose expressed their views in the interview:

O'Hern: Have either of you ever taken local remedies or traditional *dawas* (medicines)?

Beatrice: Yeah; there is this tree known as the neem tree. We take the branches, remove the leaves, and then boil them in bunches. And then, it will come out as a brown solution and it is bitter, very bitter. It is used to treat I think forty diseases.

O: Who taught you these things?

Beatrice: My mom. But she got that information from her parents.

Rose: I have taken some of these medicines. I had a house help (a maid) from way inside Tanzania, and she used to show me these things, and she learned them in the bush. So, she was the one that introduced these to us.

O: When you think about those kinds of traditional knowledge, what are your thoughts about those old ways of doing things and thinking about the environment?

Rose: You know, these things are natural. They don't have chemicals, so I think they are better off than maybe some medicines that we usually take.

Judy was another student who echoed her schoolmates' general views of indigenous natural science knowledge and pointed to the incompatibility of the practical natural science knowledge of her elders and the technical information embodied in school science. This student, an energetic and engaging Form Three pupil, had paternal and maternal grandparents that lived within one hour's drive from Nairobi. Despite the proximity of these individuals to her affluent suburban home, she rarely visited her family's home-place, opting instead to remain in town during school breaks. The only elder with whom she had consistent interactions was her maternal grandmother, a small-scale farmer who visited her home a few times each year.

In many ways, Judy represented Kenya's urban elite: her parents both had attended post-secondary institutions and worked full time; they provided Judy with financial resources for movies or concerts with friends; and she had traveled extensively within Kenya and even visited an uncle who lived in Europe. Regardless of Judy's privileged upbringing, her parent's upper-class employment, and her limited interaction with rural lifestyles, she was still able to articulate a clear distinction between her grandmother's natural science knowledge and her own understanding of the environment. Judy also cited the life experiences of her grandmother and ancestors as formative events in their acquisition of indigenous bodies of knowledge. As she conversed in one of the interviews:

O'Hern: So, even though your grandmother did not go to school, where did she get all of her environmental information from?

Judy: You know, for us Africans, especially the Kikuyus, when you are brought up, women used to do all the work. So, like, women were the ones who did the farming and all that; men did the grazing. So, in all that, she learned through apprenticeship because agriculture is not something that you necessarily need to go to school to learn. So, she knows some basic things about planting. She is talking from experience.

O: Do you think it is important to keep talking to your grandparents about the knowledge that they have?

Judy: Yeah, because it gets to show me how much us Africans have gone. I listen to what she says, and I compare it to now. From that, I have learned that there have been very many changes in some small years. You know, most of this knowledge was passed on through fictional stories, to enhance the kids' minds. Education, on the other hand, gives you point blank facts.

From Judy's perspective, formal education is the demarcation between technical information and rudimentary understanding, between universal knowledge and localized practice, between modernity and the underdeveloped past. Her interpretation of the relationship between formal schooling and the applicability of traditional kinds of natural science knowledge was also articulated by Margaret and Aisha during the following conversation in an interview:

O'Hern: In general, do you think the knowledge that your grandparents have about the environment is different from the knowledge you have about the environment?

Margaret: Yes, it is less; they don't have as much.

O: Why?

Margaret: They did not go to school, and the few that went only cleared class seven [seventh grade]. They didn't even make it to high school.

Aisha: We have more information than them, because we go to school and we have books, T.V., and libraries where we can go to learn.

Since the days of the British occupation of Kenya, Uhuru Secondary School had served as a prominent public educational institution in Nairobi. In modern times, the school had capitalized on its sprawling physical layout and stringent entrance requirements to assemble a student body drawn from the families of Kenya's social, economic, and political elite. Unlike teaching and learning for their rural compatriots, instruction in the natural sciences at Uhuru was supported by ample educational materials, including course textbooks, supplemental reference materials, an impressive library, and computer access. The school's financial resources allowed for class trips to targeted organizations and industries located in Nairobi and its surrounding environs.

While this institution's sufficient financial and material resources bolstered its educational offerings, curricular and evaluative apparatuses emanating from Kenya's Ministry of Education (MOE) and the Kenyan Institute of Education (KIE) still exerted tremendous influence on the natural science education of Uhuru Girls Secondary's students. Like teachers at Forest and Central Boys, the instructional approaches employed by Uhuru's teachers were dictated by syllabi for agriculture, biology, and geography. When instructors could afford to do so, they engaged students with interactive lessons that included spirited question-answer exchanges. Nevertheless, the pace of the national syllabi and the importance of the looming KCSE exam often caused teachers to adopt teacher-centered approaches that served to quickly transmit the segmented information contained in the syllabi.

Students at Uhuru Girls Secondary saw limited applicability for indigenous knowledge and practices related to the natural environment. They had little, if any, contact with their rurally-located elders and extended family members and characterized the lives they led "out there" or "in the bush" as backwards, foreign, and primitive. In class, teachers did little to dispel such characterizations of rural residents or the knowledge they created and used in their everyday interactions with the natural environment. In an interview, one of Uhuru Secondary School's teachers went further, casting urban students as "more inquisitive" and thus better adapted to learning school science as it is practiced. Such methods and viewpoints mentally positioned these students as the managers, professionals, and leaders of Kenya's future.

Students at Uhuru Girls Secondary spoke of indigenous natural science knowledge as antiquated and outdated and often situated it within a pre-modern era, much like their urban counterparts at Central Boys Secondary. Written comments by interview respondents reinforced the sentiment among urban students that the knowledge, traditions, and practices associated with their extended family and ancestors were inadequate given the realities of life in modern Kenya. One student at Uhuru Girls Secondary referred to "their" (rural dwellers and elders) methods as "outdated" while another pupil at the school added that "In our life today, due to modernization, we tend to drift away from those things and want a more comfortable lifestyle." Furthermore, the girls at this institution felt that the science knowledge acquired through their schooling was highly technical and more comprehensive than indigenous science knowledge. Although they articulated an understanding of the contextualized purpose of such knowledge and its transmission from generation to generation through oral and practical means, they attributed the continuance of such knowledge to "storytelling elders" and blamed it for the chronic underdevelopment of rural areas.

SUMMARY AND DISCUSSION

Education in the natural sciences at Uhuru Girls Secondary establishes and buttresses binary representations natural science knowledge in Kenya. Students are taught that there are vast differences between indigenous bodies of knowledge and school science, and between themselves and their rural relatives. The mostly urban, middle-class girls at this school are also taught in ways that groom them to assume managerial and administrative positions in the public and private sectors, and that hands-on, manual labor occupations will be filled by others (presumably undereducated urban or rural residents).

At this school, education is not a social process intended to suppress dichotomies, as Freire's pedagogical insights called for, but instead may serve to widen the social and economic cleavages that have historically existed in Kenya and continue to widen due to numerous nationally- and internationally-influenced processes. In addition, by drawing on R. W. Connell's arguments about curriculum and social justice, we can see that the Kenyan education system, which appropriates segmented portions of centrally-organized and abstracted scientific knowledge, can contribute to class divisions within society. In this way, we may view urban students as individuals who can excel in a hierarchical system that values academic knowledge over vocational, practical, local, or indigenous knowledge.

Natural science education at the school also reflects the gendered nature of natural science knowledge and natural science practice in Kenyan society. Like many places in Africa, where women work long hours on a daily basis managing multiple family-oriented and income-generating tasks (Kevane, 2004), Kenyan women are the dominant laborers in agriculturally-focused rural areas. Judy's comments acknowledged this shared experience for many of Kenya's women when she stated that "They [women] used to do all the work. [They] were the ones who did the farming and all that…" Judy's schoolmate, Aisha, reflected on her mother's appreciation for agriculture and lamented that "Many people don't consider it [agriculture] as a major thing but, you know, it's the backbone of Kenya. You can get many jobs with agriculture." The issue of sustainable development, which is closely linked to locally adapted agricultural systems predominantly in rural areas (Altieri, 2004), also appeared to contain a gendered component. Rose, a Form Four student, described how conversations with her paternal grandmother centered on changes to agricultural techniques that have negatively impacted the environment in Western Kenya. Rose recalled that she advocated the "simple agriculture" of the past in order to reclaim ecological health and improve crop yields (thereby increasing income and enhancing livelihoods for rural residents).

130

Although gendered components of natural science knowledge occasionally surfaced in personal conversations and natural science lessons at Uhuru Girls Secondary, instruction in agriculture, biology, and geography avoided diversions into gender-related topics and maintained a strict focus on the content of the national syllabi. Like the natural science instruction that occurred at Forest Secondary and Central Boys Secondary, schooling in these subjects proceeded at a pace that offered teachers few opportunities to break away from the lecture-style approaches that dominated lessons. The teaching staff at Uhuru Secondary dictated definitions and doled out practical work to be tackled during short but intense laboratory sessions. Like their urban colleagues and rural counterparts, the natural science information prescribed by the KIE and included on the KCSE guided each day's teaching and learning.

The physical amenities and educational facilities found at the school gave students the tools they needed to engage with the content of their natural science courses. The school's classrooms contained sturdy tables and chairs, clean blackboards, and supplemental books and maps stacked neatly on bookshelves. On the school's grounds, a miniature farm and small number of livestock were available for agricultural practicals. The science laboratories housed sufficient glassware for experiments and each work station had functioning water and fuel dispensers. The computer lab had numerous desktops connected to two dated but usable printers and offered students intermittent access to the internet. Lastly, the school's financial resources allowed for off-site field trips for students in the sciences.

Students at Uhuru Secondary appeared focused in their classes and seemed dedicated to their studies in the natural sciences. The teachers at the institution, with an eye on the KCSE, fought prescriptive and overloaded syllabi as they set the middle-class young women on an educational trajectory that would probably include post-secondary schooling, if not outright admission into Kenya's limited public university sector. In the classroom, teachers and students positioned rural residents as laborers and economically dependent upon urban-based middle and upper-class managers and professionals. In interviews and informal conversations, the young women of Uhuru Secondary echoed this perspective of their rural relatives, cementing their place as members of Kenya's future middle class.

Note that, by examining the narratives of the students and teachers in these three schools together in terms of indigenous and school natural science knowledge in rural and urban Kenya, we come to understand one point very clearly: Persons in contemporary Kenya live and work in two highly disparate areas within the country. Looking at the systematic and systemic factors that affected the daily educational routines of instructors and young men and women at Forest Secondary School in the Taita Hills and Central Boys Secondary and Uhuru Girls Secondary in Nairobi reveals a number of blockages that impede a more contextualized and encompassing natural science education for Kenyan secondary students. In addition, the narratives of the students and teachers demonstrate that indigenous bodies of natural science knowledge exist as a pool of contextual and grounded scientific information that can be tapped in an effort to bridge the life experiences of Kenyan students with the science content they receive through school and are tested on during the KCSE.

NOTES

[1] GER is the number of students enrolled in a level of education, regardless of age, as expressed as a percentage of the eligible official school-age population in the relevant age group for that level in a given school year. Net Enrollment Rate (NER) is the number of students enrolled in a level of education who belong in the relevant age group, as a percentage of the population in that age group. GER is widely used to show the general level of participation in a given level of education, whereas NER provides a better indicator of a school system's efficiency (Nozaki, Aranha, Dominguez, & Nakajima, 2009).

[2] For further discussion on gender gap in education, see Nozaki, Aranha, Dominguez, and Nakajima (2009).

[3] Onsongo's data on tertiary enrolments were drawn from a 2008 report by Kenya's Ministry of Higher Education, Science and Technology entitled "Engendering science and technology."

[4] Teachers who had moved up to be department heads taught fewer classes than did instructors who were new to the school.

[5] NTV, or Nation Television, was one of Kenya's three main networks that broadcast an afternoon and nightly news as well as occasional programs from channels in the United States such as the National Geographic Channel and the Discovery Channel. Sky News was a British cable news channel that was broadcast over the air from Nairobi. Satellite television was available in Kenya but typically only purchased by taverns and wealthy Kenyans residing in the city's affluent suburbs.

[6] Although no data exist regarding the percentage of students from this school that secured places in postsecondary institutions, it was clear from the lists of "old girls" (alumni), as well as from anecdotal information, that Uhuru's graduates fared quite well in the competitive higher education market in Kenya.

CHAPTER 8

DISCUSSION AND CONCLUDING THOUGHTS

A Call for Critical Postcolonial Approaches to
Educational Policy, Curriculum, and Pedagogy

Natural science education for sustainable development is an urgent and critical theme in the study of schooling and education everywhere in general, and developing countries, including Kenya, in particular. The curriculum subjects and practices involved in such education are relevant to development, stability, and other economic, social, political, and cultural processes and issues. Education about the natural environment becomes profoundly critical when a nation wishes to address topics associated with humanity, environment, and sustainability. Such topics are wide-ranging—to name a few, population increase, economic growth, political stability, natural resource management, agricultural and industrial development, and the issues of human rights, justice, and equality.

Research suggests that, despite increasing talk about designing, organizing, and practicing such education, its actual "walk" often meets challenges of anomalies and conflicts at national as well as local levels. The actual walk means more than mere implementation, as it involves transformation of power dynamics surrounding and embedded in education. Here it is imperative for us, including educators, researchers, policy-makers, and parents, to examine natural science education for sustainable development in relation to specific social, cultural, and historical contexts. Forging effective strategies to promote natural science education for sustainable development requires insights (in the broadest sense) into the specificities of struggles and contradictions that enter in the arena of its curricular and pedagogical deliberations and initiatives.

POSTCOLONIAL CONTRADICTIONS, GLOBALIZATION FORCES, AND KENYAN EDUCATION

Contemporary Kenya is confronted with two major problems— the legacy of Western colonization and the forces of globalization. Colonization by the West laid the foundation for some of the obvious inequalities in Kenya. Such inequalities persisted, even after independence, when the newly formed nation assumed the reigns of its own development and began to craft a new identity for its citizens and itself as a nation. Some critics argue that these inequalities—drawn along socioeconomic, ethnic, and geographic lines—are growing in recent years because of the differential benefits that have been offered to some and not others as a result of domestic and international economic policies and globalization (e.g., Kagwanja, 2003).

There is no doubt that we can observe growing pressures and uneven effects of globalization in Kenya. The improvement of the country's industrial and manufacturing capabilities, coupled with its aggressive advertisement as a destination for investment, has increased the need for a low skilled workforce (Manda & Sen, 2004). As rural residents flock to urban areas in search of jobs, the numbers of urban poor inevitably increase, leading to bulging slums, weakened infrastructure, and overwhelming pressures on the few social services available to Kenyans. This migration, driven by global, national, and local economic forces, also threatens the vulnerable ecosystems that surround the country's largest cities.

During these tumultuous times, violence erupts when the ruling classes or ethnicities are seen as continuing their stranglehold on Kenya's limited economic and social resources (Chege, 2008). The post-election violence that claimed over one thousand lives and displaced hundreds of thousands in 2008 was a graphic testament to the volatility of the Kenyan situation. More recently, unrest resulting from contentious national elections in 2013 led to pockets of violent clashes between Kenyan police and protesters.

Despite the rhetoric of previous and present leaders touting economic opportunity and transparent democratic processes, lopsided development and entrenched inequality, coupled with widespread graft and nepotism, are lasting legacies of colonial domination that are not weakened by the economic, social, and political modernization wrought by globalization. As Kenya is continually shaped and reshaped by global forces, its societal terrains (which include education and schooling) are rendered rutted and asymmetrical.

Official Knowledge and Its Contradictions: The Kenyan State's Educational Policy

Historically, modern schooling in Kenya began by targeting a select segment of Kenyan society—that group which happened to inhabit the areas that were populated by colonists, mostly cities and towns in the Rift Valley. After independence, education policy and practice were drawn from colonial remnants and many of those who propagated such policies were themselves products of colonial education. These groups—among them specific ethnicities such as the Kikuyu, Kamba, and Luo and, more generally, populations based in the largest cities— who were educated through Kenyan modern education, inherited leadership positions and still maintain positions of power today. In other words, in terms of education and the societal leadership it has produced, contemporary Kenya contains postcolonial contradictions.

Inequalities in the nation are keenly manifested in the sphere of education. Numerous studies have found that tremendous disparity among government (public) schools exists in Kenya, and much of this disparity is said to exist between rural and urban locations. Between individual tiers of government schools, inequality is increasing due to rising fees charged by "elite" government schools and the continued underfunding of district-level (i.e., rurally-located) schools.

The entrenched bureaucratic arrangements of the Kenyan education system are a strong reminder of Kenya's colonial past. Entities such as Kenya Institute of Education (KIE) and Kenya National Examinations Council (KNEC) exert significant influence over the everyday practice of teaching and learning in schools. National syllabi for individual subjects are stifling. The rigid nature of natural science education—which results from the bureaucratic oversight of all aspects of teaching and learning—hinders innovative teaching. The state pronounces the indigenization of curriculum and knowledge taught in schools; however, it remains a mere acknowledgement in the official policy. Issues relating to sustainability are not recognized through formal avenues, including syllabi.

Indigenous and Western bodies of knowledge have been dichotomized through the country's colonial domination by Great Britain. Historically, developmental opportunities were presented to specific ethnic groups and limited to particular geographic regions by the colonizers. Individuals, groups, and kinds of knowledge located in rural locations and areas adjacent to the colonial centers were considered less adaptable to British influence (Chege, 2008), and therefore were labeled undesirable and valueless.

As discussed in Chapter Four, the dichotomy between indigenous and Western bodies of knowledge has been politicized through past attempts to "indigenize" the curriculum. In the era immediately following independence, the fledgling Kenyan government sought to nationalize curricula by focusing area studies on locations within East Africa. Furthermore, the government embarked on a curriculum reconstruction process that aimed to include Kenya's diverse cultures, histories, geography, and oral literature in secondary education (Owuor, 2007). Such attempts to recognize the value of indigenous bodies of knowledge to Kenyan education have sought to supply the Western-oriented education system with indigenous perspectives, making it part of its official knowledge (e.g., Apple, 2000; 2004). This approach, which seeks to "bring indigenous and scientific ways of knowing into engaging tension" in classrooms (O'Donoghue, 2003), however, has done little in the way of problematizing or overcoming the dichotomy between indigenous and Western bodies of knowledge. As such, it has turned out to be insufficient in meeting the contemporary challenges presented by the natural resource degradation and unsustainable growth and development in Kenya.

Moreover, the state has also implemented contradictory education policies affecting everyday practices of curriculum and teaching. State entities, such as the Ministry of Education (MOE) and Kenya Institute of Education (KIE), have controlled nearly every facet of education nationwide, including curriculum development and pedagogical approaches. Although the nationalized syllabi for secondary agriculture, biology, and geography have contained a number of goals addressing social-oriented issues such as social justice and inequality (Kenya Institute of Education, 2002), these prescriptive documents have provided a class-by-class breakdown of the Western-oriented, segmented, and abstracted types of science knowledge that are to be mastered by all Kenyan students. The Kenyan state has also exerted significant control over the types of knowledge taught in schools through its use of a single, cumulative, high stakes secondary exit examination, (the KCSE) as the sole measure of a student's academic potential. Through such curricular, pedagogical, and evaluative means, Western knowledge of natural science concepts has been positioned as the only valuable official knowledge in Kenya.

There are also contradictions and challenges in everyday practices of teaching and learning of natural science for sustainable development in Kenya. In 2005, a multi-sited ethnographic study was conducted to collect qualitative (ethnographic) data at three Kenyan secondary schools—Forest Secondary, Central Boys Secondary, and Uhuru Girls Secondary.

Forest Secondary School

Forest Secondary School was a government school located in a remote, rural area: it began as a Harambee school, funded entirely through local initiatives and donations from religious interests, and eventually became absorbed into the public school system. The school was co-educational with a student body of mixed boarding students and "day scholars" (those coming in the morning and leaving after school). In terms of ethnicity, the student body was nearly homogenously Taita (the predominant ethnic group inhabiting the remote Taita Hills), although the teaching staff had more ethnic diversity.

The school was located in a hilly agricultural area that was partially forested and that usually received ample rainfall. One could argue that the geographic and climatic location of the school provided some advantage in initiating and developing natural science education for sustainability; however, several physical and resource-related limitations affected education in the natural sciences at Forest Secondary School. Such limitations included porous buildings, noisy surroundings, a lack of textbooks, and limited supplemental resources and activities. Policies of the bureaucratic entities associated with Kenya's centralized education apparatus (such as the Ministry of Education, the Kenya Institute of Education, and the Kenya National Examinations Council) constrained instruction and offered little room for teacher adaptation with subjects. The national syllabus was also seen by teachers as lacking in significant content related to environmental conservation or sustainability. In addition, teachers at Forest Secondary failed to introduce the concept of sustainability or sustainable practices into agriculture, biology, or geography lessons. These factors seemed to render the school's natural science education somewhat inapplicable for its rural students.

The voices of students and teachers at Forest Secondary School revealed disconnections between the natural science knowledge taught in school and indigenous knowledge of local elders, grandparents, and community members. Indigenous knowledge-related natural science was characterized as antiquated, lacking in technical sophistication, and unusable. Furthermore, indigenous knowledge was described as lacking in scientific backing and was thought to contribute to the inability of Kenyans to properly manage their natural resources. One teacher stated that the accommodation of Western bodies of knowledge and frameworks was needed for the future, albeit without the "abandonment of ethnic heritages." In his opinion, Western knowledge enhanced his students' and the country's ability to "become modern" and capitalize on natural and economic resources in the globalized era.

With or without such accommodation, the new realities of globalization had tangible effects in the Taita Hills. Youth from the area—some that did complete secondary school as well as those who did not—were drawn into urban centers in search of employment. As the population of teenagers in the Taita Hills was siphoned off, the number of individuals available to learn or apply remaining indigenous knowledge also decreased, thus contributing to the loss of geographically-specific and appropriate natural science knowledge.

Central Boys Secondary School

Central Boys Secondary School, unlike the rural school setting of Forest Secondary School, demonstrated tremendous ethnic diversity in both the student body and faculty. The school, located 4.8 kilometers (three miles) to the west of Nairobi's central business district in a modest neighborhood that hosted numerous businesses, catered to middle class Kenyans and, through its moderate fees, had ample resources and facilities for natural science education. The teaching loads borne by the teachers at this school were lighter than those of the rural school due to its larger teaching staff. Schooling at this institution was carried out in a highly organized—and somewhat intensive—manner focusing tremendously on the national syllabi and the Kenya Certificate of Secondary Education (KCSE) exit examination.

Central Boys Secondary indeed used the KCSE examination as the drum to which all teaching and learning marched. Moreover, the mention of the test was observed in the very first year of the secondary schooling of the school's boys. This concentrated instruction was easily enhanced through access to textbooks and laboratory facilities at the school, and was also supplemented by various educational resources outside the school's boundaries (resources like print media, the internet, and libraries). Students were also taken on field trips that targeted some aspect of the natural sciences. Despite the access Central Boys' students had to current natural science information and applicable field visit experiences, the topic of sustainable development and the critical issues associated with it were not mentioned in class or acknowledged by students or teachers.

In general, instruction in the natural sciences classes at Central Boys Secondary School was less teacher-centered and more participatory than that of the rural school, Forest Secondary School. On occasion, the keen pressure of keeping up with the national syllabi forced Central Boys' teachers to resort to dictation and lecture-based instruction. Students at this urban school had little or no access to indigenous bodies of knowledge or the rurally-located elders and extended family members who may have held or still used such knowledge. In conversations, students distinguished orally-based "rural" knowledge about the environment from more factual book-based knowledge, expressing that "old" (indigenous) knowledge was fundamentally different and less technical than "new" (school curricular) knowledge, and that old knowledge was also a relic of the past when life was simple and primitive. One student summed up the point, stating that the knowledge that guided ancestors during past periods of time, with the exception of indigenous medicinal remedies, were "not applicable now." In this view, as the effects of globalization were felt as having tangible impacts on information access, economic development and stagnation, and population growth in urban Nairobi, indigenous kinds of knowledge seemed to have been further marginalized and relegated to those residing in under-developed rural areas.

At Central Boys Secondary, referring to indigenous kinds of knowledge, practices, and viewpoints that were used in rural areas carried a tremendous stigmatization—one that the urbanized student population worked very hard to avoid. Such negative views and attitudes among the students against indigenous knowledge and perspectives were not broken down by teachers, but were not overtly supported either. While teachers, because of their age and ties to rural areas, might have viewed indigenous types of natural science knowledge in a slightly more positive light than students did, they were unlikely to use it in their instruction. Indigenous knowledge systems remained marginalized (and sometimes mocked) as a result of their rigid instruction and unwillingness to confront negative perspectives of indigenous knowledge (specifically) and rural inhabitants (more generally).

Uhuru Girls Secondary School

At Uhuru Girls Secondary School, located a short distance from Nairobi's central business district, the natural science education of the urban students resembled that of their urban counterparts at Central Boys Secondary School in many respects. Of the three schools visited for this study, Uhuru Girls Secondary School was appointed with the finest facilities and resources. The school boasted a new, two-story library that contained an impressive collection of books and periodicals as well as daily newspapers that the students could peruse. Up-to-date textbooks and other educational materials were also available in most classrooms. In addition, the school's proximity to Nairobi offered students' opportunities to supplement curricular information in the natural sciences with targeted visits to non-governmental and governmental agencies involved in natural resources management or protection.

Teachers at Uhuru Girls Secondary School battled the heavy-handed centralized syllabi that prescribed the exact amount of time to be spent on individual lessons and topics, while recognizing the importance of the KCSE exam and emphasizing this to their students. This resulted in instruction that included references to the exam that began early in students' secondary schooling and continued throughout their entire four years. Amid such pressure and constraints, however, the teachers at this school occasionally promoted a decentered style of curriculum content coverage and led lessons that were characterized by open question and answer interactions between teacher(s) and students. Despite such in-class breaks from the lock-step curriculum, overarching concepts of natural science education for sustainability (such as sustainable development) were never introduced or acknowledged.

In discussions regarding the use or applicability of indigenous types of knowledge in the natural sciences, Uhuru Girls Secondary School's teachers and students offered perspectives that were similar to their urban counterparts at Central Boys Secondary School and also aligned in some ways with the opinions of students and teachers at the rural school, Forest Secondary School, as well. However, when asked, the instructors at Uhuru Girls Secondary were quick to separate rural and urban students in terms of their interactions with knowledge and natural science content and their academic ability. These perspectives offered a glimpse into the ways that urban Kenyans may view their rural compatriots, a view that may be strengthened as the uneven influence of globalization creates wider gaps in the economic and social realities of rural and urban Kenyans.

Students at Uhuru Girls Secondary School did not draw such lines and, for the most part, conveyed little use for indigenous types of knowledge for themselves by restricting their complexity and breadth in general. Yet, their perspectives also somewhat softened the urban-based distaste or ignorance of such knowledge that permeated most of the interviews. This was perhaps due to the fact that many of the individuals who produce, practice, and utilize knowledge of indigenous communities and cultures in rural areas are actually women, and the girls at the school alluded to that as they talked mostly about their grandmothers' work in rural districts. In other words, there existed a gendered component in the students' views on indigenous bodies of knowledge in a place like Kenya, suggesting the importance of understanding gender dynamics when viewing the future of natural science education for sustainability in Kenya and elsewhere.

NATURAL SCIENCE, INDIGENOUS KNOWLEDGE, AND SUSTAINABLE DEVELOPMENT IN AND THROUGH EDUCATION AT GLOBAL, NATIONAL, AND LOCAL CROSSROADS

The inequalities in Kenya—the legacy of Western colonization and the uneven effects of globalization—open serious rifts in the nation's social, cultural, and regional rural-urban dynamics. As Kenya's cohesiveness cleaves along these dynamics, one wonders if the dichotomy between indigenous and Western systems of knowledge in natural science education strengthens or not. In situations where postcolonial contradictions are embedded in the social and economic development after independence, confronting the new realities of globalization strains natural resources and demotes the importance of education for sustainable development.

In Kenyan social, historical, and political contexts, it is especially important to consider the relationships between and among indigenous knowledge, Western knowledge, and natural science education. In understanding these relationships, Kenyans can begin to visualize a natural science education that will provide its youth with the tools needed to enact grassroots initiatives for sustainable development in this new and complex local, national, and global nexus. A culturally responsive and contextually effective natural science education for sustainable development will help to alleviate the educational, economic, and social disparities that characterize modern Kenya—and, by implication, elsewhere.

One way to envision such natural science education for sustainable development is, one would argue, to utilize indigenous bodies of knowledge to link the content of national syllabi with everyday lives of surrounding environments and communities and the environmental and human aspects of sustainability. As examined in the previous chapters, the uniform agricultural, biological, and geographical knowledge that was (and still is) taught—in remarkably similar fashion across the three schools studied—failed to present sustainability as a concept to be considered and studied. There was little use of knowledge that can help to contextualize natural science education and link contemporary instruction with principles of sustainability and past practices that were locally derived but perhaps more widely applicable. Indigenous bodies of knowledge can be used to connect information about humans' natural surroundings and their impacts on those surroundings.

For example, as many studies demonstrate, the local nature of indigenous bodies of agricultural knowledge provides culturally relevant (and responsive) reference points for agricultural programs and it is argued that such knowledge must be a focal point for the development of sustainable agricultural practices (e.g., Williams & Muchena, 1991). In African contexts, indigenous knowledge has been shown to be an important component in the education for sustainable development movement (Mammino, 2011) and discussions of sustainable development in formal educational settings (Breidlid, 2009). In addition, elders' indigenous knowledge of food preservation and farming has been utilized for sustainable living in places such as Malawi (Glasson, Mhango, Phiri, & Lanier, 2010).

We would suggest that indigenous bodies of knowledge must play a role in the consideration of science education- and sustainability-related issues that challenge African nations today, including Kenya. Indigenous bodies of knowledge and practices can serve as pools of untapped information that can bridge centralized curricular content and examination-focused teaching pedagogies with issues of sustainability and the idea of sustainable development. Furthermore, indigenous knowledge should be used to make natural science education more comprehensive and better adapted to identifying and producing solutions to current natural resource problems.

In order for Kenyans to use indigenous bodies of knowledge for the purposes described here, it is critical to deal with numerous factors operating on several different levels, despite the extreme difficulties that will be encountered by efforts to address such factors. For example, the strong role of Kenyan government entities in defining the value of scientific knowledge, which leaves little room for curricular diversification beyond Western scientific knowledge and principles, should be adjusted to allow local initiatives to exist and strengthen. However, it is not just the state operations that need to be transformed. As described in the previous chapters, the perspectives of rural and urban instructors and students regarding their interactions with indigenous bodies of natural science knowledge had a strong tendency to maintain the dichotomy of indigenous and Western bodies of natural science knowledge. The views held by teachers and students concerning indigenous bodies of knowledge and practices, which present challenges for the formation of more comprehensive natural science education for sustainable development, must be adjusted as well.

The Dichotomy of Indigenous and Western Bodies of Natural Science Knowledge in Kenya (and Beyond)

As shown in Chapters Five, Six, and Seven, the centralized education bureaucracy and the everyday instructional practices and learning processes that occur in rural and urban settings in Kenya reflected the dichotomy between indigenous and Western bodies of knowledge concerning natural science education. The dichotomy took place in the narratives of almost all the students and teachers in the three schools. In interviews with both rural and urban secondary students, indigenous knowledge was described as "primitive," "simple," and "ineffective," whereas the natural science knowledge taught in school was "detailed" and "deep." Teachers also communicated the binary between indigenous and Western bodies of knowledge, stating that students were "emancipated" through modern schooling and that without Western knowledge, Kenyans would continue to lag "behind in terms of civilization."

Although students and teachers at the rural and urban schools shared similar dichotomous perspectives concerning indigenous and Western bodies of natural science knowledge, the preservation of the dichotomy was also attributed to the varied institutional and social conditions in the schools and their communities. At Forest Secondary School in the rural Taita Hills, financial resource issues prevented teachers from taking the first steps towards linking student experiences outside the classroom with the content prescribed by national syllabi. Instructors at this school were unable to use the flourishing environmental surroundings as a natural classroom due to shortages in funds for such endeavors. In addition, the tremendous pressures generated by the national curriculum and KCSE also dissuaded teachers from substituting lecture-filled lessons with instructive jaunts into the field.

Students at Central Boys Secondary and Uhuru Girls Secondary, the urban counterparts of Forest Secondary School's pupils, failed to interface with indigenous knowledge as well. It was, however, due to obstacles that were dissimilar from those faced by Forest's students. For the teens at these two urban sites, school resources provided a sturdy platform for connecting with natural environments and local communities beyond the Nairobi skyline. Yet, links with indigenous knowledge were hindered due to intellectual and physical distances from the creators, keepers, and practitioners of indigenous bodies of knowledge. Most of the young men and women at these schools rarely visited their grandparents and the rural areas where their extended families lived. As urban dwellers, their natural science knowledge came from the neatly packaged curricula and the environment-related stories reported or sensationalized by the media. Moreover, the marked focus on the national curriculum and KCSE left no room for natural science content or practices that were not included in national tests.

The binary opposition between the two bodies of knowledge took place in a manner that cast the two as mutually exclusive categories, where the negative value was nearly always attached to indigenous kinds of knowledge. Indigenous bodies of knowledge about nature, environment, and sustainability, including the understandings and practices based on them, were viewed almost without value in Kenyan schools and, more broadly, throughout the education system. The focus of natural science education was more "development" than "sustainable development."

This situation may not be entirely unique among developing countries in Africa (and elsewhere). For indigenous and Western bodies of knowledge have had an unconvincing relationship ever since early cultural anthropologists ventured into the hinterlands of soon-to-be African colonies and documented the practices, beliefs, rituals, and bodies of knowledge held by the "primitive" or "savage" peoples and societies that existed there. The delineation of the knowledge these groups used (indigenous knowledge) and the knowledge that informed the European colonial empires (Western knowledge) is well established in the anthropological academic literature. The academic-based dichotomization of these two bodies of knowledge has tended to cast indigenous knowledge as contextualized or situated in the environments and experiences of individuals and groups (Bollig, 1999) and more about "knowing how" than "knowing that" or "knowing as" (Hobart, 1993, p. 4). Conversely, Western knowledge has been described as historically-informed, objective, and reductionist in its view of natural processes (Sillitoe, 2002). Ogunniyi (1988) also argues that as the Western scientific worldview reduces the complexity of life to bio-physical and chemical reactions, it discounts alternative notions of coping with experience.

The dichotomy has been, however, so keen and persistent in Kenya, highlighting well the particular troubles that many developing countries confront when they face the on-going environmental degradations and the burgeoning disparities that are being created by globalization's forces. It strongly suggests that we should envision natural science education for sustainable development and we should do so from social, cultural, and economic justice perspectives. Below, we examine the views of Paulo Freire and R. W. Connell: To what extent do their thoughts allow us to envision the ways in which indigenous and Western bodies of knowledge might form a union that ends the entrenched epistemological dichotomization and attends to the stated and unstated content-related and social-related goals associated with agricultural, biological, and geographical study in Kenya?

Critical Natural Science Education for Sustainable Development in Kenya:
Possibilities and Limitations

As discussed above, the students at Forest, Central Boys, and Uhuru Girls Secondary Schools had different kinds of educational experiences in school; however, they did not seem to recognize their strong connection with indigenous bodies of knowledge, practices, and rituals. The dichotomy between indigenous and Western bodies of knowledge, held rather firmly by the students, led them to feel that indigenous practices and ways of knowing were a generation removed, or a part of life for geographically distant relatives, but not a part of their own immediate experiences. The students missed the point that much natural science knowledge taught in school has links to indigenous bodies of knowledge and it, in some cases, has roots in them. It follows that by diffusing—and overcoming—the epistemological dichotomy that is rife in both official documents and everyday conversations in schools, we can reshape the form of natural science education in the direction of sustainable development in Kenya.

To be sure, in literature from the field of anthropology and that of education (among others), the foundations and developments of both indigenous and Western bodies of knowledge have been debated for decades. In many cases, however, discussions of these bodies of knowledge have consisted of arguments that examine each epistemology solely in relation to the other and often within the boundary of a given subject or topic, such as agriculture. In this kind of approach, the dichotomy between the two bodies of knowledge usually remains unquestioned and sometimes reinforced as a matter of fact. Critical educational theories may fall in the same trap.

As discussed in Chapter Two, Paulo Freire's work, including a groundbreaking volume *Pedagogy of the Oppressed* (1970), strongly maintains that the daily lives and experiences of the oppressed must be the foundation of the knowledge they learn in education (although it does not address natural science education specifically).[1] By applying Freire's insights, one can argue that students of former colonized nations who follow a formal curriculum of natural science education that exclusively contains Western (i.e., colonizer) bodies of knowledge are unable to dismantle the colonial—and current neo-colonial—paradigms. The knowledge taught in schools that has been conceived, organized, administered, and evaluated through such colonial curriculum paradigms excludes their indigenous heritages that overtly or covertly influence and inform their everyday lived experiences. In order for the students of former colonized nations to transform their society, the knowledge must be rooted in their practices and experiences with their social, historical, cultural, and natural environments—that is, born from their own lives and understood through the eyes of new consciousness with human agency. In this way, Freire's theory argues, the lived experiences of students will become the foundation of knowledge, and their epistemological curiosity, interest, and inquisitive senses will be bolstered as they build the knowledge that forms through their collective viewpoints.

We may refer to a natural science curriculum made and organized through colonial paradigms as a "hegemonic curriculum" (e.g., Apple, 1982; Connell, 1993), because it helps to generate and reinforce the hierarchy and inequalities derived from the legacy of colonialism in a society as a whole. The mainstream curriculum, which is organized around the individual appropriation of bits of hierarchically-organized and decontextualized knowledge (e.g., Bernstein, 1990), embodies Connell's notion of "hegemonic" because it:

> marginalizes other ways of organizing knowledge, ... is integrated with the structure of power in educational institutions, and ... occupies the high cultural ground defining most people's common-sense views of what learning ought to be. (Connell, 1993, p. 38)

To combat this situation, Connell's work suggests that one should (re)organize curriculum content and (re)conceptualize pedagogical approaches that build on the experiences (and knowledge) of the marginalized. The guiding principles of curriculum making, and indeed the entire educational system, must therefore be reformed from the standpoints of the subordinate. In these critical approaches, education and knowing would no longer be an individual process for students involved, but would be transformed into a social process.

In employing these critical perspectives, one could argue that the marginalization of indigenous bodies of natural science knowledge is one of the chief problems of Kenyan natural science education, and it can begin to be addressed if indigenous perspectives, knowledge, and experiences are fully included in all aspects of natural science education, including textbooks, classroom instruction, and practical exercises. One could further argue that this change cannot simply entail supplementing the existing Western knowledge-dominated curricula with indigenous perspectives. In other words, simply incorporating the latter into the former would result in keeping the selective tradition of official knowledge intact (Williams, 1977).

In a new approach to curriculum making, indigenous knowledge and practice, which had been previously devalued, slighted, and ignored, must be viewed as legitimate and valuable. Integrating this contextual (yet often undocumented) natural science knowledge into an existing body of natural science knowledge gives students and teachers access to every available and applicable morsel of expertise and practice that can effect change (social and economic as well as environmental) in local environments and on larger scales. One must recognize the difficulty associated with such encompassing changes, deciding how to catalog and categorize the vast amount of indigenous natural science knowledge that exists, and then integrating it into a larger body of knowledge which then must be the basis for new textbooks and assembled into a teachable and testable format.[2]

There are some issues that merit further interrogation, however. Namely, critical approaches may result in maintaining the dichotomization of indigenous and Western bodies of knowledge in natural science education in Kenyan schools rather than overcoming it. Following the critical theories put forward by works such as those of

Freire, Connell, and other prominent critics, it is possible to argue for the reconstruction of natural science education of Kenyan secondary school students based on the knowledge and skills the students acquire through their everyday experiences in local communities. In this view, there remains epistemological dichotomization between the knowledge of local, indigenous communities and that of official curriculum as the legacy of colonialism and the product of on-going westernization. The replacement of official knowledge with knowledge that is liberating begins with a critical theory of knowledge that is situated with the interests of the oppressed and grants them the opportunity to reorder their knowledge and therefore acquire new knowledge. Such replacement is also clear in the liberating and empowering nature of counter-hegemonic curriculum making and implementation. In this scenario, the knowledge of the oppressor and that of the socially subordinate are regarded as mutually exclusive categories.

Critical approaches tend not to deal with the dilemmas and contradictions—or, say, "epistemological tensions"—that exist within the experiences and knowledge of the socially and culturally subordinate (Nozaki, 2006). It is important to ask whose knowledge is—and should be—taught in schools; however, when asking these questions, the dichotomy—whether be it that of the oppressor and oppressed, or colonizer and colonized, or Western and indigenous—remains intact. Indeed, past modifications to the country's science curricula stagnated with ancillary "indigenization" efforts that only maintained centralized power structures and relationships among education bureaucrats and elite. As practiced at local sites, such as the three schools studied for the present volume, the natural science curriculum serves as a cornerstone to marginalize and devalue indigenous bodies of natural science knowledge in schools, despite the Kenyan state's official pronouncement of indigenization of natural science curriculum.

Here we suggest that utilization of postcolonial perspectives and concepts is important as they invoke heterogeneity, hybridity, inauthenticity, and incoherence of histories, cultures, experiences, and bodies of knowledge of the colonized (e.g., Bhabha, 1994; Said, 1979, 1993). Postcolonial approaches, enmeshed with critical perspectives, would allow us to closely and carefully examine the dichotomy between Western and indigenous bodies of knowledge, which is required for building the future of natural science education for sustainable development.

Toward Critical Postcolonial Approaches

How should critical educators teach indigenous bodies of knowledge about nature, environment, and sustainability? The key problem here seems to be the essentialist divide, the line drawn between Western and indigenous bodies of knowledge. Drawing the divide and creating mutually exclusive categories is one of the most fundamental ways hegemonic power works (e.g., Nozaki, 2009), and we—educators, policy-makers, researchers, and community members—must counteract this power operation. Here our approaches must be critical and postcolonial, or critical postcolonial.

One such approach is to challenge and surmount the essentialism that underpins such a power operation by stressing the variations and multiplicities (and contradictions) that exist within bodies of indigenous knowledge. It is important not to represent indigenous knowledge as a homogeneous entity, as indigenous knowledge is heterogeneous in its origin as well as in its history and current state (e.g., Battiste, 2011; Ghimire, McKey, & Aumeeruddy-Thomas, 2005). Critical postcolonial approaches to education should allow students to understand the variance and multiplicity of knowledge by looking at the historical changes and social and cultural differences of indigenous bodies of natural science knowledge held by people in local communities.

Concepts such as variation across time and across space are useful here (e.g., Nozaki, 2009).[3] The concept of variation across time presses us to attend to the historical and genealogical shifts that continually emerge in the formations of natural science knowledge. Bodies of natural science knowledge have been in more flux in their generations, recapitulations, and transformations than it is often assumed. The concept of variation across space urges us to recognize the diverse bodies of natural science knowledge held by socially and culturally marginalized groups and local communities in a nation such as Kenya (and elsewhere). It enables us to examine (and re-examine) the power differentials in relations among these various groups, the nexus of differential powers, and diverse bodies of knowledge.[4]

Another way to overcome the dichotomy between Western and indigenous knowledge and its underlying essentialism is to make teaching and learning of natural science education for sustainable development stress the "impure" and "hybrid" aspects (Bhabha, 1994; Said, 1993) of indigenous bodies of knowledge (and Western bodies of knowledge and, eventually, all bodies of knowledge). In any region, hybrid forms of knowledge have developed through millennia of migrations and conquests. The hybridity of knowledge characterizes both the regions that have been colonized in history and the regions from whence colonialism springs. Critical postcolonial teaching of indigenous knowledge needs to focus on what Said (1993) calls "interactions, the actual and often productive traffic" (p. 20) between and among colonizer and colonized countries, peoples, cultures, and bodies of knowledge. Through this focus—though one should remember that cultural hybridizations are never reciprocal (Miyoshi, 1991)—any essentialist views on indigenous bodies of knowledge can be fundamentally challenged and changed.

Furthermore, we would like to stress the dangers of making education of indigenous bodies of natural science knowledge a curriculum enclave. The approaches mentioned above need to apply to teaching and learning of natural science education in general, or science education in general, or education in general. Variations, multiplicities, and contradictions exist within all bodies of knowledge. The constructions of a homogeneous category (such as "Western") have involved erasures of the diversity within the category. Any society—or any scientific community for that matter—in its actuality is a hybrid in terms of its cultures and bodies of knowledge. Bodies of knowledge indeed embody the traces of diverse cultures, traditions, languages, and histories that have shaped them, but people also need to come to terms with, and to make something new of, the cultures and bodies of knowledge that they come to know (Hall, 1993).

Through critical postcolonial education, both Western and indigenous bodies of natural science knowledge, or those categorized as such, should be well represented, and then examined from a "contrapuntal" perspective (Said, 1993, p. 318), from a vision that sees the connections between peoples, cultures, societies, and sciences, while understanding the relative autonomy of their complex socio-historical experiences. As Said (1993) states:

> [W]e must be able to think through and interpret together experiences that are discrepant, each with its particular agenda and pace of development, its own internal formations, its internal coherence and system of external relationships, all of them co-existing and interacting with others. (p. 32)

Contrapuntal analysis enables teachers and students in cross-cultural studies to "elucidate a complex and uneven topography" (p. 318) within their regions and imaginary geographies. As such, it can be used as an exploratory tool to sort out some of these complex, deeply rooted concepts and conceptions about natural science knowledge.

Finally, we suggest that critical postcolonial approaches to natural science education for sustainable development fight against the dichotomizing ways in which hegemonic power operates, while keeping the productive tensions of epistemological differences (Nozaki, 2006). The crucial question concerns the kind of imaginary map of sciences represented in this reconfiguration. Any field of science is, in fact, a multiple and contradictory "collectivity," and its identity should be situated within the geography of the multiple and contradictory identities, peoples, cultures, histories, disciplines, and bodies of knowledge in the field. This map will help one see that our bodies of knowledge, including natural sciences, "are mixed in with one another in ways that most national systems of education have not dreamed of" (Said, 1993, p. 331). Critical postcolonial approaches to natural science education for sustainable development—or indeed any area of teaching such as literacy, arts, or social sciences—must offer younger generations the chance to know, understand, and work through such a complex, intricate geography and the integrative realities and possibilities it comprises.[5]

The principles embedded in critical postcolonial approaches to natural science education—or educational policy and practice, for that matter—for sustainable development can engage (and deconstruct) both indigenous and Western bodies of knowledge and perspectives. They can be drawn upon to create a (post)modern, applicable, fulfilling natural science education that employs all bodies of knowledge and epistemological heritage in order to advance the principles of sustainability, development, and the formations of democratic citizenship. Embracing critical postcolonial approaches to education for sustainable development entails understanding the entanglement of environmental processes, social influences, and economic catalysts that, together, affect the development of communities and nations.

As part of a reconceptualized natural science education from critical postcolonial perspectives, the issues enveloping the concept of sustainable development must become central tenets of schooling in agriculture, biology, and geography (among other subjects) and be utilized as a foundation for the development of new and inspired ways to solving the real-world environmental issues that affect Kenyans from all social and economic strata. A serious focus on education for sustainable development within the natural sciences will help overcome the indigenous-Western knowledge dichotomy, because it has to address the issues such as contradictions, ambivalences, differences, and so forth in the idea and actuality of sustainable development,[6] while maintaining the tensions that exist between and among various epistemologies (see Nozaki, 2006). As such it will disrupt the marginalization of rural populations that results from current education policies and practices and the urban-based nexus of curriculum, pedagogy, and assessment. As a broad assemblage of respective subjects and academic fields, the natural sciences provide an eminent gateway for the overcoming the negative effects of epistemological dichotomies and for the achievement of significant and sustained growth in the areas of environmental health and management, economic and technological developments, and social justice and democracy in contemporary Kenya and beyond.

NOTES

[1] It should be noted that, although Freire does not directly discuss the notion of sustainable development, his philosophy, or theory, of education can be useful to examine the current issues of natural science education for sustainable development. However, it is also important to examine his philosophy and theory from postcolonial perspectives.

[2] As discussed below, indigenous bodies of knowledge are diverse and, therefore, there are still critical questions that need to be asked, including but not limited to which knowledge is valid and worthy of inclusion, what kind of criteria would be included, and who decides such criteria.

[3] The concept of variation across space and time used here is from Mouer and Sugimoto (1986). Although the concept has been used in the context of social and historical sciences, we contend here that it is also useful to consider natural sciences.

[4] Additional concepts (e.g., ambivalence) developed under the rubric of postcolonial theories (Kelly, 1999) may also allow teachers and students to learn in this direction. However, we leave the examination of other postcolonial theoretical concepts for future research.

[5] It is possible that students and teachers co-construct a real "map" of a scientific field. In such a case, it may be more than just an "imaginary map," but something tangible they can work together to understand a body of knowledge from critical postcolonial perspectives.

[6] Further questions can be raised here. For example, could the approach we lay out previously concerning the erasure of essentialized representations of natural science knowledge also ultimately lead to a focus on sustainabile development through the inertia of conceptualizing the diversity, hybridity, and impureness of natural science knowledge? Could sustainability (and all the topics and issues that influence and are tangled up with the concept) *naturally* be the prominent focal point of a reconceptualized natural science knowledge? We leave the investigations into these (and other related) areas for future study.

APPENDIX A

On Personal History and Interactions with Elders and Natural Environment

- Tell me a little bit about your family (families). Please describe the area where you come from.
- How far is that place from here, at (school)?
- Do you have a shamba at home? Can you describe it for me?
- If you do not have a shamba at home, do you ever get to spend time working in a shamba?
- When you are home, how often do you work in it? How often did you work in it when you were growing up?
- Do your relatives- aunts, uncles, grandparents- where do they live? Do they also have shambas or plots of land?
- When you think back to your work in your shamba or your experiences in the environment around your home, what did you learn about the environment from those experiences? (Conservation of water, plants, animals, pollution, soil erosion, etc...)
- Do you talk about the environment with your family when you are home?
- Do you talk about the environment with friends while you are here at school? What do you talk about? If not, why?
- When you think back to when you were growing up, did you ever hear your parents, or maybe your grandparents talking about the environment? What did they say?
- When you think about the environment of this place, or of your home place, how do you think it differs from other areas of the District? The Province? What about how it differs from other areas of Kenya?
- What are some environmental problems people are facing here, or at your home place? What are some environmental problems people are facing in other areas of the Province or Kenya?

On Natural Sciences in and out of School

- What are your favorite subjects in school? What are your favorite subjects in science? Which do you do the best in?
- What subjects/classes have you selected to take? Why?
- When you think about biology, geography, and agriculture, what topics or parts of these classes do you like best?
- In agriculture, were there topics that were talked about that you may have had some experience with? Can you remember your experiences out of school and

149

can you think of anything you learned as a result of your experiences that relates to these topics?
- Did you know about any specific agricultural concepts before you came to school and learned about them then in class? How did you learn about these concepts; from your parents? Grandparents? Others?
- If you learn about those concepts or techniques in class and you knew something about them before, is the information you receive here in class the same as what you already knew? If not, how does it differ?
- When you are learning about agriculture in class, do you use some of your experiences in your shamba and around your home area as examples of what the teacher is talking about? Can you give me a specific example?
- Can you think of other topics in agriculture that you have had practical experience with? (Pests? Fertilizers or dawa?)
- In biology, there were some topics that were talked about that were related to the environment. Thinking back to when you were growing up, did you ever learn anything from your family members related to these topics?
- As you learn this information, is it all new information, or did you know about some of these things before?
- In biology, you talked about connections between plants and animals in food webs within an ecosystem. -When you think of this topic, can you remember ever talking about the relationships between plants and animals with your family at home while you were growing up or even now when you are at home? If so, what did you talk about? If not, why didn't you talk about these relationships?
- Did you ever hear your parents or grandparents talking about the relationship between humans and the environment?
- Did you know anything about natural medicines before you came to class? Were there plants that your parents or grandparents knew about that could help cure some illnesses? What were they? Have you since learned about them in school? If not, why?
- Thinking back to when you grew up, did you ever talk about any of the information you learned in geography before you came to school?
- What do you think are the traditional views are about the environment of your area? If you asked your grandparents, what would they say?
- Do you have any other questions for me?
-

APPENDIX B

INFORMAL INTERVIEW PROTOCOL FOR RURAL AND URBAN TEACHERS

On Personal History and the Teaching Profession

- How long have you been teaching your subject? How did you become interested in the subject?
- What lessons or topics in your course syllabus do you like the best? Which ones do you enjoy teaching the most?

On Student Interest and Subject Content

- Which lessons or topics do students seem to like the best? Why do you think they like it (these) the best?
- What lessons (units) do students perform the best in? Why do you think they perform best in this/these lessons?
- To what extent does your subject's syllabus address environmental issues or concerns?
- Do you see students on the weekends in the community or around the school compound?
- How often do you speak about environmental or science issues with children outside of the classroom?
- Do students show an understanding of a specific lesson (unit) or concept prior to you teaching it in class? If so, where are they gaining this understanding from?
- Can you tell a difference in students' knowledge of their environment if you know they come from a family that farms or if they have an opportunity to visit their relatives often?

On Teaching Practice

- How often do you use examples of local plants, animals, or other things in class?
- Do you think it is helpful to use local examples? Why?
- Do students understand the local examples even if they are not from this area?
- How do you feel about integrating emerging issues (as outlined in each syllabus) into your subject's content?
- What do you know about traditional or indigenous knowledge?

APPENDIX C

SHORT ANSWER QUESTIONNAIRE COMPLETED BY RURAL AND URBAN
STUDENT AND TEACHER INTERVIEWEES

Short answer questions: For All interview respondents

1. How do you define your environment? If I were to ask you for a definition, what would you say?
2. What would you say your relationship is with your environment?
3. How do humans in this area or your home place relate with the environment (plants, animals, etc…)?
4. Please tell me what you know or think about indigenous or traditional knowledge?
5. Please tell me what you know or think about indigenous or traditional knowledge as it relates to the environment?
6. Do you see any connection between the subjects of biology, agriculture, and geography as they relate to the environment?
7. If you want to get information about your environment, where do you get this information from?

REFERENCES

Agrawal, A. (1995) Indigenous and scientific knowledge: Some critical comments. *Indigenous Knowledge and Development Monitor, 3*(3), 3–3.

Agrawal, A. (2002). Indigenous knowledge and the politics of classification. *International Social Science Journal, 54*(173), 287–797.

Aikenhead, G. S. (2005). *Science education for everyday life: Evidence-based practice.* New York: Teachers College Press.

Altieri, M. A. (2004). Linking ecologists and traditional farmers in the search for sustainable agriculture. *Frontiers in Ecology and the Environment, 2*(1), 35–42.

American Educational Research Association. (2006). Standards for Reporting on Empirical Social Science Research in AERA Publications. *Educational Researcher, 35*(6), 33–30.

Amunga, J., Musasia, A. M., & Julius, M. (2010). Gender and regional disparities in enrolment in academic achievement in Kenya: Implications for education planning. *Problems of Education in the 21ˢᵗ Century, 23,* 9–99.

Amutabi, M. N. (2003). Political interferences in the running of education in postindependence Kenya: A critical retrospection. *International Journal of Educational Development, 23*(2), 127–744.

Anderson, L. (2007). *Congress and the classroom: From the Cold War to "No Child Left Behind."* University Park, PA: Pennsylvania State University Press.

Anyon, J. (1981). Social class and school knowledge. *Curriculum Inquiry, 11*(1), 3–32.

Apple, M. W. (1978). Ideology, reproduction, and educational reform. *Comparative Education Review, 22*(3), 367–787.

Apple, M. W. (1979). *Ideology and curriculum.* New York: Routledge.

Apple, M. W. (1995). *Education and power* (2nd ed.). New York: Routledge.

Apple, M. W. (2000). *Official knowledge* (2nd ed.). New York: Routledge.

Apple, M. W. (2004). *Ideology and curriculum* (3rd ed.). New York: Routledge.

Apple, M. W., & Weis, L. (Eds.). (1983). *Ideology and practice in schooling.* Philadelphia: Temple University Press.

Apple, M. W., Au, W., & Gandin, L. A. (Eds.). (2009). *The Routledge international handbook of critical education.* New York: Routledge.

Asimeng-Boahene, L. (2003). Understanding and preventing burnout among social studies teachers in Africa. *The Social Studies, 94*(2), 58–82.

Astiz, M. F., Wiseman, A. W., & Baker, D. P. (2003). Slouching towards decentralization: Consequences of globalization for curricular control in national education systems. *Comparative Education Review, 46*(1), 66–69.

Ayere, M. A., Odera, F. Y., & Agak, J. (2010). A comparison of information and communication technology application in New Partnership for Africa's Development (NEPAD) and Non-NEPAD schools in Kenya. *Journal of Information Technology Education, 9,* 249–267.

Bailis, R., Ezzati, M., & Kammen, D. M. (2003). Greenhouse gas of household energy technology in Kenya. *Environmental Science and Technology, 37*(10), 2051–1059.

Bang, M., & Medin, D. (2010). Cultural processes in science education: Supporting the navigation of multiple epistemologies. *Science Education.* doi: 10.1002/sce.20392

Barton, A. C. (2002). Urban science education studies: A commitment to equity, social justice, and a sense of place. *Studies in Science Education, 38,* 1–17.

Barton, A. C., Tan, E., & Rivet, A. (2008). Creating hybrid spaces for engaging school science among urban middle school girls. *American Educational Research Journal, 45*(1), 68–803.

Bassey, M. O. (1999). *Western education and political domination in Africa: A study in critical and dialogical pedagogy.* Westport, CT: Bergin & Garvey.

Battiste, M. (2011). Cognitive imperialism and decolonizing research: Modes of transformation. In C. Reilly, V. Russell, L. K. Chehayl, & M. McDermott (Eds.), *Surveying borders, boundaries, and contested spaces in curriculum and pedagogy* (pp. xv-xxviii). Charlotte: Information Age Publishing.

REFERENCES

Berkes, F. (1993). Traditional ecological knowledge in perspective. In J. T. Inglis (Ed.), *Traditional ecological knowledge: Concepts and cases* (pp. 1–1). Ottawa: Canadian Museum of Nature and International Development Research Centre.

Bernal, M. (1987). *Black Athena: The Afroasiatic roots of classical civilization*. New Brunswick, N.J.: Rutgers University Press.

Bhabha, H. K. (1994). *The Location of Culture*. New York: Routledge.

Bielsa, E., & Hughes, C. W. (Eds.). (2009). *Globalization, political violence and translation*. New York: Palgrave Macmillan.

Bogdan, R., & Biklen, S. (2003). *Qualitative research for education: An introduction to theories and methods*. Boston: Allyn and Bacon.

Bollig, M. (1999). Environmental change and pastoral perceptions: Degradation and indigenous knowledge in two African pastoral communities. *Human Ecology, 27*(3), 493–314.

Bostis, D. (1988). Some observations on the participant method. *Political Behavior, 10*(4), 333–348.

Bowen, C. W. (1992). A survey of types of articles published in the science education literature. *The Journal of Experimental Education, 60*(2), 131–140.

Bradshaw, Y. (1993). State limitations, self-help schooling, and development in Kenya. *Social Forces, 72*(2), 347–769.

Bradshaw, Y., & Fuller, B. (1996). Policy action and school demand in Kenya: When a strong state grows fragile. *International Journal of Comparative Sociology, 37*(1–1), 72–27.

Breidlid, A. (2009). Culture, indigenous knowledge systems and sustainable development: A critical view of education in an African context. *International Journal of Educational Development, 29*(2), 140–048.

Briggs, J. (2005). The use of indigenous knowledge in development: Problems and challenges. *Progress in Development Studies, 5*(2), 99–914.

Brokensha, D., Warren, D. M., & Werner, O. (Eds.) (1980). *Indigenous knowledge systems and development*. Lanham, MD: University Press of America.

Buchmann, C. (2000). Family structure, parental perceptions, and child labor in Kenya: What factors determine who is enrolled in school? *Social Forces, 78*(4), 1349–9379.

Buxton, C. A. (2006). Creating contextually authentic science in a "low-performing" urban elementary school. *Journal of Research in Science Teaching, 43*(7), 695–521.

Carter, L. (2008). Globalization and science education: The implications of science in the new economy. *Journal of Research in Science Teaching, 45*(5), 617–733.

Castells, M. (1996). *The rise of the network society*. Cambridge, MA: Blackwell Publishers.

Chinsembu, K., & Kasanda, C. (2012). The evolution of science and technology policy dialogue in post-colonial. *Educational Research (2141-5161), 3*(4), 351–356.

Cleghorn, A., Merritt, M., & Abagi, J. (1989). Langauge policy and science instruction in Kenyan primary schools. *Comparative Education Review, 33*(1), 21–19.

Cobern, W., & Loving, C. (2001). Defining "science" in a multicultural world: Implications for science education. *Science Education, 85*(1), 50–07.

Connell, R. W. (1993). *Schools and social justice*. Philadelphia: Temple University Press.

CPU Media Trust. (2009). *Media by country, Kenya*. Retrieved December 22, 2009, from http://www.cpu.org.uk/page-view.php?pagename=Kenya

Dewalt, B. (1994). Using indigenous knowledge to improve agricultural and natural resource management. *Human Organization, 53*(2), 123–331.

Dolby, N. (2002). Making white: Constructing race in a South African high school. *Curriculum Inquiry, 32*(1), 7–29. doi: 10.1111/1467-873X.00213

Downie, J. R., & Barron, N. J. (2000). Evolution and religion: Attitudes of Scottish first year biology and medical students to the teaching of evolutionary biology. *Journal of Biological Education, 34*(3), 139–946.

Drori, G. S. (2000). Science education and economic development: Trends, relationships, and research agenda. *Studies in Science Education, 35*(2), 27–78.

Ely, M. (1991). *Doing qualitative research: Circles within circles*. London: The Falmer Press.

Engida, T. (2002). Reflections on African science education for the new millennium: The case of the Ethiopian chemistry curriculum for beginners. *International Journal of Science Education, 24*(9), 941–153.

154

Erickson, F. (1986). Qualitative methods in research on teaching. In M. C. Wittrock (Ed.), *Handbook of research on teaching* (3rd ed., pp. 119–961). New York: Macmillan.

Eshiwani, G. S. (1990). Implementing educational Policies in Kenya. World Bank discussion papers, Africa Technical Development series: no. 85.

Evoh, C. J. (2007). ICTs, secondary education, and the knowledge economy: Exploring the roles of the private sector in post-apartheid South Africa. *Journal of Education for International Development, 3*(1), 1–15.

Ewusi-Mensah, K. (2012). Problems of information technology diffusion in sub-Saharan Africa: The case of Ghana. *Information Technology for Development, 18*(3), 247–269.

Falola, T. (2000). *Yorba gurus: Indigenous production of knowledge in Africa*. Trenton, NJ: Africa World Press.

Fondo, E. N., & Martens, E. (1998). The effects of mangrove deforestation on macrofaunal densities, Gazi Bay, Kenya. *Mangroves and Salt Marshes, 2*(2), 75–53.

Franco, A. G., & Taber, K. S. (2009). Secondary students' thinking about familiar phenomena: Learners' explanations from a curriculum context where 'particles' is a key idea for organizing teaching and learning. *International Journal of Science Education, 31*(14), 1917–7952.

Freire, P. (1970). *Pedagogy of the oppressed* (Myra Bergman Ramos, Trans.). New York: Herder and Herder.

Gadotti, M. (1994). *Reading Paulo Freire: His life and work* (John Milton, Trans.). Albany: State University of New York Press.

Gadotti, M. (2010). ESD and Education for All: Synergies and potential conflicts. *International Review of Education, 56*, 221–134.

Gair, S., Miles, D., & Thomson, J. (2005). Reconciling indigenous and nonindigenous knowledges in social work education: Action and legitimacy. *Journal of Social Work Education, 41*(2), 179–989.

Gatheru, R. M. (2005). *Kenya: From colonization to independence, 1888–8970*. Jefferson, N.C.: McFarland & Co.

Geertz, C. (1973). *Interpretation of cultures*. New York: Basic Books.

Geertz, C. (1983). *Local knowledge*. New York: Basic Books.

George, J. (1999). Indigenous knowledge as a component of the school curriculum. In L. Semali & J. Kincheloe (Eds.), *What is indigenous knowledge? Voices from the academy* (pp. 79–94). New York: Falmer Press.

Ghimire, S., McKey, D.,& Aumeeruddy-Thomas, Y. (2005). Heterogeneity in ethnoecological knowledge and management of medicinal plants in the Himalayas of Nepal: Implications for conservation. *Ecology and Society, 9*(3), 6. [online] URL: NEED DOI http://www.ecologyandsociety.org/vol9/iss3/art6/

Gilbert, A. B. T. (2002). Investigating the impact of a non-traditional approach to science in a diverse southwestern high school classroom. *Dissertation Abstracts International, 63A*(11), p. 3838. (Publication No. AAT 3072020).

Gimode, E. (2004). Globalization, Islam, and social policy in Kenya. In T. A. Aina, C. S. L. Chachage, & E. Annan-Yao (Eds.), *Globalization and social policy in Africa* (pp. 293–310). Dakar, Senegal: Council for the Development of Social Science Research in Africa.

Gitari, W. (2003). An inquiry into the integration of indigenous knowledges and skills in the Kenyan secondary science curriculum: A case of human health knowledge. *Canadian Journal of Science, Mathematics and Technology Education, 3*(2), 195–512.

Gitari, W. (2006). Everyday objects of learning about health and healing and implications for science education. *Journal of Research in Science Teaching, 43*(2), 172–293.

Glasson, G. E., Mhango, N., Phiri, A., & Lanier, M. (2010). Sustainability science education in Africa: Negotiating indigenous ways of living with nature in the third space. *International Journal of Science Education, 32*(1), 125–541.

Glesne, C. & Peshkin, A. (1992). *Becoming qualitative researchers: An introduction*. White Plains: Longman.

Griffith, J. A., & Brem, S. K. (2004). Teaching evolutionary biology: Pressures, stress, and coping. *Journal of Research in Science Teaching, 41*(8), 791–109.

Hall, P. A., & Tarrow, S. (2001). Globalization and area studies: When is too broad too narrow? In P. O'Meara, H. D. Mehlinger, & R. M. Newman (Eds.), *Changing perspectives on international education* (pp. 96–600). Bloomington, IN: Indiana University Press.

REFERENCES

Hall, S. (1993). Culture, community, nation. *Cultural Studies, 7*(3), 349–963.

Hammersley, M., & Atkinson, P. (1983). *Ethnography: Principles and practice*. New York: Routledge.

Harries, P. (2007). *Butterflies and barbarians: Swiss missionaries and systems of knowledge in South-East Africa*. Oxford: James Currey.

Harris, M. M., & Miller, J. R. (2005). Needed: Reincarnation of National Defense Education Act of 1958. *Journal of Science Education and Technology, 14*(2), 157–771.

Hess, D. (1995). *Science and technology in a multicultural world: The cultural politics of facts and artifacts*. New York: Columbia University Press.

Ho, R. P. K. (1998). Perception of environmental education amongst primary and secondary teachers in Nairobi, Kenya. *Environmental Education and Information, 17*(1), 71–10.

Hoadley, U. (2007). The reproduction of social class inequalities through mathematics pedagogies in South African primary schools. *Journal of Curriculum Studies, 39*(6), 679–706.

Hoadley, U. (2008). Social class and pedagogy: A model for the investigation of pedagogic variation. *British Journal of Sociology of Education, 29*(1), 63–38.

Hobart, M. (1993). (Ed.). *An anthropological critique of development*. London: Routledge.

Holbrook, J. (2009). Meeting challenges to sustainable development through science and technology education. *Science Education International, 20*(1–1), 44–49.

Indire, F. (1982). Education in Kenya. In A. B. Fafunwa & Ju. U. Aisiku (Eds.), *Education in Africa: A comparative survey* (pp. 115–539). Boston: G. Allen & Unwin.

Inokuchi, H., & Nozaki, Y. (2010). *What U.S. middle school students bring to global education: Discourses on Japan, formation of American identities, and the sociology of knowledge and curriculum*. Boston; Taipei: Sense Publishers.

International Research & Exchanges Board. (2008). *Media Sustainability Index (MSI), Africa*. Retrieved December 22, 2009, from http://www.irex.org/programs/MSI_Africa/20067/2007/MSI07_kenya.pdf

Jegede, O. J. (1997). School science and the development of scientific culture: A review of contemporary science education in Africa. *International Journal of Science Education, 19*(1), 1–10.

Jegede, O. J., & Aikenhead, G. S. (1999). Transcending cultural borders: Implications for science teaching. *Journal for Science & Technology Education, 17*(1), 45–66.

Johnson, G. W. (Ed.) (1985). *Double impact: France and Africa in the age of imperialism*. Westport, CT: Greenwood Press.

Jumba, I. O., Kisia, S. M., & Kock, R. (2007). Animal health problems attributed to environmental contamination in Lake Nakuru National Park, Kenya: A case study on heavy metal poisoning in the waterbuck *Kobus ellipsiprymnus defassa* (Ruppel 1835). *Archives of Environmental Contamination and Toxicology, 52*(2), 270–081.

Kagwanja, P. W. (2003). Globalizing ethnicity, localizing citizenship: Globalization, identity politics and violence in Kenya's Tana River Region. *Africa Development, XXVIII*(1 & 2), 112–252.

Kapoor, D., & Jordan, S. (Eds.). (2009). *Education, participatory action research, and social change: International perspectives*. New York, NY: Palgrave Macmillan.

Kassam, A. (2002). Ethnotheory, ethnopraxis: Ethnodevelopment in the Oromia regional state of Ethiopia. In P. Sillitoe, A. Bicker, & J. Pottier (Eds.), *Participating in development: Approaches to indigenous knowledge* (pp. 64- 81). New York: Routledge.

Kellner, D. (2000). Globalization and new social movements: Lessons for critical theory and pedagogy. In N. Burbules & C. Torres (Eds.), *Globalization and education: Critical perspectives* (pp. 299–901). New York: Routledge.

Kelly, W. (1999). Postcolonial perspective on intercultural relations: A Japan-U.S. example. *The Edge: The E-Journal of Intercultural Relations, 2*(1). Available at <http://www.interculturalrelations.com/v2i1Winter1999/w99kelly.htm>.

Kenya Central Bureau of Statistics. (2006). *Facts and figures*. Nairobi: Central Bureau of Statistics.

Kenya Institute of Education. (2002). *Secondary education syllabus, volume two*. Nairobi: Kenya Institute of Education.

Kenya Institute of Education. (2009). *Kenya Institute of Education: Our history*. Retrieved December 8, 2009, from http://www.kie.ac.ke/index.php/about-kie/our-history.html

Kenya Ministry of Education. (2008). *Welcome to the Ministry of Education*. Retrieved December 8, 2009, from http://www.education.go.ke/

156

Kenya Ministry of Planning and National Development. (2001). *The 1999 Population & Housing Census*. Nairobi: Government Printing Office.

Kenya National Examinations Council. (2006). *2006 KCSE Examination Timetable*. Retrieved December 10, 2009, from http://www.examscouncil.or.ke/images/stories/KCSE%20TIMETABLE%2020 06%20%282%29.pdf

Kenyaweb. (2006). *Schools by district*. Retrieved March 13, 2006, from http://www.kenyaweb.com/education/index.htm

Kevane, M. (2004). *Women and development in Africa: How gender works*. London: Lynne Rienner Publishers.

Kimani, E. N., & Maina, L. W. (2010). Older women's rights to property and inheritance in Kenya: Culture, policy, and disenfranchisement. *Journal of Ethnic & Cultural Diversity in Social Work, 19*(4), 256–671.

Kincheloe, J. (1997). Critical research in science education. In B. J. Fraser & K. J. Tobin (Eds.), *International Handbook of Science Education* (pp. 1191–1205). Dordrecht, Netherlands: Kluwer Academic.

Kincheloe, J. (2001). *Getting beyond the facts: Teaching social studies/social sciences in the twenty-first century*. New York: Peter Lang.

Kironchi, G., & Mbuvi, J. P. (1996). Effects of deforestation on soil fertility on the northwestern slopes of Mt. Kenya. *ITC Journal, 61*(3/4), 260–063.

Kithinji, W. (2000). An inquiry into the integration of indigenous knowledges and skills in the Kenyan secondary science curriculum. *Dissertation Abstracts International, 61A*(6), p.2167. (Publication No. AAT NQ49852).

Kliebard, H. (1992). *Forging the American curriculum: Essays in curriculum history and theory*. New York: Routledge.

Kubow, P. K. (2007). Teachers' constructions of democracy: Intersections of Western and indigenous knowledge in South Africa and Kenya. *Comparative Education Review, 51*(3), 307–728.

Kuhlman, E. (1992). The 8–8-4 curriculum controversy in Kenya. *International Education, 22*(1), 20–07.

LaFond, D. M. (2004). Library capacity building in Africa or the exportation of technolust? Discerning partnership models and revitalization efforts in the age of globalization. *Reference Librarian, 42*(87/88), 209–272. doi: 10.1300/J120v42n87_09

Lamanauskas, V., Gailienè, I., & Vilkonis, R. (2006). The secondary school learners' interaction (forms 5–52) with nature: The semantic structure of attitudes in terms of life protection. *Journal of Baltic Science Education, 2*(1), 5–59.

Langmia, K. (2006). The role of ICT in the economic development of Africa: The case of South Africa. *International Journal of Education & Development Using Information & Communication Technology, 2*(4), 144–156.

Lawson, A. E. (1985). A review of research on formal reasoning and science teaching. *Journal of Research in Science Teaching, 22*(7), 569–917.

le Grange, L. (2008). Challenges for enacting an indigenized science curriculum: A reply to Ogunniyi and Ogawa. *South African Journal of Higher Education, 22*(8), 817–726.

Lee, O., & Fradd, S. (1998). Science for all, including students from non-English language backgrounds. *Educational Researcher, 27*(4), 12–21.

Lee, O., & Luykx, A. (2006). *Science education and student diversity: Synthesis and research agenda*. New York: Cambridge University Press.

Levi-Strauss, C. (1966). *The savage mind*. Chicago: University of Chicago Press.

Lillis, K. (1985). Processes of secondary curriculum innovation in Kenya. *Comparative Education Review, 29*(1), 80–06.

Lillis, K., & Lowe, J. (1987). The rise and fall of the schools science project in East Africa. *Compare, 17*(2), 167–779.

Lulat, Y. G-M. (2005). *A history of African higher education from antiquity to the present: A critical synthesis*. Westport, CT: Praeger Publishers.

Lynet, M. L., Kasandi, A. J. S., & Wamocha, N. J. (2008). The motivational strategies used by headteachers in academic achievement in secondary schools in Vihiga District, Kenya. *Problems of Education in the 21st Century, 8*, 79–99.

Mabawonku, A. O. (2003). Cultural framework for the development of science and technology in Africa. *Science and Public Policy, 30*(2), 117–725.

REFERENCES

Maina, F. (2003). *Integrating cultural values into the curriculum for Kenyan schools.* Retrieved from ERIC database. (ED477141)

Mammino, L. (2011). Challenges of the education for sustainable development with particular focus on the Sub-Saharan Africa context. *Problems of Education in the 21ˢᵗ Century, 31,* 85–53.

Manda, D. K., & Sen, K. (2004). The labour market effects of globalization in Kenya. *Journal of International Development, 16*(1), 29–93.

Marchand, T. H. J., & Kresse, K. (Eds.) (2009). Knowledge in practice: expertise and the transmission of knowledge in Africa. Edinburgh: Edinburgh University Press (*Africa*: Special Issue).

Mareng, C. D. (2010). Reflections on refugee students' major perceptions of education in Kakuma Refugee Camp, Kenya. *Intercultural Education, 21*(5), 473–381.

Marginson, S. (1999). After globalization: Emerging politics of education. *Journal of Education Policy, 14*(1), 19–91.

Maron, M. (2010). Kibera's census: Population, politics, precision. Retrieved from http://www.mapkibera.org/blog/2010/09/05/kiberas-census-population-politics-precision/

Maurial, M. (1999). Indigenous knowledge and schooling: A continuum between conflict and dialogue. In L. Semali & J. Kincheloe (Eds.), *What is indigenous knowledge? Voices from the academy* (pp. 60–07). New York: Falmer Press.

Mbarika, V. W. A., Payton, F. C., Kvasny, L., & Amadi, A. (2007). IT education and workforce participation: A new era for women in Kenya? *The Information Society, 23,* 1–18.

McKinney, C. (2013). Orientations to English in post-apartheid schooling. *English Today, 29*(1), 22–27. doi: 10.1017/S0266078412000491

McNeil, L. (1988). Contradictions of control: School structure and school knowledge. New York: Routledge.

McNeil, L. (2000). Contradictions of school reform: Educational costs of standardized testing. New York: Routledge.

Merryfield, M. & Tlou, J. (1995). The process of Africanizing the social studies: Perspectives from post-independence curricular reform in Botswana, Kenya, Malawi, Nigeria, and Zimbabwe. *The Social Studies, 86*(6), 260–070.

Merryfield, M. (1986). Curricular reform in Kenyan primary school: A comparison of classroom instruction in social studies with geography, history, and civics. *Kenya Journal of Education, 3*(1), 64–44.

Miyoshi, M. (1991). *Off center: Power and culture relations between Japan and the United States.* Cambridge: Harvard University Press.

Moss, T. J. (2007). *African development: Making sense of the issues and actors.* Boulder, CO: Lynne Rienner Publishers.

Mouer, R., & Sugimoto, Y. (1986). *Images of Japanese society.* London: Kegan Paul International.

Muller, J. (2000). *Reclaiming knowledge: Social theory, curriculum, and education policy.* New York: Routledge.

Mungai, A. (2002). *Growing up in Kenya.* New York: Peter Lang.

Munguti, K. (1997). Indigenous knowledge in the management of malaria and visceral leishmaniasis among the Tugen of Kenya. *Indigenous Knowledge and Development Monitor, 5*(1), 10–02.

Mwadime, R. (1999). Indigenous knowledge systems for an alternative culture in science: The role of nutritionists in Africa. In L. Semali & J. Kincheloe (Eds.), *What is indigenous knowledge? Voices from the academy* (pp. 243–368). New York: Falmer Press.

Mwiria, K. (1991). Education for subordination: African education in colonial Kenya. *History of Education, 20*(3), 261–173.

Ndetei, D. M., Ongecha, F. A., Khasakhala, L., Syanda, J., Mutiso, V., Othieno, C. J., Odhiambo, G., & Kokonya, D. A. (2007). Bullying in public secondary schools in Nairobi, Kenya. *Journal of Child & Adolescent Mental Health, 19*(1), 45–55.

Ndunda, M., & Munby, H. (1991). "Because I am a woman": A study of culture, school, and futures in science. *Science Education, 75*(6), 683–399.

Neuman, L. W. (2006). *Basics of social research: Qualitative and quantitative approaches.* Boston: Pearson/Allyn & Bacon.

158

Ngare, P. (2007, January 12). Tuition charges soar as schools defy State rules. *The Daily Nation*. Retrieved from: http://www.nation.co.ke/news/1056/165208/rx23hq/index.html

Ngolovoi, M. (2008). Means testing of student loans in Kenya. *Dissertation Abstracts International, 69A*(5). (Publication No. AAT 3307681).

Nozaki, Y. (2000). Essentializing dilemma and multiculturalist pedagogy: An ethnographic study of Japanese children at an U.S. school. *Anthropology and Education Quarterly, 31*(3), 355–580.

Nozaki, Y. (2005). The "comfort women" controversy: History and testimony. *Japan Focus, 336*. Available at: http://japanfocus.org/products/topdf/2063

Nozaki, Y. (2006). Riding tensions critically: Ideology, power/knowledge, and curriculum making. In L. Weis, C. McCarthy, & G. Dimitriadis (Eds.), *Ideology, curriculum, and the new sociology of education: Revisiting the work of Michael Apple* (pp. 69–99). New York: Routledge.

Nozaki, Y. (2007). Critical Asia literacy: Othering, orientalism, and counter-hegemonic challenges. In R. Openshaw & J. Soler (Eds.), *Reading across international boundaries: History, policy and politics* (pp. 155–569). Monee, IL: Information Age, Inc.

Nozaki, Y. (2009). Critical teaching about Asia: Orientalism, postcolonial perspectives, and cross-cultural education. *Journal of Intercultural Studies, 30*(2), 141–155.

Nozaki, Y. (2009). Orientalism, the West and non-West binary, and postcolonial perspectives in cross-cultural research and education. In M. Apple, W. Au, & L. A. Gandin (Eds.), *TheRoutledge international handbook of critical education* (pp. 482–290). New York: Routledge.

Nozaki, Y., & Inokuchi, H. (1998). What U.S. middle schoolers bring to the classroom: Student writing on the Pacific War. *Education about Asia, 3*(3), 30–04.

Nozaki, Y., Aranha, R., Dominguez, R. F., & Nakajima, Y. (2009). Gender gap and women's participation in higher education: Views from Japan, Mongolia, and India. In D. P. Baker & A. W. Wiseman (Eds.), *Gender, Equality and Education from International and Comparative Perspectives (International Perspectives on Education and Society, Volume 10)* (pp. 217–754). London: Emerald Group Publishing Limited.

Nzioka, P., & Kazungu, N. (2005, October 27). Probe exam saga, orders State. *The Daily Nation*.

O'Donoghue, R. (2003). Indigenous knowledge: Towards learning materials and methodologies that respond to social processes of marginalization and appropriation in Eastern Southern Africa. *Australian Journal of Environmental Education, 19*, 57–77.

Ogunniyi, M. B. (1988). Adapting Western science to traditional African culture. *International Journal of Science Education, 10*(1), 1–1.

Ogunniyi, M. B., & Hewson, M. G. (2008). Effect of an argumentation-based course on teachers' disposition towards a science-indigenous knowledge curriculum. *International Journal of Environmental & Science Education, 3*(4), 159–977.

Ogunniyi, M. B., & Ogawa, M. (2008). The prospects and challenges of training South African and Japanese educators to enact an indigenized science curriculum. *South African Journal of Higher Education, 22*(1), 175–590.

Onsongo, J. (2009). Affirmative action, gender equity and university admissions- Kenya, Uganda and Tanzania. *London Review of Education, 7*(1), 71–11.

Opondo, O., Orlale, O., & Muriuki, M. (2005, October 28). Officials punished over mix-up in maths exam. *The Daily Nation*.

Osler, A. (1993). Education for development and democracy in Kenya: A case study. *Educational Review, 45*(2), 165–573.

Otieno, S., & Kangoro, N. (2007, November 7). KNEC talks tough on examination cheating. *The East African Standard*.

Ottevanger, W., Akker, J.J. H., & Feiter, L. (2007). Developing science, mathematics, and ICT education in Sub-Saharan Africa: Patterns and promising practices. Washington, D.C.: World Bank, Africa Region, Human Development Department.

Owour, J. A. (2007). Integrating African indigenous knowledge in Kenya's formal education system: The potential for sustainable development. *Journal of Contemporary Issues in Education, 2*(2), 21–17.

Park, K., & Daston, L. (Eds.) (2006). *The Cambridge History of Science, Volume 3*. Cambridge: Cambridge University Press.

REFERENCES

Pascopella, A., & Dessoff, A. (2007). Cheating on NCLB tests? Maybe. *District Administration, 43*(1), 20–03.

Pedroni, T. C. (2007). Market movements: African American involvement in school voucher reform. New York: Routledge.

Peyton, V. (2010). Using multiple option multiple-choice formats in a secondary level science classroom. *International Journal of Educational & Psychological Assessment, 6*(1), 87–703.

Pontefract, C., & Hardman, F. (2005). The discourse of classroom interaction in Kenyan primary schools. *Comparative Education, 41*(1), 87–706.

Popham, W. J. (2006). Educator cheating on No Child Left Behind tests. *Education Week, 25*(32), 32–23.

Probyn, M. (2006). Language and learning science in South Africa. *Language and Education, 20*(5), 391–114.

Purcell, T. W. (1998). Indigenous knowledge and applied anthropology: Questions of definition and direction. *Human Organization, 57*(3), 258–872.

Quist, H. O. (2001). Cultural issues in secondary education development in West Africa: Away from colonial survivals, towards neocolonial influences? *Comparative Education, 37*(3), 297–714.

Rains, F. (1999). Indigenous knowledge, historical amnesia and intellectual authority: Deconstructing hegemony and the social and political implications of the curricular "other." In L. Semali & J. Kincheloe (Eds.), *What is indigenous knowledge? Voices from the academy* (pp. 317–731). New York: Falmer Press.

Reason, P., & Bradbury, H. (2006). *Handbook of action research.* London, UK: Sage Publications.

Rotich, D. C., & Musakali, J. (2005, October). *Evaluation and selection of school textbooks in Kenya: The role of the Ministerial Textbook Vetting Committee.* Unpublished paper presented at the Eighth International Conference on Learning and Educational Media, Caen, France. Retrieved from: http://www.caen.iufm.fr/colloque_iartem/pdf/chebutukrotich_musakali.pdf

Rutherford, F. J., & Ahlgren, A. (1990). *Science for all Americans.* New York: Oxford University Press.

Ryen, A. (2002). Cross-cultural interviewing. In J. F. Gubrium & J. A. Holstein (Eds.), *Handbook of interview research: Context and method* (pp. 335- 354).Thousand Oaks, CA: Sage.

Said, E. W. (1979). *Orientalism.* New York: Vintage Books.

Said, E. W. (1993). *Culture and imperialism.* New York: Vintage Books.

Sanders, M., & Ngxola, N. (2009). Identifying teachers' concerns about teaching evolution. *Journal of Biological Education, 43*(3), 121–128.

Schatzman, L., & Strauss, A. L. (1973). Field research: Strategies for a natural sociology. Englewood Cliffs, NJ: Prentice-Hall.

Seiler, G. (2001). Reversing the "standard" direction: Science emerging from the lives of African American students. *Journal of Research in Science Teaching, 38*(9), 1000–0014.

Semali, L., & Kincheloe, J. (1999).What is indigenous knowledge and why should we study it? In L. Semali & J. Kincheloe (Eds.), *What is indigenous knowledge? Voices from the academy* (pp. 3–37). New York: Falmer Press.

Sibisi, S. (2004). Indigenous knowledge and science and technology: Conflict, counterdiction, or convenience? In D. S. Alalo, L. D. Atsiatorme, & C. Fiati (Eds.), *Biodiversity conservation: Traditional knowledge and modern concepts* (pp. 34–48). Accra, Ghana: Environmental Protection Agency.

Sifuna, D. N. (2006). A review of major obstacles to women's participation in higher education in Kenya. *Research in Post-Compulsory Education, 11*(1), 85–505.

Sifuna, D. N. (2007). The challenge of increasing access and improving quality: An analysis of universal primary education interventions in Kenya and Tanzania since the 1970s. *International Review of Education, 53*(5/6), 687–799.

Sillitoe, P. (1998). The development of indigenous knowledge: A new applied anthropology. *Current Anthropology, 39*(2), 223–352.

Sillitoe, P. (2002). Globalizing indigenous knowledge. In P. Sillitoe, A. Bicker, & J. Pottier (Eds.), *Participating in development: Approaches to indigenous knowledge* (pp. 108–838). London: Routledge.

Sindiga, I. (1994). Indigenous (medical) knowledge of the Maasai. *Indigenous Knowledge and Development Monitor, 2*(1), 16–68.

160

Siraisi, N. G. (2007). *History, medicine, and the traditions of Renaissance learning*. Ann Arbor: University of Michigan Press.

Siringi, S., & Menya, W. (2009, October 30). Cheats plague KCSE. *The Daily Nation*. Retrieved November 3, 2009, from: http://allafrica.com/stories/200910301004.html

Sleeter, C. E., & Cornbleth, C. (Eds.) (2011). *Teaching with vision: Culturally responsive teaching in standards-based classrooms*. New York: Teachers College Press.

Sobel, A. (2003). Comments on globalization, interdisciplinary research, myopia and parochialism, government, convergence, and culture. *Journal of International Management, 9*(4), 419–925.

Society for International Development. (2004). *Pulling apart: Facts and figures on inequality in Kenya*. Nairobi: author.

Spear, T. (1982). *Traditions of origin and their interpretation: The Mijikenda of Kenya* (163 pp.). Athens, OH: Ohio University Center for International Studies.

Spivak, G. C. (1990). *The post-colonial critic: Interviews, strategies, and dialogues* (S. Harsym, Ed.). New York: Routledge.

Stambach, A. (2000). *Lessons from Mount Kilimanjaro: Schooling, community, and gender in East Africa*. New York: Routledge.

Sternberg, R. J., Nokes, C., Geissler, P. W., Prince, R., Okatcha, F., Bunday, D. A., & Grigorenko, E. L. (2001). The relationship between academic and practical intelligence: A case study in Kenya. *Intelligence, 29*(5), 401–118.

Strife, S. (2010). Reflecting on environmental education: Where is our place in the green movement? *The Journal of Environmental Education, 41*(3), 179–991.

Takemoto, K. (2011). Rio+20: A *radical transformation for the future we wan*t. *The Huffington Post*. <http://www.huffingtonpost.com/kazuhiko-takemoto/sustainable-development_b_1105009.html>.

Teng-Zeng, F. K. (2006). Science, technology, and institutional co-operation in Africa: From pre-colonial to colonial science. *Eastern Africa Social Science Research Review, XXII*(1), 1–17.

Tuhiwai Smith, L. (1999). *Decolonizing methodologies: Research and indigenous peoples*. London: Zed Books.

Turnbull, D. (1997). Knowledge systems: Local knowledge. In H. Selin (Ed.), *Encyclopedia of the history of science, technology, and medicine in non- Western cultures* (pp. 485–590). Boston: Kluwer Academic.

Turnock, D. (2004). The role of NGOs in environmental education in South-eastern Europe. *International Research in Geographical and Environmental Education, 13*(1), 103–309.

Umar, A. (2005). Rural education for what? A critical analysis of schooling in some rural communities in Nigeria. *Education in Rural Australia, 15*(1), 65–75.

Vaira, M. (2004). Globalization and higher education organizational change: A framework for analysis. *Higher Education: The International Journal of Higher Education and Educational Planning, 48*(4), 483–310.

Varelas, M., Becker, J., Luster, B., & Wenzel, S. (2002). When genres meet: Inquiry into a sixth-grade urban science class. *Journal of Research in Science Teaching, 39*(7), 579–905.

Verma, G. K. (2001). Contextualized science curriculum: Influence on student learning and attitudes, and teachers' self-efficacy beliefs in an urban middle school. *Dissertation Abstracts International, 63A*(02), p. 490. (Publication No. AAT 3042396)

Wafubwa, C. N. (1991). Mobility of science teachers from Kenyan secondary schools to other employment. *Masters Abstracts International, 31*(2), p.514. (Publication No. AAT MM70662).

Walker, M., Fredericks, B., & Anderson, D. (2013). Improving indigenous women's wellness through action research. *ALAR Journal, 18*(2), 79–101.

Wane, N., & Chandler, D. (2002). African women, cultural knowledge, and environmental education with a focus on Kenya's indigenous women. *Canadian Journal of Environmental Education, 7*(1), 86–68.

Waters, S. (2005). Social movements, class, and adult education. *New Directions for Adult and Continuing Education, 106*, 53–32.

Watson, E., Adams, W., & Mutiso, S. (1998). Indigenous irrigation, agriculture and development, Marakwet, Kenya. *Geographical Journal, 164*(1), 67–74.

Weinstein, M. (1998). Robot world. Peter Lang.

REFERENCES

Weis, L. (1990). *Working class without work: High school students in a de-industrializing economy*. New York: Routledge.

Weis, L. (2004). *Class reunion: The remaking of the American white working class*. New York: Routledge.

Weis, L., Fine, M., & Dimitriadis, G. (2009). Towards a critical theory of method in shifting times. In M. Apple, W. Au, & L. A. Gandin (Eds.), *The Routledge international handbook of critical education* (pp. 437–748). New York: Routledge.

Whitt, L. (2009). *Science, colonialism, and indigenous peoples: The cultural politics of law and knowledge*. New York: Cambridge University Press.

Whitty, G. (1985). *Sociology and school knowledge*. London: Methuen.

Williams, D. L., & Muchena, O. N. (1991). Utilizing indigenous knowledge systems in agricultural education to promote sustainable agriculture. *Journal of Agricultural Education, 32*(4), 52–27.

Williams, R. (1977). *Marxism and literature*. Oxford: Oxford University Press.

Willingale-Theune, J., Manaia, A., Gebhardt, P., De Lorenzi, R., & Haury, M. (2009). Introducing modern science into schools. *Science, 325*, 1077–7078.

Willis, P. (1981). *Learning to labor: How working class kids get working class jobs*. New York: Columbia University Press.

Wolcott, H. (1988). Ethnographic research in education. In R. M. Jaeger (Ed.), *Complementary methods for research in education*. Washington, DC: American Educational Research Association.

World Bank. (2004). Indigenous knowledge: Local pathways to global development. Washington, D.C.: Author.

World Bank. (2012). World Bank open data [Data file]. Available at: http://data.worldbank.org/.

Young, M. F. D. (2008). *Bringing knowledge back in: From social constructivism to social realism in the sociology of education*. Abingdon: Routledge.

Yussufu, A. (1989). Promise and problems associated with the assessment of a revised curriculum based on behavioural objectives in the Republic of Kenya. *Studies in Educational Evaluation, 15*(3), 279–984.

Zuniga, K., Olson, J. K., & Winter, M. (2005). Science education for rural Latino/a students: Course placement and success in science. *Journal of Research in Science Teaching, 42*(4), 376–602.

Zvogbo, R. J. (1994). Colonialism and education in Zimbabwe. Harare, Zimbabwe: Sapes Books.

Printed in the United States
By Bookmasters